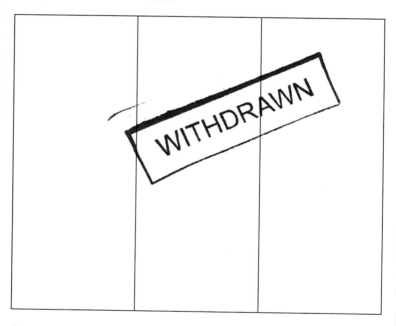

Sister Sleuths

Female Detectives in Britain

Nell Darby

PEN & SWORD
HISTORY

First published in Great Britain in 2021 by
Pen & Sword History
An imprint of
Pen & Sword Books Ltd
Yorkshire – Philadelphia

ISBN 978 1 52678 025 6

Typeset by Mac Style
Printed and bound in the UK by CPI Group (UK) Ltd,
Croydon, CR0 4YY.

Pen & Sword Books Limited incorporates the imprints of Atlas,
Archaeology, Aviation, Discovery, Family History, Fiction, History,
Maritime, Military, Military Classics, Politics, Select, Transport,
True Crime, Air World, Frontline Publishing, Leo Cooper, Remember
When, Seaforth Publishing, The Praetorian Press, Wharncliffe
Local History, Wharncliffe Transport, Wharncliffe True Crime
and White Owl.

For a complete list of Pen & Sword titles please contact

PEN & SWORD BOOKS LIMITED
47 Church Street, Barnsley, South Yorkshire, S70 2AS, England
E-mail: enquiries@pen-and-sword.co.uk
Website: www.pen-and-sword.co.uk

Or

PEN AND SWORD BOOKS
1950 Lawrence Rd, Havertown, PA 19083, USA
E-mail: Uspen-and-sword@casematepublishers.com
Website: www.penandswordbooks.com

Contents

Acknowledgements

I would like to express my appreciation of all the archivists, librarians, archives and libraries for providing me with advice and archival material – especially at The Women's Library of the London School of Economics, The National Archives, the Bodleian Library, Oxford Brookes University Library, Mary Evans Picture Library, the Metropolitan Police Heritage Centre, London Metropolitan Archives and, online, the British Newspaper Archive, Findmypast, The Genealogist and Ancestry. Thanks and appreciation are also due to Susannah Stapleton, the author of a recent biography of private detective Maud West, for her help, advice, and good company. Thanks too to Rosemary Collins, Sarah Williams and Andrew Chapman for commissioning me to write about various aspects of the private detective's work for their magazines.

Lastly, thanks as always to my family – John, Jake and Eva Darby – for their support and for putting up with my numerous tales of lady detectives.

Introduction: 'At least as good detectives as men'[1]

In a close-knit community, a stranger one day appears, a lone woman, moving her meagre possessions into a vacant apartment. She is unmarried, or perhaps widowed; respectable, articulate, and pleasingly well-mannered. She makes an effort to get to know her new neighbours; she calls on them, she invites the wives over to take a cup of tea with her. There is one local woman, in particular, who she quickly becomes friends with. They regularly take afternoon tea together, and start to gossip together, as ladies do. They show each other photographs of their loved ones; the local lady feels comfortable enough with this new resident, her new confidante, to let her read the love letters she has been sent.

Then, as quickly as she moved in, the new resident moves out again, the friendship suddenly cut off. A few months later, though, the other lady who made her friendship sees her again – but this time, it is in the Divorce Court, and the lady is being divorced by her suspicious husband. A witness appears in the courtroom to tell of the lady's indiscretions and her love life, and the married lady flinches in recognition. The witness is her former friend – a woman who now tells the court of her real identity, that of the lady detective.[2]

This is what happened in 1907, when the female detective Kate Easton was engaged to watch Violet Mabel Wigglesworth, a company director's wife from Marylebone. Her husband, Francis, had suspected Violet of having an affair with clerk Frederick Simpson, although this was the latest in a litany of complaints that centred around Violet's alleged extravagance and intemperance. In 1906, she had admitted to having been 'indiscreet' with another man, and Francis had left her. The following March, he told her he would take her back – 'if she would behave herself'. She refused.[3] Francis's response was to engage Kate Easton to live in the same rented lodgings as Violet, at Ennismore Avenue in Chiswick.

The male detective Francis had previously engaged to watch his wife was now let go, and in a fit of jealousy over a woman being given his job, wrote to Violet to tip her off about her new co-tenant:

Kate Easton, a woman detective, has been engaged to watch you. If she or one of her satellites has managed to get into your house, get Mr P or one of your gentlemen friends to chuck her out immediately. So beware of any strange woman who tries to make your acquaintance. They are anxious to find out what takes place at night at your apartments. Beware![4]

Violet failed to listen to this warning; instead, she was soon discovered in bed with her lover by the female detective. She pleaded with her husband to divorce her quickly; he refused, and it wasn't until April 1909 that a divorce was duly granted.

Violet was discovered by just one of several female detectives operating at this time, but this book looks at the development and growth of the 'lady detective' since the 1850s, using the lives of real women working in this field to bring the hitherto somewhat sidelined history of female detective work to life. The fictional 'lady detective' of the 1860s is recognised here as representing a new career path for women in real life; the fiction was not sensational in depicting women as private detectives, but was reflecting what was happening in real life. The book tracks the development of the 'amateur' detective, and how she differed from her professional counterpart, as well as looking at the pride felt by women who had been involved in amateur work and how this embodied a frustration with their usual day-to-day lives in a patriarchal world. It also explores why and how women became detectives, from Scotland Yard's recognition of women's particular skills in detection work and subterfuge, to women seeking to escape the confines of middle-class Victorian life. It also looks at press coverage of these women and how these reflected, at times, a wider concern about women's independence that heralded complaints about the women's suffrage campaign. The egalitarian nature of detective work – a job that was open to women from different backgrounds and of different marital status – is shown through specific case studies.

Although this is a history of female private detectives in Britain, there are a couple of caveats. Firstly, the book takes, by necessity, a comparative approach at times, in considering similarities and differences on opposite sides of the Atlantic. It looks at the influence of America in determining the possibilities for female detectives in Britain, but also shows how this was a symbiotic relationship. Interestingly Allan Pinkerton – a Scot – is regarded as the first man to formally employ a female in his Chicago-based detective agency; it was arguably the obituaries of this woman, Kate Warne, copied from the US press by British newspapers, that helped stimulate the profession in Britain. Even in 1901, one newspaper in Yorkshire was stating that the increase in the number of British female detectives meant that 'if we cannot keep up to American methods of enterprise, we are not altogether lagging hopelessly behind'.[5]

The second caveat is in the exploration of female private detectives across Britain. There is an unavoidable emphasis on London, as this is where the private detective world was centred, for both men and women. The proximity of the divorce court, of London's Theatreland, its shopping district around Regent Street and Oxford Street, and the City and its financial institutions, meant that there were a glut of competing detectives and agencies in the capital by the early twentieth century. These were also the professionals who were most frequently mentioned in the press, either in terms of coverage about their cases, or in the classified adverts they paid for to promote their businesses. However, I have attempted to look at the existence and role of the female detective in the provinces and regions, where evidence exists for them. The female detective, like her male counterpart, is likely to have existed across Britain, but the job could be both peripatetic or temporary, and some women chose to take a low-key approach – working from their homes or by personal recommendation, rather than advertising their services in the press, or establishing a separate office for their work. If they did not get named as witnesses in divorce petitions, or work on cases newsworthy enough to get recorded in the press, or come before magistrates or judges to give evidence, their lives as private detectives may not have been preserved in the archives. In this, as with so many other aspects of female lives in history, there is an imbalance in the archival evidence of male lives compared to their female counterparts.

Sister Sleuths takes both a thematic and chronological approach, focusing on individual female detectives in order to look at wider issues. Therefore, the life and work of Antonia Moser, working in London from the 1890s to 1910s is used to explore the political awareness of female agents working for themselves in a male-dominated world, and their involvement in the suffragist movement. Others, such as Kate Easton and Dorothy Tempest, illustrate the popularity of detective work for former actresses, highlighting the links between the two professions. Another key theme is spiritualism, its popularity in the early twentieth century leading to private detectives being employed in exposing spiritualist frauds, while some spiritualists and palmists – such as Midlander Rosalie Thompson – in turn became detectives.

Key themes explored within these chapters also include the impact of the 1857 Matrimonial Causes Act on women's work; and how the Jack the Ripper murders and subsequent criticism of the Metropolitan Police's failure to catch the perpetrator led to calls for women to be employed to find him instead. I have also included a brief history of store detectives, as this proved an increasingly important source of work for many female detectives from the early twentieth century onwards. Some took on store work alongside other private inquiry work, while others moved from one field to another. What emerges from these women is their adaptability and versatility – they came from different backgrounds, and came into detective work in different ways, but they took on a variety of jobs with alacrity.

Time, and the concept of a society gradually changing over a period of time, is important here. *Sister Sleuths* takes in the key developments and changes in wider society over the course of the nineteenth and twentieth centuries, looking at the language and terms in which female detectives were described in the press, to see whether this reflects changing attitudes towards them, or whether, despite the other changes in society over the course of the Victorian and Edwardian periods in particular, women continued to be perceived in terms of their novelty and looks – one particular report, for example, concentrating on the 'stylishness' of the female detective.[6] Throughout, reference is made to the books, stories, plays and, later, films that have appeared at different points and that feature female detectives to study whether these accurately reflect the reality of the female detective – or, if they differ, *why* they differ.

Both fact and fiction can tell us much about the society in which these enterprising women operated.

Kathleen Gregory Klein, in deciding what constituted a female detective for the purposes of her research into fictional sleuths, decided to limit her analysis to 'the paid, professional woman detective', excluding 'amateurs and policewomen'.[7] Although I concentrate more on the professional private detective rather than the numerous women who were reported in the press as having helped catch a criminal (keen amateurs, but amateurs nonetheless), this book does take a slightly broader approach, in that in some cases, it is not clear what the financial remuneration was, if any, for some women, who may have been helping their detective family members out rather than being formally employed. However, if they were taking on 'traditional' private detective tasks, then they are considered here. The focus is on the private detective – otherwise known as the private inquiry agent and, later, the private investigator – as opposed to the development of the female police detective. Having said this, though, it is necessary to involve some discussion of the police, as several female detectives learned their skills from husbands who were either serving police officers, or former policemen or police detectives who had moved into private detective work themselves. Women also faced competition particularly from these former police detectives, who opened agencies or worked as private detectives after they had retired from police work, and who could use their experience to publicise themselves and their skills.

Researching and writing a female-centred history of an already shadowy profession has been a challenge, and there are inevitably gaps, both in the archival record, and in this book. Even as I was finalising the final draft, I was still uncovering further details of these shadowy sleuths, and I'm sure that more is still to be found out. However, I hope that what I have discovered so far helps to shed light both on this necessarily private, stealthy activity, and on some of the pioneering women who made it their job. What it also shows, though, is that women have always had a role in maintaining the stability of society, long being involved in tracking down those who have been seen to have transgressed in some way, whether in committing crimes – as we understand the term – or in flouting moral or religious standards. To find out more, we first need to go back to seventeenth-century London.

On Friday evening, about half after nine o'clock, the inhabitants of Cockey-lane were alarmed by the cry of 'Stop thief! Stop thief!' – Excited by the impulse of curiosity, several of them hastened to their doors, where they beheld an unfortunate fair one, almost bare-headed, in pursuit of a boy, who, it seems, had made a snatch at her bonnet…

Bury and Norwich Post, 2 September 1789, p.3

Chapter 1

Early Detective Work

Crime, and the detection of crime, depends on watching. Criminals watch for an opportunity – as Sarah Good did in 1680, waiting for the opportunity to steal a silver tankard from Roger Reading in St Botolph's, London.[1] Wary locals watch for evidence of a crime, as Richard Wilson did when he saw two women act suspiciously in St Paul's Churchyard in 1756, soon seeing Catherine Griffiths and Mary Evans pickpocket another man, stealing his handkerchief.[2] In 1758, a pawnbroker named Bunn reported how he had been watching Mrs Jane Wylae, who was standing at her front door on Petticoat Lane; when she saw him watching her, she 'went backwards and went out the back way'. He was watching her, and watched her watch him.[3] Over centuries, people have watched others, in order to commit crime, or in order to detect crime. Prior to the nineteenth century, personal property was the basis of one's standing in society: people had fewer possessions, and those possessions were therefore highly valuable both in a financial and a personal context. Possessions were also sought after by those without them, as well as being guarded and watched by those with them.

From the late seventeenth century, and the passing of the Old Poor Laws, individuals in England and Wales were deemed to have a place of settlement, a parish where they were seen to belong, either by birth, parentage, work, or marriage. Many stayed living in their parish for their whole lives, or ventured little further than the neighbouring parishes. Others attempted to migrate, and the creation of places of settlement was designed to restrict this ability to migrate, and to establish responsibility for individuals if they fell on hard times and needed to seek financial relief. But the relative lack of mobility compared to today also led to suspicion. In a rural community, particularly, if a stranger appeared, one would instantly be on one's guard: who was this individual, and what did he or she want? Even in London, a bustling metropolis, strangers within a parish could immediately find themselves regarded with suspicion. If an item was lost, one might suspect it had been stolen by a stranger seen recently in the village, and attempts be made to locate that individual. Others might have seen something they felt to be suspicious, and pass those concerns on. Those inhabiting that community took it on themselves to act as law enforcers – as watchers, as witnesses, as detectives, and as police.

Many of those watching were women. Wives were at home more than many men, either supervising servants and household tasks, or undertaking them themselves. If they were lucky enough to have some downtime, they might sit or stand at their door, conversing with neighbours, or simply watching the world go by. They had keen powers of observation, noticing unusual activity, spotting neighbours arguing, or doors being left open. Women appear in court records as prosecutors, as offenders, but also as vital witnesses. In one case heard at the Old Bailey, for example, 16-year-old Elizabeth Cooper was accused of stealing linen sheets, aprons, bedgowns, shifts and Holland caps belonging to Edward Williams. Yet it was Edward's wife, Mary, who gave evidence, and she showed that she had a keen eye. Mary ran a lodging house from her home at Castle Street in Bloomsbury. She kept a linen basket in her kitchen, and when she woke up one morning, noticed that the items were missing from it. Using her detective skills, she suspected a female apprentice employed by one of her neighbours; she had approached Mary the previous evening asking for a night's accommodation, but Mary had refused. Mary went to where she worked, and asked her to 'tell me who she saw go out at my door', and 'whether she knew anything of the matter'. The apprentice initially said that her mistress had ordered her to steal from her neighbour. Mary Williams marched the girl, Elizabeth, to the local magistrate – the infamous Justice Fielding – and obtained a warrant to search the home of Elizabeth's mistress, but nothing was found.[4] Despite this, Elizabeth Cooper was found guilty of theft, and sentenced to transportation. Although both Mr and Mrs Williams gave evidence at the trial, it was Mary's that was the detailed account, and it was Mary who identified a suspect, questioned her, obtained a search warrant, and took the suspect before the magistrate. She was a good detective, and her search for the person who stole her linen saw a young girl sent to the other side of the world as punishment.[5]

As the case of Mary Williams shows, detectives of some kind or another have always existed, even if they have been amateurs following their instincts, rather than professionals with training: and these amateur detectives have frequently included women among their ranks. Prior to the formation of the police – the Metropolitan Police Act was passed in 1829, followed by the Rural Police Act in 1839 – there was a clear need for individuals to act as detectives. In criminal cases, the onus was on a victim to act as detective and prosecutor, tracking down an offender and taking him to a parish constable, then to the local magistrate. If the victim did not do so, there would be no case at court, whether at summary proceedings, Quarter Sessions or the Assizes. The victim had to get the help of neighbours and his community – getting others to take part in a hue and cry – the common law precept of summoning local people to give help or witness information in the event of a crime such as an assault, or an act of theft. The victim of such a crime had to find out information, and track down offenders to help bring a prosecution. Even back in medieval times, as Janka Rodziewicz has noted, women were involved in local hue and cry activity because it was a means by which they could become 'involved in regulating their own community, participating in the formal mechanisms of the law' – and in Great Yarmouth, women were almost as active in the hue and cry as the men in their community.[6]

This activity continued, enabling women to participate in the law and policing in various ways. Surviving magistrates' notebooks from the seventeenth and eighteenth centuries clearly show the involvement of women in such cases; widows and single women had their own property to protect, and some had businesses – shops, or other work conducted from their own homes – where goods were needed, and expensive to replace. Even some married women who, under the common law of coverture, saw their legal entity subsumed by that of their husbands, meaning that legally, their property was owned by their spouse, still took on an equal role in questioning neighbours, or snooping round their yards and rooms if they suspected them of being involved in a theft.

By the early nineteenth century, both men and women had recourse to the *Police Gazette, or Hue and Cry*, a publication that enabled those in different parts of the country to share information about crimes and suspected perpetrators. For example, in 1828, Ann Scott, a widow living in Soho, accused her one-time lodger of having stolen numerous articles of clothing from her. Ann's powers of recall and description were clear from her detailing of the accused woman, 'Betsy':

> She wears a green gown with a white spot, very much washed, an old light-grey shawl, a green and grey plaid handkerchief round her neck, and Denmark satin boots, with leather fronts; she is of the middle stature, rather marked with the smallpox, shows her teeth when smiling, and is a Yorkshire woman. She said she had an uncle living at Blackheath, and was brought up, from seven years of age, by Lady Downs, and married a ship carpenter [sic] at Portsmouth.[7]

Elsewhere in the *Police Gazette*, female property owners gave equally detailed descriptions of the items that had been stolen from them – from Martha Merrewether of Newbury's description of her five shifts embroidered with her initials to her stockings, which were numbered so that the number five on one stocking would enable her to find the other of its pair, to Miss Dicks of Woodford, and her 'six new plain tea-spoons, six old ditto, much worn'.[8] The *Police Gazette* was a modern form of the traditional hue and cry, but could reach more places, more quickly; and these female victims made sure they made the most of the opportunities it presented to get their property back, by providing it – even if via others – with the most precise detail they could bring to mind. Ann Scott's power of recall shows that such women had the skills that were utilised in subsequent generations by the detective.

The hue and cry proved an often effective means of community policing, such as with the case in 1735, whereby a cheesemonger robbed one of his competitors in Coleshill, Warwickshire, of £235 but was 'pursued by a hue and cry, was taken 2 miles from Coventry and committed to gaol there' and sentenced to stand in the pillory at Warwick in addition to being fined £50.[9] The same year, a Dublin innkeeper's wife, Mrs Wood, was murdered, her throat cut, while her husband was at church; before she died, she was somehow able to whisper the name of the man who had attacked her, and 'there was a hue and cry raised immediately, so that it is supposed the villain is taken'.[10]

However, by this time, there was increasing recognition that a more formal system of policing was needed, certainly in the expanding urban areas of the country. The Bow Street Runners, formed in London in 1749 by the magistrate and author Henry Fielding, were the first organised police force, and started the move away from victims of crime having responsibility for finding an offender and bringing a prosecution against him or her. Fielding had been 'vociferous in campaigning for some sort of criminal intelligence network', and the Runners – who were attached to the magistrates' office, and travelled across the country in order to catch criminals – were the culmination of his ideas.[11] By the late eighteenth century, the Runners' task was made easier by the employment of clerks in the magistrates' offices whose tasks included the collecting and recording of information about offences and offenders. The crime rate began to increase by the end of the century, though, and this led to parliament attempting to reorganise and strengthen the system of law enforcement. However, the crime rate in London then decreased, and the Runners' work slackened; much of their work in the early nineteenth century was spent on helping cases from outside the metropolis.

In 1829, the biggest change occurred to date, when the Home Secretary, Robert Peel, established the Metropolitan Police, under the Metropolitan Police Act.[12] Ten years later, the Rural Constabularies Act enabled organised police forces to be established across England and Wales. Once there was an organised system of policing in Britain, one might expect that this need for individuals to carry out detective work would disappear, but there is little sign of that. Local people worked for the police carrying out their own detective work on the police's behalf, or simply finding out information and reporting it to the constables to aid their own work; and, for the first decade of the Met's existence, their role was to prevent crime, not to act as detectives.[13] The Metropolitan Police established its own Detective Department in 1842, following a recommendation by its police commissioner at the time, Sir Richard Mayne, a recognition of the need for, and value of, detection work that followed on from the work of Fielding's Bow Street Runners.[14] The Detective Department was the subject of much discussion, and criticism even, as the creation of a detective force was seen as incompatible with individual liberty – a precursor of modern fears over a surveillance state.[15]

However, the new detective department certainly gained the public's attention as well as rousing their curiosity. The newspapers from the 1840s onwards contain many stories of London detectives, such as the story, in 1848, of 'Mr Thornton, of London detective police' going in transatlantic pursuit of an Irish fraudster, and, after a long journey on board the ship *Caledonia*, catching up with the fugitive in New Brunswick, Canada.[16]

The following year, the Bermondsey Horror caught the nation's attention. Maria Manning and her husband Frederick were suspected of having killed Maria's lover Patrick O'Connor. Both fled the scene of the crime, and the press was full of accounts of their eventual apprehension. In the case of Mr Manning, 'two officers of the London Detective Police', one being Edward Langley, who had had previous contact with the man, helped locate him, hiding out in a house on the St Aubin's Road at Beaumont on Jersey. Manning said to Langley that 'he was glad he had come'.[17] So alongside the suspicion of police detectives, and the perceived restriction on individual freedoms that followed, came a fascination with the issue, and an eager following of stories involving manhunts and transnational criminal detection work.

Alongside these police detectives, but largely lurking in the shadows in the earlier part of the nineteenth century, were the private detectives, or private inquiry agents, as they were also commonly known. Early examples were entrepreneurs, usually with little or no police experience, striking out on their own. They were individuals who undertook detective work as one in a series of employments, using their cunning, contacts and fearlessness to try and solve cases. But in the first half of the century, and into the second, these old school detectives were mainly focused on the mundane – the returning of money, the investigation of financial crimes. Ignatius 'Paddington' Pollaky – a Hungarian immigrant to London – was the most well-known example, but he was not the only one.[18] Charles Field, a former Metropolitan Police detective turned private detective, claimed to be heavily involved in the case of the 'Rugeley Poisoner' – murderer William Palmer – in 1856. However, his claiming of involvement in this high profile case was likely to be more the desire to publicise himself and his availability as a private detective rather than a major collaboration with the police investigating that case.[19] Yet beyond the likes of Pollaky and Field, the work of these early Victorian private detectives remains murky.

Heather Shore has suggested that 'agent provocateurs' – in effect, private detectives – were used during the first half of the nineteenth century, but that, as little exploration has been undertaken into this area, our knowledge of it relies on what was happening in the late part of the century.[20] In addition, where private detectives have been studied, the emphasis has been on the male experience; female private detectives, it has been assumed, did not exist until the latter half of the nineteenth century, and then, they were an anomaly, or a novelty at best. Yet, given women's role as witnesses and complainants in crime cases earlier in history, and their involvement in the hue and cry or other neighbourhood detection of crime and criminals, surely it is unlikely that they would not have been involved in detective work in the first half of the nineteenth century? Detective skills involve secrecy or the ability to be unobtrusive, to avoid drawing attention to one's self. In the light of this, women would be ideal detectives, expected by a patriarchal society to be unassuming, discreet, low-profile, while actually taking in their surroundings, observing, noting. The secrecy inherent in much detective work makes it hard to identify individual women involved in such tasks, but not always impossible. What is similarly hard is to separate fact from fiction. As the next chapter discusses, the woman regarded as the 'first female private detective' is largely known thanks to her male employer's attempt to memorialise her. Kate Warne was not British but American; but although she was certainly not the first woman to be involved in crime fighting – as this chapter has suggested – the reports about her life and death certainly publicised private inquiry work as an option for women, and came at just the right time for women in Britain.

Up to that time he had not thought of employing females, but the novelty and utility of the thing quickly banished what he supposed might be the prejudices of society.

On Allan Pinkerton employing Kate Warne –
Northern Standard, 18 July 1868, p.4

Chapter 2

It Started with Kate

It is a day for languid tea-drinking, for a stroll in the park, perhaps, a chat with friends; anything more, on this humid summer's day in 1856 would make one glow, the heat of the roads and the sidewalks reflecting up and almost into one's soul. In any other city, in any other place, it would be a time for quiet, for rest, for torpor – but not in Chicago.

Thousands of miles away, in England, it has only been five months since Charlotte Brontë was buried, leaving her elderly, eccentric father and her taciturn husband awkwardly sharing a Yorkshire parsonage together. In Boston, Eliakim Littell, the man behind literary magazine *The Living Age*, has published some summer reading for the city's tourists that includes three stories about women: Margaret Oliphant's 1855 romance *Zaidee*, *Kate Coventry*, by George Whyte-Melville, and the short story *Sister Anne*, by Fitz-James O'Brien.[1] Meanwhile, in the Catskills, the weather is not like Chicago: there has been four days straight of torrential rain, causing lumber to be swept off docks and along the river, and the cancellation of steamer services. The rain only stopped at midnight the previous night; it had caused the destruction of houses and shops, and the loss of large amounts of business goods.[2] Flooding also hit Louisiana, and only a few weeks ago, thousands of party-goers were killed at Last Island due to the storms. Flooding seems an impossibility in Chicago, though, in the heat of an Illinois summer. In three months, the presidential election will take place in this state, and Illinois will duly vote for the Democrat candidate, James Buchanan.[3]

On this particular Saturday, 23 August 1856, one of Chicago's Scottish émigrés is busy at work in his office, a small, wooden building at 89 Washington Street, when he is suddenly disturbed by his secretary knocking on his door. To his surprise, she tells him that there is a young woman waiting to see him.[4]

The man in question was Allan Pinkerton, born and raised thousands of miles from Illinois, in Glasgow's poor Gorbals district. By 1842, aged only 23, he was a married journeyman cooper.[5] However, Pinkerton was ambitious, and hot-headed. Shortly after marrying, he had left Scotland forever, making his way to Illinois.[6] Settling initially in the Scottish émigré settlement of Dundee, he had resumed his old occupation of cooper, before finding that he was rather adept at tracking down miscreants – soon, he had become something of an unofficial police officer, there being no state-wide law enforcement organisations at that time.[7] After realising that his detective skills were somewhat under-utilised in Dundee, Pinkerton relocated some 40 miles south-east to Chicago, initially becoming Deputy Sheriff of Cook County. It was then a natural development, in the early years of the 1850s, to form his own private detection agency.[8] In 1855, he was awarded a major contract to police the local railroad network, which required the hiring of other operatives to help police the rail lines.[9] His reputation was growing, as were his successful cases; hence his need to work a full week when necessary, including weekends, however much his family wished for his company. His image as a fearless investigator of crime had now, on this summer's day, led to a stranger, this young woman, turning up at his office, having heard of his career and his agency.[10]

Little is known for sure about Kate Warne. She was said to be a widow, childless, but with parents who needed supporting. She was also said to have been born Kate Hulbert in Erin, New York State, in 1830.[11] At the time of Kate's birth, Erin had a population of just under 1,000; even at its nineteenth-century peak, in 1880, it would fail to reach 1,600 before decreasing to under the thousand again by 1900.[12] Her parents were not well off, and she and her siblings had to work from a relatively young age to help the family fortunes.[13] Marriage offered women such as Kate a chance for financial security, but it often happened that this security failed to materialise. Such was the case here, for when Kate married and became Mrs Warne, she found herself widowed by the age of 26. In search of a regular job, she moved, with her parents and brother, to Chicago, and came knocking on Allan Pinkerton's door.[14]

Although Kate could have simply turned up at Pinkerton's door that day, apropos of nothing but the desire to get a paying job, it is more likely that she had seen one of Pinkerton's newspaper advertisements, and noted Pinkerton's obvious ambition in making his agency not just a local concern, but a national one.[15] A growing business was likely to need a growing number of employees, and so her decision to visit Pinkerton's office was not based on an explicit vacancy at the agency, but on the hope that an ambitious business might need more staff, even if it was not advertising for such. In addition, even a cursory read of the local papers would have instilled Pinkerton's name in her mind; earlier that month, he had made the headlines after exposing what was described as a 'grand swindling scheme' involving four men who had started their own bogus bank near to Pinkerton's own office. Pinkerton's testimony in the subsequent court case was reported by the *Chicago Tribune*: it highlighted his investigation methods and how he had been able to arrest and examine one of the suspects. For anyone with a taste for excitement and intrigue, such tales of the private detective's work were sure to whet their appetite for a similar job.[16]

Up to this point, Pinkerton had employed only men – but this was because it was men who had answered his calls. Understandably, therefore, he assumed that the young lady in front of him was seeking secretarial work.[17] When she corrected his assumption, she made clear that she had particular skills that a man might not, as a private detective: 'I can go and worm out secrets in many places in which it is impossible for male detectives to gain access,' she told him. Pinkerton was impressed by the fact that she had obviously thought about the matter, and when she gave him numerous other reasons why she could be of service to him, he found himself increasingly convinced that he should employ her.[18]

Allan Pinkerton was unusual when it came to male employers in the mid-nineteenth century. He was able to see beyond the crinolines popular at the time, and look objectively at the needs of his agency. He recognised that what Kate Warne said was true: women might be able to infiltrate situations where men were too obvious. They could play on their gender, encouraging men to trust them and confide in them – what we would see as a form of honey-trapping. Subsequent generations of male detective agency proprietors would similarly see women as offering unique skills in detection and infiltration, but Pinkerton was arguably the earliest. Although he asked Kate Warne for time to think about her request to join his agency, by the time she returned to the office the next day, he had made up his mind to employ her. She met his rigorous moral standards in appearance, being polite, honest, and respectably dressed. In addition, her inexperience was a bonus in Pinkerton's mind; he preferred to take on those with little or no previous detective experience, as he could then train them himself, the way he wanted them to work. He therefore became known for his willingness to find, and gift at finding, operatives in unusual ways, and create expert spies out of them.[19]

Kate Warne joined what was then still a small-scale agency, with around nine male agents on its books, including George Bangs – Pinkerton's second in command following the departure of Rucker – Timothy Webster, a former New York police officer, and Adam Roche, a German native.[20] Kate joined, however, as the agency was about to expand further. The Chicago office was joined by ones in New York, Baltimore and Wisconsin, and Pinkerton's National Detective Agency was being written about in the press as a highly successful agency with close links to the police, that meant they could operate across America.[21]

In 1858, Kate was assigned her first major case, working as part of a team on what became known as known as The Adams Express Case. It centred round the theft of rail company secured bags by employees, but it needed a woman to befriend the wife of Nathan Maroney, the man accused of the theft, in order to find out where the money stolen had been stored.[22] Kate's role would be one that female detectives would find very familiar half a century later: for Pinkerton noted that when an individual had a secret, he (or she) inevitably needed someone to confide in, and to talk to about that secret. Nathan Maroney must surely have confided in his wife, and so now Kate was required to 'ingratiate herself into the confidence of Mrs Maroney, become her bosom friend, and so, eventually, be sure of learning the secret of her overwrought mind by becoming her special confidante'.[23] Kate took on this new role with alacrity, posing as a southern woman, the wife of a jailed forger, and sticking to her complex back-story. She told her boss, 'I feel sure I am going to win,' and Pinkerton commented, 'She always felt so, and I never knew her to be beaten.'[24]

Kate was in effect being asked to take advantage of another woman's loneliness and desire for company; Pinkerton admitted that Mrs Maroney had few friends, and seems to have struggled to get other women to like her. It was no wonder that she sought out Kate's company, and appreciated her company and confidences. This would become a regular feature of female private detectives' work – the need to manipulate other women's insecurities or friendlessness in order to gain information. Yet in both Pinkerton and Kate's view, this was not a betrayal of other women, for the women they targeted were suspected of knowing about a crime, even if they had not committed one themselves; in addition, in Pinkerton's mind, Mrs Maroney was immoral, and judgemental, and therefore deserved everything she got, just as her husband deserved punishing for his crimes. The ends justified the means.[25]

In early 1861, Kate was assigned her most high profile case, working alongside her boss. The president–elect, Abraham Lincoln, was in Philadelphia, preparing to make his way by train to Washington to be sworn in as president. It emerged that there was a plot to assassinate him as he headed from Baltimore to Washington, and so Pinkerton was dispatched, 'with a large force of detectives, male and female', to protect him.[26] This account was produced in the 1890s allegedly from Pinkerton's own archives – but given that many archives relating to the early years of the agency had not been preserved, or had been destroyed, it seems more likely that the account originates with Pinkerton's own memoirs, which were not averse to a bit of exaggeration. Pinkerton does not appear to have had a 'large force' of female detectives at this time, and of the agents who were named in 1894 as being involved, all but one were male.[27]

According to legend, it was Kate who was tasked with intercepting Lincoln and his team, and telling Norman B. Judd, Lincoln's security chief, about the plot, before persuading him to change Lincoln's plans. She also went undercover in a Baltimore hotel lobby, doing needlework and making polite conversation with other guests.[28] Pinkerton said that Kate was adept at getting information out of strangers: 'she had an ease of manner that was quite captivating' and was a 'brilliant conversationalist when so disposed, and could be quite vivacious'.[29] In other words, her 'womanly' skills in talking, and encouraging confidences, enabled her to get vital information about a plot to kill the president–elect.[30] These skills would be frequently noted in female private detectives during the nineteenth century.

In the desire, perhaps, to fully recognise Kate's role as Pinkerton's first female detective and, by implication, being America's first female detective, her position in the Lincoln story has been made much of in recent years; yet accounts over the nineteenth and early twentieth century differ in how much credit she is given. Some reports refer to her dress, her manner and personality, detailing how she was able to extract information out of individuals that ultimately helped her foil an assassination plot. Yet in others, she is only mentioned a couple of times, and one of those instances is to show her booking three rear carriages for her 'party' on the train. This suggests more of an administrative role for Kate, as though Allan took charge and gave Kate specific instructions for tasks he wanted her to complete as his underling. The truth is probably somewhere in-between. If anything can be concluded, it is that finding an objective account of what happened in February 1861 is hard to come by as each narrative has its own agenda: even Pinkerton's own first-hand accounts were written decades later, and with the aim of marketing or publicising his agency and its numerous 'firsts' to a new, modern audience. But across the accounts, the name of Kate Warne survives.

The woman herself, of course, didn't. In a very cold week in 1868, she succumbed to pneumonia, still aged only in her thirties. She was buried in the Pinkerton family plot within Chicago's Graceland Cemetery. Some six weeks later, on 13 March 1868, the news had reached her home state of New York, with the *Buffalo Daily Courier* reporting that day:

Mrs Kate Warn [sic], a celebrated female detective, and head of the female department of Mr Pinkerton's agency for 13 years, has died lately.[31]

The Buffalo paper then referred to the many 'stories' of Kate's detective skills that had been reported by the Chicago newspapers; news of her death had also been covered by the local papers initially, which is how other publications from further afield then came to learn of it. The first newspaper in Illinois to have covered the news of her death may have been the short-lived publication *Chicago Republican*, whose fulsome report, possibly furnished by Allan Pinkerton himself, was copied in its entirety by an Ohio newspaper on 19 March.[32] This early obituary noted the facts which have become part of the Kate Warne mythology – in particular, the poor upbringing that meant she took on 'many of the household cares of a numerous family' from a young age. The obituary also challenged, though, the preconceived ideas of a woman's value lying in her looks and her quietness; it made clear that Kate was notable because of her refusal to behave in a conventionally 'feminine' way:

> She was a marked woman amongst her sex, with a large, active brain, great mental power, an excellent judge of character, and possessed of a strong, active vitality ... She was always equal to any emergency that came. Her firmness, will and character enabled her to subject everyone who came within range of her mind to her ideas.[33]

Although the Buffalo paper only included a couple of sentences on Kate, other American newspapers soon built on the news, including full obituaries, using a combination of fact and myth, and concentrating on what was known of Kate from the time of her joining Pinkerton's onwards; her life prior to that would always be somewhat sketchy. Her achievements as a detective, however, were fully recognised from this time onwards; it was noted that she had shown that women could do so much more than they had previously been assumed.

By the time Kate Warne died, she had taken on numerous other jobs for Pinkerton, and had become superintendent of his female section. This seems to have meant, in reality, overseeing a home that was provided for his female agents, where one of her roles was to ensure that the female detectives behaved in an appropriately 'moral' way (Pinkerton had a 'strict rule of moral probity').[34] It appears to have been a task akin to being a matron – one wonders whether this 'domestic' role was requested by Kate, or whether she was placed in it against her wishes.

Although she was known both within Pinkerton's agency, and within Chicago, she was little known outside of this local arena, however, and it was her death that propelled her into the national consciousness – and then the international. The cut-and-paste nature of journalism for much of the nineteenth century meant that the UK press took its American news largely from the American press, it being cheaper to copy their news than to employ a correspondent themselves. When the US press published Kate Warne's obituary, the British press learned not only of her death, but of her life as well, and started to republish her obituaries to entertain their own readers with this tale of an unconventional American heroine.

The news of Kate's death took six months to reach Britain, and so July 1868 saw a spate of identical, or near identical, obituaries appear in newspapers across England, Scotland, Wales and Ireland. Possibly the first newspaper to include an obituary was the *Morning Advertiser* of 7 July 1868 – which itself utilised an account of Kate's life that had appeared in the *New York Revolution* – with the bulk of British news stories then appearing between 9 and 13 July.

The British coverage of Warne's death focused on the Adams Express robbery committed by Nathan Maroney, laying the solving of the case purely at Kate's feet and thus contributing to a mythologising of her story – in this version, she was not only in 'charge' of the case, but also, after the loss of $10,000, she undertook a 'long and intricate search' and 'followed the package step by step until she finally recovered it except 485 dollars, at Jenkintown'. There was no mention of the male agents involved in the case – including Pinkerton – and no mention that Kate had been charged with following 'Mrs Maroney', rather than a package of money, even if it was hoped she would find the money by following the woman. She was also given the credit for foiling the plot against Lincoln – thanks to her 'precautionary steps as to her intimate knowledge of the plot and ready judgement suggested'.[35] It was stressed that she took on a role far different to traditional gender roles, with it being noted that 'whilst in Washington [during the Civil War], her experience was varied and startling, she having to combat with the whole army of female spies and secret agents of the rebels'.[36]

This 'army' shows that women in America were taking on an active role in subterfuge, detection and spying work during the 1860s. As with the case of British women during the First World War, during times of conflict, women were able to work outside of accepted gendered positions in aid of the greater good. The likes of Rose Greenhow, a notorious female spy who evaded Allan Pinkerton for some time, proved that women's accepted skills of persuasion and communication were not all they had: they were also good at tasks such as deciphering codes and transmitting messages, and this could be something of an eye-opener, showing that intellectually and physically, they could be the equals of men.[37] So although Kate Warne may have been an early, or indeed the first, example of a female operative in America, it was not long before she was joined by others. They were working for different people or organisations, and perhaps for differing reasons, but they were united by their gender and their desire to do something extraordinary with their lives.

The early female detectives in Pinkerton's agency are shadowy for more reasons than the simple nature of their job. Little is known about either Kate Warne or Hattie Lawton, another woman employed by Pinkerton.[38] This lack of concrete information has helped create a somewhat ghostly image of a brave female spy – an image helped by Pinkerton's later descriptions of her and her operations, as detailed in his memoirs. Much of Kate Warne's career, like the basic facts of her life, has also been mythologised over. This is as though her value and newsworthiness lies in the myth as much as the reality: a curated image of a woman as created originally by a man, Pinkerton, in his memoirs. This reflects the oft too common fact that women in history have tended to be portrayed by men, created in the shape that men have wanted to see them, or conversely, ignored; the facts of their lives remaining less known than those of their male counterparts.

In reality, Kate Warne was likely to have been less prominent than Pinkerton suggested; again, he was an able publicist, and it was in his interest to promote his use of a female detective in the mid-nineteenth century to get publicity and to show how his agency was innovative and creative. However, by the time Kate Warne died, opportunities for female detectives were also growing on the other side of the Atlantic, and she was not the first female detective to appear in print in the United Kingdom. Instead, new opportunities in England and Wales led to a series of stories about fictional female detectives being written that reflected the dawning of a new reality.

The stranger leaves, and in the Divorce Court in due course she appears – as witness to the indiscretions of her too confiding friend. She is the Lady Detective.

Cardiff Times, 13 March 1897, p.7

Chapter 3

Monitoring Morality

In obituaries of Kate Warne in the American press, it was noted that as she was 'undoubtedly the best female detective in America, if not the world', she would leave 'a void in the female detective department which it will be difficult to ever fill'.[1] Over the coming decades, many women in both America and Britain would attempt to fill that void, and show that Kate Warne's exploits and career could be achieved by anyone with the need or desire to break free of conventional gender roles. Is it true, though, that we should thank Kate for women working as private detectives by the late 1860s in countries outside of the US, such as in the UK? The absence of news stories about Kate in the UK press during her lifetime suggests that her career did not reach across the Atlantic, and the coverage after her death also implies that she was a rarity in being a female detective.

However, she was not alone, although prior female detectives had been either employed on an unofficial basis, or as part of police activities.[2] For example, in 1851, the Great Exhibition at the Crystal Palace required undercover police work to help detect thieves. Both men and women were employed to pose as ordinary visitors, walking around the site to monitor the behaviour of others. The 'female detectives', as they were even then described, were employed to walk arm–in–arm with undercover policemen, posing as their wives or sisters, so that any potential thieves would believe that this was an ordinary couple and be lulled into a false sense of security. The female detective was here recognised as serving a vital purpose and not just a decorative one, for she would study onlookers, and discuss with her male companion who looked suspicious, and which passers–by might have ulterior motives.[3]

Although the employment of women as detectives in such contexts did exist in England, it appears to have been on this kind of basis – working for the police on specific 'projects', serving as much as foils or distractions as serious spies. They were also employed by specific organisations or companies, usually to help detect thieves at work; in 1855, the Eastern Counties Railway, which ran services between London and Colchester, started to employ female detectives specifically for this purpose.[4] These were unusually progressive employment schemes, however, and the fact that we know about them is because they were deemed so unusual that they made the news across Britain.[5]

Male private detectives also employed females to help them, but these women were often employees not of the detective, but of a household being investigated by that detective. For example, in 1854, a Cheltenham magistrate, Omwell Lloyd Evans, then aged 37, suspected his younger wife, Mary Sophia, of criminal conversation with Robert Ansley Robinson.[6] The couple had married only four years earlier, but had soon found that they were not compatible, and separated. Mrs Evans was allowed a substantial annual allowance, and returned to her father's to live. However, in 1853, she moved to London and her husband suspected her of meeting with Mr Robinson. Charles Field – the former Met Police detective turned private detective – was duly engaged to investigate, but he chose to pay the cook at Mrs Evans's lodgings, Sarah Grocott, to spy on her. Sarah used a hole in the drawing room door to spy through, and reported back to Field that she had seen Mrs Evans sitting on Robinson's knees, and that they had been in 'a position which left no doubt of a criminal intercourse taking place'.[7] Sarah had called over two other female servants to look through the hole and corroborate her evidence.

When the criminal conversation case was heard at the Liverpool Assizes, all three servants gave evidence, but the jury 'placed no value on their oath' and acquitted Mary Sophia Evans and Robert Robinson of any untoward behaviour.[8] Doubts about the women's evidence centred on their social background: one of the witnesses, Mrs King, in whose house Mrs Evans had lodged, had formerly run a cigar shop near Covent Garden Theatre and admitted that at one time, she had been a 'kept woman'. The second woman, a Mrs Price, was described as 'a person very much below' Mrs King, while Sarah Grocott was not only a butcher's wife and a cook, but had been 'hired to act as spy'. Their testimony, then, was 'worthless'.[9]

These women were not professional private detectives, but they had been paid to undertake investigative work, and show that women might be involved in such tasks while also engaged in other paid work – detective work was often one of a series of temporary, short-term jobs. The dismissal of these women's findings was typical of a society that focussed on social position and gender roles; their evidence was not believed firstly because they were women, and secondly because they were women from the lower social orders. They were not seen as respectable, and that would be an issue for the wider private detective world even at the end of the century and into the twentieth.

This example of the doubt as to the ability of female detectives was not unique in the 1850s. It was also expressed elsewhere, as when the Eastern Counties Railway's female detective was asked to help identify a thief who was stealing property from the first-class waiting room at Bishopsgate Station, the railway's terminus. The thief was eventually tracked down, but when he appeared at Worship Street Police Court in December 1855, the female detective's vigilance was called into question, as the thief had managed to steal a portmanteau from 'under her very nose' while she was supposed to be on surveillance duties.[10] A suspicion of the abilities both of working-class individuals, and women, combined to instil a doubt of the capabilities of the limited number of female detectives in the minds of the public, following such cases being reported in the press. However, by the time Kate Warne started work for Allan Pinkerton in Chicago, a change had taken place on the other side of the Atlantic that opened up the opportunities for British women to similarly take on new roles as female 'private enquiry agents'. That change was the passing of the Matrimonial Causes Act in 1857, which came into effect in January 1858, and this piece of legislation is largely responsible for opening up the world of private detection to women in England and Wales.

Prior to 1857, in these countries, divorce was only possible by means of a private Act of Parliament, thus making the legal end of a marriage out of reach for all but the wealthiest members of society. Indeed, in the years between 1700 and 1857, there were only 314 Acts for divorce, mostly started by husbands, showing the limitations of such a form of divorce.[11] In the absence of divorce, many unhappy couples either continued living in the same property but with little interaction, or underwent an informal separation. Some simply abandoned their spouse or family, moving elsewhere and later being found living with a second family.

Change came with the Matrimonial Causes Act, but this was a system weighted in favour of men. The Act introduced divorce by means of filing a petition for divorce in court. Although this would still cost money, it was immediately more affordable than by the previous parliamentary means. However, divorce was only allowed on the grounds of adultery; and if you were a woman, you had to prove additional complaints against your husband in order to be allowed a divorce. Your husband had to have committed adultery, and that adultery either had to be incestuous, or else you had to prove that in addition to adultery, a husband had also been guilty of bigamy, cruelty, or desertion. Cruelty could be violence, rape, sodomy or bestiality, and any desertion had to be of two years' duration or more.[12]

When the Act was passed, there was horror in some quarters at the idea of more couples ending their marriages. For months, there were stories in the press regarding the opposition of the clergy to divorce. Then, in December 1857, hundreds of clergymen signed a petition opposing the Act, stating that they believed such an Act could not be used to stop the 'indissolubility of marriage' and that they could refuse to marry any divorced person.[13] For some unhappily married couples, though, the Act was a lifeline. One of the early cases to reach the courts was that of Omwell Lloyd Evans, who, after his criminal conversation case failed, successfully petitioned for a divorce in February 1858.[14]

However, although the rates were far higher than the previous century, the number of divorcing couples was still small. In 1858, just 24 divorces were granted, although the figure jumped to 114 in 1859. By the end of 1868, a full decade after divorces were permitted in the civil courts, 1,302 had been granted.[15] In this first decade, 1861 saw the highest number of granted petitions at 196; this would not be exceeded until 1873.[16] Part of the reason why the number of divorces was relatively small was undoubtedly due to the necessity of finding evidence that would prove adultery – and, in the cases of women petitioning for divorce, the additional poor behaviour on the part of their husbands that was required by the law, in addition to the cost of providing this.

The 1857 Act brought women more freedom, but at a cost. To seek a divorce was to see their private lives played out in court, to have to prove sometimes horrific behaviour towards them by the person who was supposed to love and care for them, to gain some kind of notoriety for their decision to seek that divorce. It had financial implications, but it also led to a growth in one particular industry that could help them prove allegations against their spouse. That growth was in the field of private detective, or private inquiry, work.

The Matrimonial Causes Act became an opportunity firstly for men to establish themselves as private inquiry agents, and then, gradually, for women to start being used and then formally employed by them. However, it also became the main reason why private detection was viewed with suspicion, and even distaste, amongst some parts of society, including the private detective industry itself – a distaste that has remained to this day. In the 1990s, for example, a survey of private detectives noted that matrimonial enquiries 'could accurately be termed "the policing of personal relationships" and many investigators find it somewhat distasteful for this reason'.[17] Yet, given that such cases have been amongst the 'most frequently requested services' in the private detective world since 1857, it is clear that only the most moral of detectives (and those able to afford to turn down work) would be able to reject such cases.[18]

Between 1850 and 1859, there are just thirty-one mentions of private inquiry agents in the newspapers included in the British Newspaper Archive. This number increases to eighty-eight in the following decade – nearly a threefold increase, as the Act started to result in more individuals being granted a divorce.[19] These 1860s' private inquiry agents were not solely concerned with divorce cases, as the relatively small number of divorces granted during this decade would indicate that such specialising would not be financially viable for agents, but this era did see the start of a new branch of work for them.

In the 1860s, those working in private inquiry work would have been unlikely to advertise their services in the press, or even boast about it among friends and associates, because of this 'disreputable' connotation of the job title. It appears that it had already, by this stage, become associated with grubbing around in search of people's secrets; of following married men and women round in the hope of finding them in flagrante with others, in order to prove adultery in the courts. The disreputable nature of such work, or perceived disreputability, had been identified on the other side of the Atlantic – despite the existence of a Divorce Act – by Allan Pinkerton, when he stressed that his agency would not undertake such work. He wanted to set out his respectable credentials, suggesting that monitoring morality, as others saw it, was seen as an occupation only worthy of the lowest of the low.[20]

Because of this link, in part, there was a perception that private inquiry agents must be lower-class individuals, although this was clearly not the reality. Ignatius Pollaky was a Hungarian immigrant who, once established in London, lived a solidly middle-class life – but his fellow detective, Frederick Smith, for comparison, had formerly been a wine merchant in Manchester, and was the son of a county magistrate.[21] It was certainly true that anyone could afford to set up as a private detective, for Smith was once asked whether he had needed any capital to start up, and answered:

> None at all. I was employed by gentlemen to make inquiries… In June 1850, I began to work on my own account.[22]

However, the stories about women undertaking detection work on an amateur basis tend to involve women from the emerging lower middle class – the daughters or wives of tradesmen and shopkeepers, for example, rather than being women from labouring backgrounds. A piece in the *Morning Advertiser* in 1861, for example, headed 'Juvenile Delinquents and Lady Detectives', notes the efforts of Miss Louisa Gillott and her sister in protecting their father's shop on Fetter Lane from teenage thieves. Having monitored the behaviour of the suspects, Louisa set up a watch through a curtained window at the back of the shop, and told her sister to take up position in the hallway of the private entrance to their living quarters, to watch the shop's interior through a glass door. They both waited there patiently until the youths entered, and watched them carefully until they saw one take a fishing rod from the shop. At that point, 'Miss Louisa darted from her place of concealment and detained him, while her sister informed her father', who chased the other thief and caught up with him in nearby buildings.[23] This daughter was both resourceful and brave, as well as being strong enough to hold a teenaged boy until he could be taken into custody. The willingness of these women to take part in the apprehension of offenders, and to help protect their family's businesses, highlighted that many Victorian women were not gentle, domestic creatures but able to take an active part in maintaining an ordered society. However, unlike the 1853 case mentioned before, Louisa Gillott's actions were implicitly approved of by the press, because she was helping her father, and thus acting out of a sense of responsibility rather than out of a desire for financial reward.

The Matrimonial Causes Act provided the impetus for existing private detectives to expand their work, undertaking the surveillance of husbands or wives alongside their existing cases. It also enabled others to start a new career, one that was open to all classes as it involved nosiness, persistence and an attention to detail more than the need for money. There were few overheads, but plenty of potential. The accounts of the 1860s show men diversifying and making a living working on divorce cases – but women were starting to make an impact too: indeed, 'from the beginning women operatives worked in arenas inaccessible to men'.[24]

Women were primarily recruited to become domestic servants in order to spy on their employers. Besson and Hemming, a mid-century agency supplying domestic servants, were struggling to find staff as their reputation for charging high fees from those on their books had spread. When divorce petitions started to be filed in 1858, they saw the chance to diversify, now recruiting men and women to work ostensibly in domestic service, but actually to find out information about them that could be used in court cases.[25] Although they were neither professional nor discreet, employing former criminals or poverty-stricken individuals desperate for money, they were an early example of how agencies could exploit the Matrimonial Causes Act – and how the Act provided new work for women as undercover servants; the smaller detective agencies relied on matrimonial work, which became 'the metier of female investigators'.[26]

As with the story of Kate Warne, it is hard to be sure of facts when it comes to the number of women working as private detectives in England and Wales in the 1860s; certainly, if you go by press coverage alone, you would be forgiven for thinking that there were no women working professionally in the field at that time. As John Walton has phrased it, 'surprisingly, given the central place of the private detective in popular culture, very little evidence exists about who played this part in reality. There are plenty of stereotypes . . . but almost no evidence.'[27] However, by looking at literature of the time, it is possible to see how the career was seen as a real possibility for women, and not a fantasy. For, from the early 1860s, stories and books started to be published that featured female detectives – and they were not viewed by their readers as tales of make-believe, but rather, as something both realistic and aspirational. I believe that the fact that these books could be written and published, and at this time, during the first Golden Age of the female detective in fiction, is evidence that the female detective was both a realistic prospect, and a reality by this time.

At [my father's] death, there was nothing for me, so far as my relatives could see, but to become a governess or a companion. The idea of such dependence was hateful to me, and so were the two or three situations I filled before my mind travelled elsewhere. I had always been particularly fond of detective stories, like a good many other people whose own life is uneventful... I applied at a certain detective agency and... perhaps my self-confidence, or something in my appearance, was in my favour, for I was soon after given a trial.

Unnamed lady detective in *The Sketch*, 24 January 1894, p.704

Chapter 4

The Female Detective: Fact or Fiction?

In 1864, while Kate Warne was on active service for Allan Pinkerton, Andrew Forrester's *The Female Detective* was published in the UK, followed some months later by William Stephens Hayward's *Revelations of a Lady Detective*. These were the precursors not only of a range of books about the female detective over the next half a century, but also of the British detective novel itself.[1] Wilkie Collins' *The Moonstone* (1868) has been perceived as the first of this kind, yet it is the female detective in British fiction who came first, albeit written initially in serial form.

Forrester's *The Female Detective* avoids the mundanity of the real detective's divorce cases, in his depiction of female detective Miss Gladden and her criminal cases, although she herself recognises that 'in a very great many cases women detectives are those who can only be used to arrive at certain discoveries'.[2] An important part of her job is to ascertain people's real characters, and to step in undercover when police have failed to solve a case.[3] Female intuition, the ability to strike up acquaintances with other women and get them to open up about their lives, and to utilise one's own curiosity about people are seen as vital skills for the female detective – skills that are seen as 'different' from those of the male police force, and perhaps reasons why they fail to solve some of their cases.

Joseph Kestner has suggested that the female protagonists of Hayward and Forrester were able to be created as the result of a 'complex interaction of social, moral, institutional and gendered practices' over the course of the nineteenth century.[4] Yet he also sees these lady detectives as works of the imagination, for:

Some [protagonists], contrary to all historical actuality during this era, are detectives at Scotland Yard. Others are employed by private enquiry agencies, while some work independently of either an official or private institution, being self-employed.[5]

This is echoed in the introduction to a modern edition of *The Female Detective*, in which Mike Ashley notes, 'when *The Female Detective* was first published in May 1864 there were no women detectives in Britain'. He notes that Kate Warne had been employed as a detective in 1856 across the Atlantic, but then segues back to Britain with the formation of the Women Police Volunteers in 1914.[6] He thus ignores half a century of female private detectives in Britain. Although Mrs Gladden is a fictional creation in so far as she is asked to work on cases by the police, and refers to the need for 'female detective police spies', her working methods and skills are those of the private detective, together with her recognition that hers is seen as an unrespectable job.[7] Similarly, Mrs Paschal, the lady detective of Hayward's *Revelations of a Lady Detective*, clearly states that she is employed on cases through the head of the Metropolitan Police's detective department, noting that 'it was through his instigation that women were first of all employed as detectives'.[8] However, her comment that she 'became one of the much-dreaded, but little-known people called Female Detectives' clearly brings the private detective to mind; those who have to carry out investigative tasks secretly, and who, when discovered, are reviled by the public.[9] In addition, although she is tasked with projects by the Met, she is clearly not a member of the force, per se, but works on her own initiative – a self-employed private detective whose main client is the Metropolitan Police, rather than a police detective. In this light, Hayward did not imagine a female detective; he was creating a character who was already starting to emerge in Victorian Britain.

The fact that Forrester and Hayward were able to publish their stories, and gain an audience for them, suggests that the idea of a British female detective in the middle of the nineteenth century was not perceived as something unbelievable, or preposterous. It was unusual, perhaps, to be what Forrester calls the 'petticoated police', but not impossible.[10] It is tempting to see the advent of these stories as being a reaction to the exploits of Kate Warne and her American colleagues, but also as a recognition that in Britain, too, women were being recognised as having skills that made them able detectives, not just in an amateur sense, but also professionally. There is also the possibility that these two 1860s female detectives were created as private detectives, but given a police association in order to justify the wider variety of criminal cases they were engaged to help with; in reality, a private detective would have been engaged more on civil cases than criminal, and more petty cases than murders or major thefts. A literary creation, of course, would utilise the more extreme cases, the more newsworthy types, rather than the often more mundane reality of the private detective.

Is it correct to say, as Kestner implies, that these female detectives could not exist in Britain, and did not exist there, in the middle of the nineteenth century? One of the historical problems in assessing the involvement of women in detective work during this middle period of the nineteenth century, as mentioned in the previous chapter, is in finding the evidence for it. There may not be women in the staff records for the Metropolitan Police for this time – with several historians all repeating the assumption that 'there were no women attached to the Metropolitan Police until 1883', when two women were appointed to oversee female prisoners – but does this mean that women were not employed by Scotland Yard in any capacity, informally?[11] I would suggest that they might well have been employed, but not on a formal basis. Rather, they may have been employed on an ad hoc basis, in secrecy, for specific tasks: as, indeed, was William Stephens Hayward's female detective. Certainly, there were press allusions to women carrying out detective work for the Met police by the 1870s, as will be discussed later.

The evidence is always going to be elusive, and shadowy, because of the very nature of women's employment in this area, and the job itself; it should not be taken as fact that women were not working for the police, just because the paperwork does not exist to prove it. However, where Kestner is particularly interesting is where he suggests that although female detectives in literature were fantasies, they also 'accorded with cultural aspirations'.[12] This suggests that women were seeking, wanting, occupations beyond the home. Of course, working-class women had been taking on work outside the home for a long time, but for middle-class, educated women, the choices had been more limited – teaching or governess work, for example; those few occupations deemed to be suitable for unmarried women from families that were educated but not wealthy.

The fictional female detectives were similarly impoverished but intelligent, and imbued with skills seen to be particularly associated with women – the ability to observe, unseen; to note details, for example, of someone's looks, or actions; to assimilate into a household and develop friendships with suspects, putting them at ease, with the female ability to converse (or, in its more pejorative form, to gossip) enabling the gaining of valuable information. In addition, the recognition that women had a valuable part to play in detective work, whether in reality or fiction, challenged the patriarchal hierarchy. It gave women power by the recognition that she could undertake surveillance, watching men as well as women, rather than men watching women.[13] This was a subversion of traditional stereotypes, and reflected a growing awareness that women had skills that could be used for jobs not previously perceived as 'ones for the women'. The newspapers of the 1850s and 1860s record women tackling thieves and undertaking surveillance work, showing not only that Victorian women were able to carry out detective work – they wanted to, as well.

This challenge to the status quo, to the Victorian ideal of the 'angel in the house', was clear even in these early fictional representations of the female detective. These were independent women – whether by necessity or choice. Even their names were not necessary; it was their professional achievements rather than their personal lives that were depicted as important. These were women who were portrayed in terms of their jobs, their successes, rather than in terms of their domestic achievements. They may have been seen as fictional, with the reality of the female detective not widely known, perhaps, but they were certainly aspirational fictional heroines. Indeed, in 1868, it was noted, in relation to detective work, that 'females are useful in the sphere to which the wants of society have long been loath to assign them'.[14]

Male private detectives, as this newspaper comment suggests, clearly saw how women had skills that had uses far beyond the domestic sphere. Maurice Moser, a Scotland Yard detective who later became a private detective – and whose own wife, Antonia, will later be discussed in terms of her own career as a female detective – stated that:

A woman has a much greater command of herself [than a man]. She can disport herself with less obtrusiveness, [and] her sex in itself is a species of protection. She possesses a certain unexplainable power of always ... defending herself, often with great success, by clever fending and finesse.[15]

What the male owners (such as Maurice Moser) of detective agencies also understood was that financial insecurities, for example, as a result of a husband's death, might necessitate an intelligent, educated woman seeking employment as a lady's companion or even as a domestic servant – and such a servant might invite more confidences from a wife than one from a lower background might. These factors can be seen in both Andrew Forrester's *The Female Detective* and in the *Revelations of a Female Detective*. Forrester starts his narrative being deliberately vague as to the motivations of his detective:

> It may be that I took to the trade ... because I had no other means of making a living; or it may be that for the work of detection I had a longing which I could not overcome. It may be that I am a widow working for my children – or I may be an unmarried woman whose only care is herself.[16]

But all characterisations and backgrounds clearly sound feasible; this is a woman who has no man to provide for her, so she has to find the means to do so herself. She stresses that as 'criminals are both masculine and feminine', detectives need to be of both genders as well, because women have 'far greater opportunities than a man of intimate watching, and of keeping her eyes upon matters near, which a man could not conveniently play the eavesdropper'.[17]

These detective novels of the mid-1860s were both a reaction to the growth of the private detective industry following the Matrimonial Causes Act and to the increasing professionalisation of policing, which had led to the creation of the police detective in the 1840s.[18] In turn, the success of fictional stories about British female detectives, and the obituaries of Kate Warne reaching the pages of the British press, created a growing awareness of, and interest in, the life of a private detective, alongside an awareness that women could offer a great deal to the world of policing.

On both sides of the Atlantic, the mid-century saw coverage of amateur female detectives; just as shopkeepers' daughters and intrepid wives in Britain were fighting crime, so too were American women, such as Mrs Mary Cox of New York, who, in 1866, found an Irish migrant named

Patrick O'Connell in her front room, stealing her cutlery, and chased him up Flushing Avenue, where she found a police officer who could take him into custody.[19] In Detroit, in 1869, a local journalist travelled to Chicago to visit the base of Allan Pinkerton's National Detective Agency, to see for himself how it operated – resulting in a report that was soon copied and published in the Scottish press. Although an Oban and Argyllshire paper made clear that it was repeating the story because it would be of interest to its readers 'who remember its organiser [Pinkerton] as a boy in our own city' (despite Pinkerton being from Glasgow, not Oban or Argyllshire), it did not comment pejoratively on its employment of females as a 'private police force', and so made it appear a usual employment for women, rather than the relative novelty it still was by this time. It stressed the high moral standards that Pinkerton insisted on, and how this was reflected in how male and female detectives worked at the 'office':

> It frequently happens that women can be employed far more advantageously than men; and, indeed, there are places where women can be employed with success, as Mr Pinkerton's experience has fully proved. In this establishment they are employed as frequently as men; and the rule as to intelligence and moral character applies to them as well as to the rest of the establishment. They have separate apartments, and occupy a separate floor ... The compartments for the ladies comprise a kitchen, bedrooms, offices, and all equipments necessary for an effective police force. Both the male and female service are in charge of a chief, to whom they render an account of their work, daily, in writing. These statements are then entered in a regular record book, indexed, filed, and put away safely for future reference.[20]

With British newspapers covering the employment of female detectives in America, and the popularity of stories and novels about the 'lady detective', the profession was becoming normalised, to some extent at least. In England, this reflects the after-effects of the Matrimonial Causes Act in requiring not only men, but women, to 'snoop' on married people and to find evidence of adulterous liaisons; although there was concern at women being employed in this manner, there was also a pragmatic recognition that both men and women could commit adultery, and that if proof was needed of this in the divorce courts, then there needed to be people who could help prove (or even disprove) allegations made against them.

In America, as in Britain, the exploits of Kate Warne, covered by an eager press, helped publicise the possibilities of private detective work to others. America was just ahead of the game, for before the 1860s were out, women were being identified as detectives in professional work. In one article from 1869, the *New York Times* reported how $40,000 of jewellery had been seized from passengers on a Cunard steamer on its arrival into port. Two men were searched by the customs surveyors, who found the smuggled goods on their bodies. Only in the final lines were the readers told that on the same ship, 'two elegantly dressed young ladies came in the way of the lady detectives, and upward of $10,000 worth of jewellery was found upon their persons'.[21]

In Britain, the Matrimonial Causes Act gave women a gendered role in detective work that men could not do, by gaining the confidences of wives; in America, female detectives were becoming recognised for spotting and searching female smugglers. Even in 1869, their work was being reported without comment, as though an accepted part of life, but it would take a while more for the lady detective to become a regular feature of life both in London and New York.

In the early days of my youth, I possessed a most curious hobby, namely, watching people. I used to haunt railway stations and other public places, and, so to speak, try to frame in my imagination the pursuits of the passers-by.

Kate Easton, in the *Northern Scot and Moray & Nairn Express*,
12 February 1910, p.2[*]

---

[*] The longer letter this extract comes from was described in the newspaper as being by an anonymous 'lady correspondent', but it has been ascribed to Kate Easton by Susannah Stapleton

Chapter 5

From Amateur to Professional

In the following decade, the initial tales of fictional detectives continued to be advertised, sold and read, suggesting that their stories were attractive to an audience who presumably included women wanting to learn of more exciting lives than theirs, perhaps, were.[1] Some women continued to work for male detectives, going undercover to find out salacious information for divorce cases, but without necessarily making a full-time profession out of the work; others took on work for the police, where a woman's 'touch' was seen to be necessary. Other women were not detectives per se, but eagerly took on the role when they saw an opportunity, suggesting a desire for excitement and challenge that had not quite manifested itself as a desire for a career.

In 1873, for example, Rose Chippendale was shopping when she saw three youths hanging around the shops on Denmark Street in Bristol. Thinking them suspicious, she moved nearer, and heard one of them say, 'It's all square now.' She watched them go over the road to a shop run by grocer Mrs Alder, and, from her vantage point in the lobby of another shop, where she couldn't be seen in the shadows, she saw two of the men go into the shop, where one put a box – containing some 33lbs of raisins – onto his shoulders, and then all three ran off. Rose duly gave evidence in the subsequent committal hearing of the three for theft.[2] As in previous eras, the Victorian world, with its shops and consumerism, provided ample opportunity for women – unsuspected, for they were expected to be in such environs – to use their eyes and ears to monitor the behaviour of others, and to report crimes being committed.

Other women were given the opportunity to work as private detectives as a result of their own prior reputation on the other side of the law – as consumerism increased throughout the late nineteenth century, so too did the temptation to shoplift or otherwise steal fashionable items for oneself. On occasion, a woman who had been tempted in this way might be used by police to net a larger fry. This occurred, for example, in 1877. Bradbury Greatorex was a long-established London textile merchants and warehouse that stored and delivered cloth.[3] After 88 yards of silk and 7 yards of cloth were taken from the factory, three men were charged with theft. One of the accused, 18-year-old Robert Clough, worked for the company, and another, George Blacker, 24, had been the firm's porter. The two men had met another, Edward Slow, aged 26, in a local pub eight months earlier, and soon the three were accused of workplace theft. Robert Clough immediately pleaded guilty, and gave evidence against his two friends.

What was interesting about this case was not the theft itself, or the guilty plea, but the evidence that came from a woman named Eliza Bissell. She was a married woman, who lived locally.[4] She also knew the accused men, Slow and Blacker. Eight weeks earlier, Slow had asked her to buy some silk, but she told him she couldn't afford it. He eventually persuaded her that it was a bargain; and she pawned it for £2, giving Slow the money. So far, so usual. But then the police, who had become aware of the theft, got in touch with Eliza and employed her to engage Slow in a honeytrap. She got in touch with him, and bought 16 yards more of the silk, seeing him take it from a box under his bed. Slow told her he had another 70-odd yards, and so Eliza returned to his house the next day and bought the rest 'under the instructions of the police, who gave me the money'.

The police officer who had got in touch with Eliza was William Osborne, a detective from the City of London police, who had been notified of the crime by Bradbury Greatorex. Under cross-examination, Eliza stated that:

'I knew Osborne before, and knew perfectly well what I was sent for – he did not threaten to take me in custody for pawning silk – I knew that I was going as a species of female detective.'[5]

In Eliza's case, she was from a working-class background, and had been willing to buy stolen silk – receiving stolen goods. She didn't have enough money to buy the goods, and had to pawn them in order to pay Slow for them in the first place. She clearly struggled to maintain herself and her family, but was tempted by cheap silk to commit an offence: perhaps she imagined it someday becoming a fashionable item of clothing that she could wear, making her look something other than she was. Imagine her feelings when a police detective she knew (and how did he know her? Had she come to his attention before as an offender?) suggested that she play detective, trapping the thief into confessing his crimes. She was given money that she *had* to spend on the silk, enabling her to feel as though she was rich. But more than that: she was clearly proud of the fact that she had been commissioned to be a 'female detective', given a role, a title, and a job that sounded both glamorous and dangerous. Eliza took on this temporary role eagerly, finding a temporary boost in taking on this title. It's clear that many other women must have felt the same, as it gave them a sense of usefulness and importance both within their community and to those in positions of social power or respect.

This is also clear by looking at what other women were concerning themselves with during this decade. The issue of baby farming – where women promised to look after other women's babies for a fee, but then either neglected them or even killed them for the money – would be an area of concern for the police and public for much of the late nineteenth and early twentieth centuries, with Amelia Dyer being perhaps the most notorious of these figures. These baby farmers were predominantly female, and so their placing of money over womanly care of infants was seen as particularly abhorrent, and against nature. Margaret Waters was hanged for the murder of a child in her care, John Walter Cowen, in October 1870, and her case preoccupied the press and the police. Both press and public felt that the police were failing to get to grips with the issue and to charge these baby farmers with offences. The alleged crimes of Margaret Waters – given the nickname of 'the Brixton ogre' – particularly concerned one 'amateur lady detective', who took it upon herself to investigate the issue of baby farming. She engaged various other agents to help her make inquiries, and found that 'children are murdered in scores by women like Waters in Brixton, and that "adoption" is only "a fine phrase for slow or sudden death"'. This female detective uncovered the methods used to kill the children – by giving them unsuitable food, drugs, or simply starving them – and went undercover to befriend one such baby-farmer, pretending to be a potential farmer herself. This woman told her:

> 'Take my advice: don't see the child, and then you don't feel its loss at all. As I always says, if you once see it and hear it cry, you may want to keep it; but the best saying is, "What the eye never sees, the heart never strives for," and it's true, my dear.'[6]

The baby-farmer told the detective the details of how she killed her charges, and the latter also uncovered evidence of collusion with medical men, who knew what was going on but agreed with the baby-farmers' assertions of the baby refusing to eat, or of being weakly. This detective duly reported her findings, and the press expressed horror and 'humiliation' at the 'insufficiency of the law under which such things can exist'. *The Times* went further, as it 'urges the importance of volunteer investigations as the only way in which the dreadful mysteries of baby-farming can be detected or exposed; yet surely the law should do something too'.[7]

This points at a wider issue in the 1870s – that of trust in the police and the criminal justice system. Press reports point to the feeling, in some sections of society at least, that the police were slow to do their jobs, and did not make enough effort to investigate cases deeply enough. Cases covered in the press show women increasingly carrying out their own investigations, feeling perhaps that it would be quicker than trying to engage the police. One Belfast woman in 1870 took it on herself to track down a 14-year-old in her service who had absconded; she tracked him down to the docks, where he was preparing to get on the Glasgow-bound boat. Instead of calling the police at any point, she located him herself, and seized him by his collar, taking him away with her to mete out her own form of punishment.[8] Her skills as a 'lady detective' who had found and punished a youth all on her own were singled out as worthy of respect.

Of course, these women were detectives in a looser sense of the word; others called them detectives, and they did not describe themselves as such, nor did they work as detectives or inquiry agents. Others did, in this decade, though, and – reflecting the female detective novels of the time – some appear to have been working for the police. The *Pictorial World* in 1877 covered the death of a London woman whose career as a female detective 'furnishes incident enough for half-a-dozen sensation novels'.[9] This unnamed individual had been employed by the 'authorities of Scotland Yard' as a detective for several years. She went undercover, cultivating a friendship with a local parish doctor, and pretending to be a nurse. She was duly asked to nurse local families – but these families were ones suspected by the police of dishonesty. She became a trusted figure in the background of these families' lives, and they forgot to be restrained in front of her.

Just as with divorce cases, where female detectives took advantage of the trust placed in them to encourage confessions of adultery from their 'friends', or to let incriminating details pass their mouths, here, the nurse listened carefully as the sick and fever-ridden patients, or their relatives, admitted to crimes committed, or the whereabouts of fugitive contacts. In another case, the police asked the woman to try and find out which local house a gang of coiners operated from; she pretended to be ill, and persuaded a child who had emerged from the door of one of the suspected houses to take her indoors for a moment. As she made her sudden entrance into the house, she heard 'metallic sounds' from an unseen coiners' workshop – the money-makers had not heard her come in, and so were still at work. When they realised they had been found out, the gang leader threw a ladle of molten lead at her head, but she was wearing a poke bonnet, and although the lead burnt her hat, and her hair, down to the roots, she was not more seriously injured.

This still unnamed woman also apparently disguised herself as a boy to infiltrate various thieves' dens, and faced danger on many occasions – on some, having to take part in hand-to-hand fights, and in another case, being discovered and beaten, fracturing her skull. Her story indeed sounds like a sensation novel, and the fact that she is not identified even in an obituary gives some reason to believe this might be a work of fiction. However, a very familiar story had been published in an Irish newspaper the preceding year, and this initial report suggests that this was the same woman whose obituary had subsequently appeared. In this account, the female detective – then, of course, very much alive – was interviewed by the newspaper's reporter, who told his readers that 'it is not generally known that a certain number of females are employed by the Scotland Yard authorities to track thieves of the lowest and most dangerous type'.[10]

The reporter described an 'unwomanly', 'low-class female detective' who lived in a poor neighbourhood and posed as a nurse, having no fear of entering contagious households in order to gain information on local thieves. Although she was described as lower class, this appears to have been a subterfuge – 'she is able to study and adapt herself to all the habits, coarseness, and foul language of her low-bred clients'. This small, muscular woman frequently wore boys' clothing and taught herself self-defence. As in the 1877 *Pictorial World* report, she had received a fractured skull during a case, and the police – who had been watching from outside – rushed in when they heard her spring her rattle. An 1876 account has some more specific information, which suggests that the obituary leaned on this earlier account for some basic details; it even states that her poke bonnet had cost 24 shillings and was a 'formidable erection of silk and flowers' and that her involvement led to the French gang leader being arrested on the Continent and condemned 'to the galleys' for eighteen years. The female detective's personality and attitude was summed up by a quote about the burns she received from the coiner's ladle:

The female detective complacently remarked that as nearly all her hair was burnt up by the roots, and the little she wears is fixed on by artificial means, it is easier for her to dress up as a boy.[11]

Although the story might have been dramatised or embellished by the press, it is likely to have had some truthful origin; it had been established that people trusted women, that they were good at adopting false personas and encouraging confidences, and so it is not unreasonable to assume that the police, needing someone who could convincingly sit in a sick person's home and encourage them to talk, might choose a woman for that role. The press, though, also recognised that women wanted to hear of others of their sex who had 'dangerous jobs' (as the female detective's role was termed), and found tales of these women exciting. The fact that this individual was armed with a whistle, rattle and other tools by the police, and knew that she only had to use these to summon the men of the law to her aid, helped make the tale more acceptable: women could have a role in detective work, as long as they could be rescued by the male police.[12]

By the time the 1870s ended, the female detective was being accepted as a reality, with the first newspaper advertisements appearing relating to them – a male inquiry agent, Mr Ward, for example, was publicising his 'male or female detectives' who clients could 'engage at a moment's notice' to work on divorce, financial losses, and robbery cases, in 1879.[13] In addition, the first professional lady detectives were being named, rather than remaining anonymous figures.

In one of the earliest press reports, however, from 1880, the naming was in connection with a court case that indicated some of the problems such independently minded women had in starting their own businesses – certainly when they were married. The case came before Clerkenwell Police Court in June 1880, and was brought by Mrs Caroline Smith, who lived at 29a Beaconsfield Buildings, on the Caledonian Road in north London. Caroline 'obtains her livelihood by making private inquiries for solicitors' as a female private inquiry agent, reported the press, making clear that this was no amateur concern to occupy a bored wife, but a professional, paid, career to keep her and her family solvent. As with many women in the subsequent decade, Caroline had learned her skills from her husband William, who had been a police constable before himself becoming a private detective. But now her marriage was over, and she was trying to ensure that her estranged husband could not get his hands on her earnings, or on the property she had been able to buy with these earnings since he had left her.

The former Caroline Greenwood, a bootmaker's daughter, had been born in 1846, and married twenty years later in Lewisham.[14] At the time of their marriage, husband William was a police constable based in Lewisham, but the couple settled initially in Greenwich, before relocating further north, and had several children.[15] However, William was not a reliable man, and deserted his family on more than one occasion. The first time he had also taken £40 – the family's savings. On the last occasion, in December 1879, he deserted her without a word, and failed to pay her or her children any maintenance then or later. The resourceful Caroline, having seen her husband at work, utilised the skills she had seen him use, and set up herself as a private detective, in order to keep her and her children from the workhouse.

However, Caroline was aware that her position was not secure. As a married woman, she was deemed the property of her husband. They were not legally separated or divorced, instead, although he had deserted her and clearly had no intention to try and resolve matters, he could still threaten to take the property she had come into the marriage with, unless she took legal steps to prevent this. The Matrimonial Causes Act not only set out that the property and future earnings of a divorced wife would remain her own, but also, in cases of desertion, women were similarly able to protect their earnings and property.[16] Therefore Caroline, rather than settle for her current situation, went to the police court to ask for an order under the Act to protect the property she had acquired, and the earnings she had made, since the time her husband had deserted her. She made clear her position, stating that she 'made her money by private inquiries and she now wanted her furniture and earnings protected. She was afraid, if an order was not made, her husband would again want to come home, and would take her things.' The order was duly granted.[17]

Although detectives had a varied career in terms of longevity, Caroline Smith was a relatively early known example of a professional female private detective working on a fairly long-term basis – she made a success for herself in terms of managing to support her family on her one income. The 1881 census – carried out on the night of 3 April, so ten months after her court case – shows that she was still working as a private inquiry agent at that point, although this is not to say that she earned a lot; it may have been simply enough to keep the wolf from the door.[18] For Caroline, and numerous more women who would follow, though, becoming a private detective was no longer seen as simply an amateur role – it could form part of a longer term, paid, career.

In fiction the woman detective is always young and fascinating; her skill in handling delicate situations and solving the most puzzling mysteries arouses admiration. She is fearless and knows how to handle an automatic pistol. Prepare to be astonished; greet one in real life!

The San Francisco Call, 3 August 1913

Chapter 6

The Emergence of the New Woman

It is clear that by the time the 1880s dawned, women on both sides of the Atlantic were increasingly taking part in traditionally male preserves of life, seeking and gaining more challenging and rewarding roles outside of the home or traditional 'female' jobs. This change has been seen as the result of what Patricia Marks has described as a 'variety of social forces [that] propelled the late nineteenth-century woman out of the doll's house created for her protection and light'.[1] The New Woman, described as a 'free-spirited and independent [woman], educated and uninterested in marriage and children' has been more associated with the 1890s.[2] However, the changes in women's lives were becoming evident in this previous decade, as single women competed for jobs, and when competition for the usual jobs – as governesses, teachers and nurses, for example – was either too much or not what these women desired, they looked elsewhere for satisfying work.

This change in how women wanted to live their lives was recognised in parts of the press, but the changes were seen as part of a feminine desire to improve the world and its inhabitants. This can be seen as a patriarchal society seeking to rationalise women's changing roles by portraying them as part of their natural 'caring' instincts rather than a need to exist on an equal basis to men, or as the result of a desire to be challenged in their daily lives. Therefore, in June 1881, the *Birmingham Evening Post* detailed various roles being taken on by the modern woman, stressing that 'the ladies are everywhere working with tremendous energy for the benefit of their fellow creatures'. There is a distinctly patronising, mocking tone taken in such reports, it being noted that such 'ladies' were constantly organising fancy bazaars, picnics, and private theatricals in aid of charity.[3]

These women were seen as the successors to Josephine Butler, the famous social reformer and friend of fallen women; other women had read about her example and followed suit, picking their favoured causes to fight for, from the consequences of drunkenness to supporting soldiers. These women can be seen to be rallying against the boredom and tedium of traditional women's roles, to be fighting to have a more physically or intellectually demanding life than that ascribed to them historically. Yet to the male-dominated press, they were latching on to any cause and annoying men in the process. The *Birmingham Daily Post* focused on one woman in particular, who they didn't name but described as 'the daughter of one of our mathematical scholars, and has studied mathematics herself with great success'. She had established herself as a 'lady detective' with her role being rather different to the other female detectives written about in the press of the previous decade. She had decided to focus on improving the lives of animals, and acting as an agent for the Society for the Protection of Animals, she would investigate those who used animals in their daily lives, such as wagoners or carters – transport being, of course, horse drawn at the time – and check that they were treating the animals humanely. She thought nothing of tracking individuals for miles until she could get help to bring them to justice, apparently on one occasion running alongside a butcher's cart from Harrow Road to the Willesden Police Station in order to make the butcher answerable to the police. This lady was said to have 'taught herself by observation to know from the very gait of a horse whether he is suffering from any injury which however cunningly concealed by the driver cannot escape detection by her vigilant eye'.[4]

This 'lady detective' was a brave and determined individual, using detective work for a more unusual cause than others, and was happy to appear before the magistrates as a witness in cruelty cases. However, her activity and her physical fitness made her the subject of amusement – she would think nothing of walking 14 miles a day, paid to establish animal drinking troughs throughout London, and even hired a paddock to house sick animals while they recovered. This, to the press, made her a curiosity, an eccentric, even while she saw herself simply as a detective tracking down those who were guilty of animal cruelty. It has been noted that the press in the late nineteenth century took an 'apparent delight in the incongruity between the common notion of feminine weakness and submissiveness and the actuality of women's strength of purpose', but there is also evidence that the press attempted to reduce women's status back to weakness by portraying her as odd, obsessive, or compulsive in her actions.[5]

When lady detectives were not being seen as eccentric, they were being portrayed as of negligible social status. It was clear that there was uncertainty as to where in society they belonged. A serialised story – *The Hand of Destiny, or, The Mysterious Tenant of Francton Holme*, by Henry Frith – in the press in 1889 made this evident. In Chapter 15, Phyllis discusses the occupation of female detective Miss Hamilton with her servant. Phyllis has previously described Miss Hamilton as 'only a detective', which amuses the latter; but after she goes to bed one night, Phyllis's servant comments,

'As nice a young lady as ever stepped, Miss … She is a lady born, no matter what her business is.'[6]

As with the lady detective looking out for animals, Miss Hamilton confuses people by being well educated and polite, yet also taking on a job that is perceived to be the preserve of more lower-class, rougher, men. There is a confusion in the press and literature of the 1860s to 1880s about where these lady detectives belong, and whether or not the profession is 'respectable' for women. However, there is also a gender divide at play in terms of male private detectives being perceived as inherently duplicitous, lower class and akin to conmen, whereas women are depicted as more genteel but down on their luck financially, or without a man to look after them. The reality did not always reflect the fictional or press representations: male private detectives were increasingly, as the nineteenth century progressed, from the burgeoning lower middle class, with former solicitors or bank clerks well represented among the ranks of private detectives. Others were former police detectives, which explained part of the suspicion towards them; opinions differed on whether policemen were to be respected, or mocked for their perceived failures or their lack of imagination. But coverage of private detectives' lives and jobs reflected uncertainty in Britain about social class and strata; the previously well-established classes were fragmenting, society was becoming more egalitarian (although still stratified) and the press coverage can be seen in terms of concerns over social stability and how moves into these more democratic or classless jobs might threaten that.

This conflict between the value of private detective work in giving single or widowed women the opportunity to earn money without sacrificing their social standing, and the perceived threat of working women using both their intellect and physical ability to the gender status quo can be seen in detective literature of the 1880s. The most significant work to address the female detective was Leonard Merrick's book *Mr Bazalgette's Agent*, which was first published in 1888. It showed the change in depictions of lady detectives, and suggested a growing awareness of the profession for women in this decade. In part, Merrick's book was a result of detective fiction as a genre increasing in popularity by the latter decade, but it also suggested the growing popularity of detective work as a career for women, and its decreasing novelty.

The period between the publication of Andrew Forrester's and William Stephens Hayward's books about the female detective in 1864, and the publication of *Mr Bazalgette's Agent* two decades later had seen a steady rise both in works of detective fiction, and works involving women in an investigative capacity. In Britain, Wilkie Collins had, of course, created the character of Sergeant Cuff in *The Moonstone,* published in 1868, and a year later, in France, Emile Gaboriau's novel about the eponymous detective *Monsieur Lecoq* was published. Both these characters were, however, police detectives rather than private inquiry agents. Most famously, Arthur Conan Doyle's first Sherlock Holmes story, *A Study in Scarlet*, was published in 1887 in *Beeton's Christmas Annual.*[7]

Also in Britain, the 'penny dreadful' had been revolutionising literature, making exciting tales of detective work accessible to all classes by making publication cheap and widespread.[8]

On the other side of the Atlantic, the dime novel was the American equivalent of the penny dreadful, and Harlan Page Halsey – who created the dime novel detective Old Sleuth in 1872 – had, eight years later, also created his own fictional female detective, Kate Goelet.[9] The female detective was therefore being written about in literature, not just in the 1860s but through into the 1880s, as part of a wider, and increasingly popular, detective fiction genre.[10] Alongside this was the growth in detective memoirs, which offered the excitement of 'real life' tales and were seen as complementing the fictional stories. When former Parisian detective Gustave Macé's memoir, *My First Crime*, was published in English in 1886, it was compared to Gaboriau's works:

> Monsieur Lecoq doubtless worked upon a framework of fact, but in this case we have an account of a real crime, traced out by a real Lecoq ... It is a novelty, and shows that reality is often as strange as fiction.[11]

Alongside this interest in detective fiction and memoirs was an interest in 'women's fiction'. Adverts in the press in the mid-1880s listed new editions of 'popular works' that all focused on women's lives: these included *Formosa, or, the Life of a Beautiful Woman*; *Skittles in Paris: a Biography of a Fascinating Woman*; *Agnes Willoughby: a Tale of Love, Marriage, and Adventure* – and *The Experiences of The Lady Detective*.[12]

Although a real-life memoir such as Macé's appealed partly because of its curiosity or 'foreignness', the fictional detective, both male and female, was becoming less of a novelty. This was reflected in the construction of Leonard Merrick's book. Unlike the works of Andrew Forrester and William Stephens Hayward two decades earlier, *Mr Bazalgette's Agent* is not a sequence of short stories, each one looking at the different jobs taken on by the female detective, but a more traditional single narrative. It doesn't need to comprise several melodramatic stories focusing on the novelty of the protagonist's career and the unlikely cases she is involved with, but instead is more akin to the male-led detective stories, allowing the female detective – in this case, 28-year-old Miriam Lea – to be represented in a more three-dimensional way.

However, there is clearly some ambiguity in how the female detective is depicted. Just as press stories of the time debated the 'problems' of women seeking charitable missions or physical exercise, and debated what 'class' detectives, especially female detectives, were from, so too does Merrick try to portray Miriam and her world as conventional. It is stressed in the book that she has to become a detective only out of financial need, rather than desire, and this is the focus of one contemporary press review of the book: 'the story deals with the fortunes of a young girl who left to her own resources is driven to accept an engagement as a female detective'.[13]

Miriam is allowed to take part in her adventures and her detective work – which are seen as being necessary for her financial survival, rather than out of enjoyment – as long as she reverts to type at the end by falling in love and marrying.[14] The focus of the narrative becomes love rather than work, duty rather than excitement. It reflects concerns about the New Woman subverting traditional stereotypes and challenging the stability of conventional society that would grow over the course of the following decade.

It should not be suggested that in the 1880s, the female detective was common, either in fact or in fiction, but she was becoming better known, and thus the profession was becoming a possibility to women who previously might not have been aware of it. Tales of female detectives increased in the British press, although they often focused on the 'foreignness' of these detectives, with stories from America, for example, being popular. One story that originated in the States, but was copied by provincial newspapers across Britain, involved a female detective in Chicago, and was published in 1888. The way this woman's story was written again suggests a confusion about how to depict such women, and to estimate how common it was for a woman in the 1880s to be a private detective. The location of this story suggests that the individual in question might be employed by Pinkerton's agency; it starts by stating that 'Chicago has many female detectives' but then later refers to the fact that there are 'so few female detectives'.[15]

The female detective is not named, because the concealment of lady detectives' names is seen as a vital part of their role – 'There are so few female detectives that it would not do for them to become known. Their occupation would be gone, and it would be a difficult matter for their employers to fill their place.' This reads as an attempt to portray the occupation as one not many women wanted to have – when the evidence, certainly within a decade, suggests otherwise. It was also stressed that the female detective would 'rarely, if ever' appear in court to give evidence – thus opening her up to identification and publicity – because 'her evidence is carefully collected, and then corroboration secured before the case is brought to trial'. Although this might provide a reason why so few female detectives are named in press reports of divorce cases, for example, prior to the 1890s, it also, again, serves to try and reduce women's roles: their evidence is not sufficient for court – it always needs backing up with corroboration (from men?). The report claimed to have interviewed the Chicago female detective, a 50-year-old inevitably described as 'motherly', who started out by posing as a domestic servant in order to investigate the wife who lived there without her husband, and had also posed as 'a strolling fortune teller, and as a book agent, and a pedlar of patterns'. She stressed how much 'domestic misery' was out there for her to investigate, particularly in the 'fashionable world', and drew attention to the importance of social rank:

> Women will suffer every imaginable indignity and insult rather than let the facts be known, for exposure means almost invariably the loss of social position – dearer to most women than life itself.[16]

Although this stress on rank was used to explain why women might prefer to remain in an unhappy marriage to going through a divorce case, it can also be seen as highlighting the importance of social position for women in late-Victorian society, and how female detectives might be subverting that traditional focus on maintaining one's rank. The female detective was feared by authority – and the male-dominated press – because nobody was sure how rare or common she was, what social status she had, whether she was subverting gender roles (in *The Hand of Destiny*, Henry Frith had a character describe a female private detective as 'a policeman in woman's clothes') and how duplicitous she was capable of being, in secreting herself into households.[17] She also reflected wider fears about women 'acting' a role, even if that meant pretending to be a happy wife when in reality, she was anything but.

The concern over women taking over men's roles, of confusing both gender and class stereotypes, and of having the potential to be more successful in investigating cases than men was brought to the fore in the autumn of 1888. This was the year of Jack the Ripper: the series of murders committed on women in the East End of London by an unidentified perpetrator. The perceived failure of the Metropolitan Police to capture the killer and guarantee the safety of women in London led to substantial public concern and press criticism.[18] The police had attempted to utilise different methods to help track the killer, but were perceived to have bodged the investigation, such as by failing to secure crime scenes (the public are often detailed as being present), get evidence, and communicate effectively. The attempt to use bloodhounds to sniff evidence was depicted as a comedy in some ways, with the police failing to pay to use the dogs they had organised, and then failing to tell colleagues involved in the investigation that there were no dogs available to go to a crime scene, leaving others waiting some time for dogs that never turned up.[19]

It is not surprising, then, that others sought to make suggestions as to what the police should do. Frances Power Cobbe, a social reformer and women's rights campaigner, saw the failure of the police as being due to the gender of policemen and detectives. Prior to the murder of the final victim, Mary Jane Kelly, she had argued that the employment of female detectives within the police would help solve the case, and in coverage of her argument, one provincial newspaper, at least, agreed with her ('the suggestion is not half a bad one').[20] She summarised the skills of the female detectives, stating that:

> She would pass unsuspected where a man would be instantly noticed; she would extract gossip from other women much more freely; she could move through the streets and courts without waking the echoes of the pavement with a sonorous military tread; and lastly, she would be in a position to employ for whatever it may be worth the gift of intuitive quickness and 'mother-wit' with which her sex is commonly credited.[21]

These were all skills already used by the female private detective, and Cobbe clearly saw their value. Women were already employed by the police on an informal basis, and so Cobbe's views were not a complete novelty – but here, she was arguing for the formal employment of women within the police force, on the highest profile case that existed. The press, although recognising that her suggestion had its merits in relation to the Whitechapel murders, were keen to highlight the drawbacks of then continuing to employ women on other, subsequent cases:

> There are moments in the detective's life when a lady would probably – to put it mildly – feel embarrassed. How, for instance,

would she set to work if she found herself alone inside a dark room, with a couple of burly burglars? Or how would she set about pursuing and capturing them, supposing they took to flight over successive walls, or shinned along the sloping roof of a house? The lady detective, or even the lady policeman, would be rather at a loss on such emergencies. The world is doubtless rude and unfeeling, but it harbours the suspicion that, except in special cases, where she is already employed, the fair one would lack the courage and activity so absolutely essential in the detective profession.[22]

Women were physically weak; scared; embarrassed. This was the press reflecting conventional views about women that were already being challenged in the private detective world. The tales of female detectives in the press and in fiction showed that women actually had physical and mental strength, and skills that enabled them to investigate cases in a more effective way than their male equivalents. There was acknowledgement that some women were already working, and working well, as private detectives, but the 1880s was not fully ready to commend them, or even give them individual recognition. Instead, their anonymity was justified on the grounds that women didn't want to be identified out of modesty or because it would make them unable to do their jobs; they were seen as few in number, or foreign, or an anomaly. Other women, such as Frances Power Cobbe, knew their capabilities and tried to promote them, but others wanted to preserve the status quo. While women were perceived as working on a part-time or amateur basis, they were seen as a novelty or unthreatening; when they became more in number, the attitude towards them in sections of the press, at least, became more negative.

It was only a matter of time, however, before the female private detective started to reject the anonymity that others insisted she wanted, and to appear, by name, in court and in the press. Others established themselves as detectives in the 1880s but did not become more widely known until later. One such woman was 'Madame Paul', or Paulowna Upperley, a woman who became a private detective in the same year as the Whitechapel Murders. This was perhaps a coincidence, but given that it was in this year that she was employed by Henry Slater, the famous London detective agency proprietor, and that Slater was always quick to leap on a new phenomenon, or to take advantage of what was going on in the world, it is possible that he saw Frances Power Cobbe's comments about the need for female detectives, and immediately engaged at least one example of the type.[23]

This lady detective was adept at taking on different identities, and was also assertive – although, as the next chapter will show, she was also capable of subterfuge in other ways. She was also able to stay working in this field for at least seven years, and it seems unlikely that she was the only woman who started work as a detective in the late 1880s, perhaps as a result of the Whitechapel Murders and the frustration felt by many at the failure of the (male) detectives and policemen who could not, apparently, catch the killer. Combined with the start of Sherlock Holmes' fame in fiction, the 1880s heralded the start of the Golden Age both of detectives and their female counterparts.

Her appearance is so deceptive that she has gone to every place a man may appear in and never has been suspected as a masquerade with a purpose. See her lounging about with a cigarette between her lips and even the most observing would find nothing in her walk or carriage to betray her sex. But withal she has retained her natural charms. The first impressions of a visitor to Miss West's offices ... is of the pervading air of femininity .... [it has] the aspect of a woman's boudoir rather than that of a detective bureau. Always modest, her womanliness bubbles to the surface in her conversation.

San Francisco Call, 3 August 1913, describing Maud West

Chapter 7

The Golden Age Dawns

Miss Isadore Rush, then aged 31, posed before the *Sunday World*'s camera, manipulating her face into a fierce expression, hoping that she looked both determined and alert. After checking that the photographer had captured her, she then adopted a look of what would later be described as 'feminine feverishness', imagining herself finding a clue. After a series of poses, each as melodramatic as the first, the actress, who described her main hobby as collecting china, collapsed into a chair to be interviewed.

This 1890s photo shoot was to promote Isadore's latest role as a female detective in a theatrical production. Yet her portrayal was not based on fact, and she admitted she had done no research for her role, simply hoping that a combination of 'good sense' and her own personality would make her believable. In response to a question from the *Sunday World*'s reporter, she said,

> 'I really have no reply when I am asked how I studied the part of a woman detective ... such characters are so infrequently met with in real life that they can hardly be said to constitute a type. No, I did not haunt detective agencies or criminal courts. I simply sat down and studied my lines.'[1]

Her portrayal, though, owed something to the literature of the 1890s. She imagined the detective being employed to track a man down, but 'no sooner has she accomplished her purpose than, womanlike, she regrets it ... The victim of the detective's professional zeal captures the heart of the woman. The woman detective finds she is in love.'[2]

Taken at face value, this American actress's response to playing a female detective suggests both that the job was a rarity still in 1897, when the interview and photographs were done, and that the female detective could not be successful in her job because she was liable to fall in love with any man she had to investigate – because, obviously, all women really wanted to do was settle down and get married. A closer investigation, however, shows that Isadore Rush needed to do a bit more research. The fact that she refused to 'haunt' detective agencies or courts – her response made after a question from the interviewer – suggests that, in fact, female detectives could be found in both places. Her portrayal of the female detective falling in love suggests a cursory reading of books such as *Mr Bazalgette's Agent* – books that did not reflect the reality of private detectives either in America or in Britain. For the 1890s saw a significant growth in the number of female detectives operating in Britain, and being named in press reports or giving evidence in court. These were not women who expressed any desire to fall in love during their work – they were of different marital statuses, and had different motives, but none appear to have worked with the aim of romantic love.

Indeed, three years before Isadore Rush's interview, a British newspaper, *The Sketch*, had published an interview with a real female detective. She was unnamed, but the interview was accompanied by a recognisably real woman, labelled as 'a lady detective'. This individual was a young, single woman, who the interviewer made clear did not look as he expected, from his (presumably 'his') experience of 'yellow-covered novels'. He found it hard to believe that 'the quietly dressed, essentially refined-looking, blonde young woman' he was looking at could really be a female detective, but his interviewee recognised his surprise, and rather than ignoring his discomfort in a 'feminine' way, immediately 'asserted':

> 'You are astonished to see a woman under thirty, with claims to being considered a lady, in intelligence, refinement, and a certain amount of good looks so necessary towards attaining an end, unless, perhaps, in the profession of husband-hunting, which, I confess, isn't in my line.'[3]

The interviewer professed himself suitably embarrassed by the lady detective's directness, especially when she added that she could see he felt she was 'degrading' her womanhood by 'putting it to such practical uses'. She added, 'It is no–one's duty to wrap his or her talents in a napkin and bury them.'[4]

The mere fact that these two interviews appeared in the 1890s – an actress playing a private detective, and a private detective talking about her work – suggest a change that had been occurring over the previous few years. The female private detective was becoming more of a known quantity, rather than an urban myth, and she was coming out from the shadows. The actress knew of the female detective's existence; the female detective knew she was of interest, and was willing to talk about her life and job, and to justify it.

Why such a change at this point? In part, it was a progression from the earlier decades of sleuthing; a job that had been carried out on an amateur basis, or temporarily for the police or other agencies, was now becoming professionalised, an opportunity for women from different walks of life to take on a professional role that offered different tasks to those traditionally open to them. Their skills in investigative work were recognised and thus, to some extent at least, accepted. This was not always the case, of course; there remained remnants of older, more socially conservative views as British society struggled with how women were increasingly seeking careers that had previously been seen as largely male. In the satirical publication *Ally Sloper's Half-Holiday*, in 1890, a comment piece relating to an interview given by a lady detective, criticised her lifestyle. This woman had been proud of her job, seeing it as 'exciting and well-paid'. She had also advised other young girls to 'embrace the profession', highlighting how it enabled women to experience different occupations (as part of their disguises) and to challenge themselves:

'I have been a waitress, charwoman, lady's maid, and have attended numerous fancy balls in costume in pursuit of my prey, and don't see why women should have more fear than men.'[5]

Ally Sloper's writer was concerned about her lack of fear, however, seeing it as a sign of immodesty. Private detectives came into contact with thieves, profligates, the debauched and the degenerate: these people were not 'fit company for our girls' and because female detectives had to associate with these people, it made them 'cease to be a woman any longer'.[6]

The views of Ally Sloper were not unique, but such opinions could not hold back the tide of social and political change. More opportunities were available to women now – not just in terms of employment, but also in education, thanks to the improvements in schooling and literacy. The burgeoning women's movement was gaining traction, and legislative change, reflecting women's growing involvement in work, also took place over the 1880s – from the Married Women's Property Acts of 1882 and 1884 (following the earlier Act of 1870), and the repeal of the controversial Contagious Diseases Acts in 1886, to the establishment of the Women's Trade Union League in 1890 and the National Union of Women's Suffrage Societies in 1897.

Women were now increasingly recognising that marriage and motherhood was not the only option for them; they could get jobs and make their own money instead – gaining a financial security that was not dependent on men.[7] The New Women were, by the 1890s, 'a force to be reckoned with'.[8] Not only were they independent, and arguing for female emancipation, they were confident – and this confidence meant that an increasing number were willing to emerge from the shadows of sleuthing and proudly admit to being female detectives. The tales of fictional female detectives continued to be published in the 1890s, but their stories were now being written by women as well as men. Although known as 'Mrs George Corbett' rather than by her own name, Elizabeth, this feminist and journalist created a series of 'lady detective' stories in this decade, including *When The Sea Gives Up Its Dead* in 1894, featuring detective Annie Cory. In 1893, the *Burnley Express* was advertising its serialisation of ten of her detective stories, called *Behind the Veil, or Revelations by a Female Detective*.[9] Elizabeth Corbett had, in 1889, written an explicitly feminist work, *New Amazonia*, in protest at Mrs Humphrey Ward arguing that parliamentary suffrage shouldn't be extended to women. Given her support for female suffrage, it is not surprising that she should, in the 1890s, appeal to other supporters by crafting tales of independent, detective women for their delectation. Alongside her work came the adventures of Loveday Brooke, the creation of author Catherine Louisa Pirkis, in 1894. Loveday was in her thirties, and over a period of around five years, had worked her way up from the 'lower walks' of detective work until she was spotted by Ebenezer Dyer, the 'experienced head of the flourishing detective agency in Lynch Court [Fleet Street]'.[10]

The first British female detectives started to announce themselves as such on the census in 1891. Mary Annabella Burridge was one. She was a solicitor's daughter originally from Wellington in Somerset, but by 1891 was living in Lambeth, south London, with a female housekeeper and a young male lodger.[11] She was from a well-to-do family, and, after the death of her mother when she was 14, it was also a very male family: Mary was living with her father and three older brothers. She was therefore raised in a rather masculine environment, and also an educated one. It may also be significant that she became a private detective after her father's death in 1885. Perhaps he left her money which she used to establish herself in business; or perhaps she wanted to make her own way in life. However, it is not clear how long she remained in this profession; the 1901 and 1911 censuses simply record her as being of 'private means', but it could be either that she only worked for a brief time, or conversely, that she retired from business before the taking of the 1901 census (which could mean that she had worked for a decade or more). Certainly, the fact that she had relocated to Cheltenham by 1901 might suggest a retirement rather than an unsuccessful stint at investigative work.[12]

Whereas Mary Annabella was from a financially stable background, the daughter and sister of solicitors, and remained single all her life, another early 1890s detective was from a very different background, illustrating how the occupation was open to all, regardless of finances or family. Mary Addey was the wife of a Yorkshire-born clerk who worked in the Nottingham lace trade. Born in Nottingham in 1847, she had a taste for adventure fostered after her marriage, when she and her husband moved to the other side of the world – to New Zealand, where their three children were born. It appears that William Addey, Mary's husband, may have been working in the goldfields there, as their daughter Essie's birth, in 1879, was recorded as having occurred in the Thames Goldfield.[13]

The Addeys were back in England by 1891, where they were recorded in the census as living in Holborn, London. William was again working as a clerk, but Mary was clearly listed as a private detective. Her son Gordon, aged 17, was also listed as such, so it is possible that the mother and son were working together from home (particularly as daughter Essie was still at school at the time).[14] Mary's profession enabled her to continue to make a living after William died – the 1901 census records her now living in south London, a widow, but still a private detective.[15] This time, it is clearly recorded that she was the proprietor of her own business, although this probably still means that she was a sole trader – there are no newspaper adverts for her online, and no mention of staff working for her, which you might expect if she had her own agency, rather than simply working as a self-employed detective. While Mary appears to have been able to make a living for some time in this manner – although it's not possible, of course, to know whether there were gaps in the period 1891–1901 in which she wasn't working, or working in a different field – by 1911, she was unable to do so any more.[16] This is likely to be because of age – she was now in her seventies, and working from home making and selling knitting.[17] To be a private detective involved often long hours of mental and physical activity, and by her seventies, Mary was likely to be slowing down and unable, or unwilling, to take on this type of work anymore.

Mary Burridge and Mary Addey were very different women: one was in her thirties, independent, and single, when she gave her profession as a private detective in 1891; the other was older, married, and from a less secure financial background. Mary Burridge wanted a job; Mary Addey needed one. But both chose to work not in the more traditional fields that had been opened to women, but in one that offered something different, and something more: a challenge, variety, hours that fitted in around other commitments, and independence. This was an egalitarian profession, open to anyone with the gumption and determination to do it.

In the 1890s, female detectives were giving interviews – albeit anonymously – in the newspapers, where they detailed the type of work they undertook. The job was clearly fascinating to newspaper readers, who wanted to know who these women were, what they did, and why they did it. In 1896, one newspaper in Wales noted that women had done a lot of detective work in large cities since at least 1870, but because they were not formally recognised by the police, they did not receive regular salaries. Instead, as self-employed individuals, they were paid by commission, or 'payment by results'. The paper was keen to note that this did not mean that lady detectives only earned a small amount.

This publication then interviewed a lady detective – whose name was not given, but who was described as 'a demure person of about 40'. She gave one of the most detailed explanations of her work in a practical sense:

> 'It is only now and then that we are employed by the police, the bulk of our work coming from private inquiry agents or from county courts. For instance, as a writ-server, a woman is obviously ten times better than a man. In such cases we are paid by the regular officials of the law for work they are supposed to execute themselves. But it is private inquiry work that pays us best.'[18]

The interview showed that women were still often engaged by other private detectives – presumably the established male ones – when a woman was needed for a specific job. The private inquiry work was likely to be predominantly shadowing work for divorce cases, but it was supplemented by the less well-paid writ-serving work. The lady detective's comments show a keen awareness of financial issues, and the need to balance different work and different rates, but also a confidence about the skillset of women that made them valuable in the private detective's workplace.

However, it was also a profession that was open to fraud, or at the least, negative perceptions amongst certain sections of society that gave rise to allegations of dubious work practices. Some women, such as Paulowna Upperley, genuinely worked as private detectives, but, when they received confidences from clients, or had clients who did not want it known that they needed a private detective, took the opportunity to try and blackmail them. Paulowna was employed by an Albert Cole in 1891 to make inquiries into an Elizabeth Price, who had homes in both Bristol and London. In order to do so, she established a 'friendship' and confidences with both Elizabeth and her husband, a captain, which led eventually to the Prices borrowing money off her. When Paulowna did not receive all the money she said was owed to her, in 1895, she took them to court. However, in court, it was alleged that Paulowna had deliberately taken advantage of the terminally ill Captain Price, that she used her job to try and extract money from those lives she 'wormed' herself into, and that she was now trying to blackmail Mrs Price.[19] As a result of this case, it emerged that not only had she adopted a fake name – Madame Paul – when she had worked for Henry Slater, but that her 'real' name of Mrs Paulowna Upperley was also fake. She claimed to be the wife of Major Upperley of the Bengal Cavalry, but although this individual existed, he was not her husband, nor had any links to her.[20]

Another 1890s private detective, 26-year-old Ellen Lyon, was employed by George Clarke, a detective based on Cockspur Street in London. George usually operated on his own, but recognised the need for a woman's skills, and so would employ women on occasion to assist him on cases. That term, 'assistant', was typically Victorian in its patriarchal assumptions: these female assistants were very much detectives, and utilised the same skills as their male counterparts and employers. George had, on this occasion, employed Ellen to work on a divorce case. The wife, Gertrude Barrett, had already left her husband and moved into a boarding house, but her husband suspected she was committing adultery. George Clarke asked Ellen to pose as 'Mrs Watson', and to persuade Gertrude to become friends with her. Ellen later reported back that she had seen Gertrude pawn her diamond rings – but Gertrude then accused Ellen of stealing them, as well as having borrowed money and clothes from her. She duly prosecuted Ellen for theft, after employing her own private detective – William Hamilton, who worked for the [Henry] Slater's Detective Agency – to track down Ellen and unmask her real identity.[21]

The prosecution did not succeed; the case against Ellen was not proved, and she was discharged. However, three years later, in January 1895, both Ellen and George Clarke were charged with conspiracy to prevent justice in connection with the Barretts' subsequent divorce case. Ellen had disappeared after the 1892 theft case against her, and it had taken over two years for the police to track her down, despite the fact that she had only moved from east London to south. Ellen and George appeared at the Old Bailey in March 1895, charged with keeping a brothel – the charge based on the allegation that they had 'procured' a man to commit adultery with Gertrude. They were both found guilty; Ellen was sentenced to a year's hard labour, half the punishment given to Clarke.[22]

The case, and its second act, presents the private detectives' work in a rather dark light. Ellen's job had been to form a friendship with a wife as part of a divorce case's gathering of evidence, which was standard fare. However, she was also told to manufacture evidence of adultery, by finding a man who she could persuade Gertrude to have sex with. Prior to the involvement of Ellen and George Clarke, there was no evidence, because Gertrude had not done anything wrong, apart from being a young woman who wanted to leave her marriage.

Once Ellen was involved, though, there commenced a campaign to introduce her to a variety of men, usually at various London theatres and music halls. They would be wined, dined and flattered, with Ellen then suggesting that Gertrude go back to a private hotel with one. Each time, Gertrude – to Ellen's annoyance, presumably – refused. The imputation is clear, though: Ellen was being paid to try and persuade Gertrude to prostitute herself to strange men in strange hotels, and hence the charge of keeping a brothel that was recorded in the Old Bailey records.[23]

The case summed up the concerns of some elements of press and public regarding the employment of women detectives in divorce cases: they behaved in a way that betrayed others of their sex, using confidences and 'friendships' to spy on vulnerable women, and, at their most immoral, to try and make them behave in a way they would not usually. Ellen was unlucky in that Gertrude, although young and fairly naïve, was strong-willed, and was not easily coerced into a sexual relationship; it took time and a lot of effort before she finally succumbed to another man's charms, and the divorce court recognised that she had been 'persuaded' into this action by the private inquiry agents.

Although Ellen had been described in the press as 'assistant to a private detective', she was clearly working as a detective herself, adopting a fake persona, befriending the client, and inveigling her into behaving in an incriminating manner. Her role clearly shows the value of female detectives, and that the male heads of detective agencies clearly recognised this value. It also shows how important disguising one's identity was for both male and female detectives, although this also has the result of making it difficult to ascertain the real names and identities of some of them. Ellen Lyon admitted to police that she used fake names, and of 'Ellen Lyon', she said, 'That is the name I am known by in this case.'

She had told one of her former landlords that she had to change her name and address frequently because of her job as a private detective; her real surname may have been Lawrence, but this might simply have been another pseudonym. She had also been said to have been living as a couple with George Clarke, but was this real or part of their acting exercise for the Barrett case?[24] After the case, Ellen fades from the archival record, her pseudonyms and changes in location making it difficult to track her down, as is so often the case with women whose professional lives were spent trying to hide their identities.

Despite the likes of Ellen Lyon drawing attention to instances of unscrupulousness, and the fact that the detective industry was not regulated (a fact that would continue to be an issue throughout the following century and beyond), female detectives were undoubtedly becoming an increased focus of news during this decade. The 1890s saw a recognition by male agency owners that the employment of women was at the least a good marketing strategy, with London detectives such as Henry Slater, Charles Attwood and Maurice Moser, and provincial detectives including the Sheffield-based Charles Keeling, and his competitor George Harrington being just some of those who eagerly highlighted their use of female detectives.[25] Moser, in 1896, made clear their value, stating that his 'lady clients can consult, in the strictest confidence, the ladies employed and also have the advantage of their experiences in the conduct of cases'.[26] It was clear that women liked being able to talk to other women, trusted them, and were keen to use them; the unscrupulous were seen as a minority and did not appear to put women off employing their own female private detective.

Ladies who 'go shopping' in the West End of London, or in the great suburban emporiums, never imagine that they are narrowly scrutinised by detectives, not, however, by those belonging to the police.

Preston Herald, 23 October 1905, p.7

Chapter 8

Fashionable Females

Although this book is primarily about the female private detective who worked for herself or for an agency on a range of tasks, such as divorce or blackmail, such a history cannot exclude what would become an important source of work for women – the job of the private detective located in shops and department stores. This role itself could not have existed if it were not for the development in the 1870s of a new kind of shopping experience, and the resultant growth in consumerism.

Prior to this time, shops had been a combination of properties, from small, local shops specialising in a single type of product, to the salubrious arcades of Regency and early Victorian England, some of which still survive in cities such as London and Birmingham. The first department store in Britain is likely to have been Harding, Howell and Co's Grand Fashionable Magazine in London's Pall Mall, which opened its four departments in 1796, but this was something of an anomaly for decades.[1] Although historians have looked at how the growth of the 'shopping experience' started to take place earlier, in the late eighteenth and early nineteenth centuries, they have also acknowledged that the drive towards mass consumption was a later nineteenth-century phenomenon, helped by population growth, rising wages, and better transport systems that could supply goods quicker and more easily than before.[2] By 1872, as Erika Rappaport has noted, London, certainly, had become so commercialised that it was described as a 'city of pleasure', and in the second half of the nineteenth century, the culture of shopping was a legitimate 'feminine' occupation. In the city's shops and stores, women could find pleasure through consumption, and from the 1870s onwards, fashion and other female-orientated journals were encouraging women to see shopping as 'women's work'.[3]

This was a phenomenon, again, taking place on both sides of the Atlantic; in America, Elaine S. Abelson has described the new type of emporium that was developing:

The large dry-goods bazaars were ... infused with the images and symbols of the aspiring middle class: the breadth of merchandise, the methods of display, the prices, the physical surroundings – each one proclaimed a similar message. Shopping had transcended functionalism, and the middle-class shoppers were expected to want, if not to purchase, what was visibly arrayed all around them.[4]

The problem with this growth in consumerism is that more women felt under pressure to keep up with others – to consume, to buy more and more. If they could not afford to purchase the multiplicity of must-have clothes and accessories, then the temptation was to steal. Unlike the older family-run shops, where there was an assistant situated behind a desk or counter, positioned between the shopper and the goods, here, items were openly on display, and needed to be taken to an assistant. There was opportunity to secrete an item within one's clothes, or in one's bag or basket, without an employee spotting you. The increase in thefts from stores led to women being employed to detect shoplifters.

Initially, detectives were drawn from the ranks of the shop's existing staff, and undertook their usual work alongside informal investigative or monitoring activity, although as time went on, women were explicitly and separately appointed as detectives, or employed through external agencies (or in their own previously existing guise as self-employed private detectives).[5] That women were not well known as full-time store detectives by the 1890s, though, is perhaps evident through an interview that appeared in an 1896 Welsh paper. A female detective was interviewed about her earnings, and she made clear that most were not in 'receipt of regular salaries'. Instead, they worked on commission primarily for other private inquiry agents, or obtaining work directly through the county courts, such as serving writs. The latter work was particularly popular as it was well paid – the male officials who were supposed to execute the writs finding it easier to outsource the work, and finding that women were good at the job. Occasionally, female detectives would get work from the police, but it was the private inquiry work that paid the best. The 40-year-old detective being interviewed noted that a six-month job shadowing a society woman's rival, and researching her past history, brought her £150 and a gold watch. Her average earnings during the winter could reach four guineas a week, but during quiet times, she might not even earn a sovereign.[6]

This detective did not even mention work in shops and stores: she appears to have differentiated her type of work from that of the store detective. If the store detective was originally a sales assistant who had been asked to take on extra responsibilities in terms of spotting thieves and stopping them from leaving the store, this is understandable. However, by the early twentieth century, women were being clearly described as being store detectives, or being employed on behalf of both stores and charity bazaars. Their jobs involved specifically monitoring other women, who might be tempted by the array of goods and clothing on sale.

That shoplifting was seen as a particularly female crime was made clear in a newspaper report in 1903, which stated that:

> The great majority of shoplifters are women, another example of Darwin's theory of the 'survival of the fittest', the feminine attire being obviously far better suited to conceal a quantity of more or less bulky articles than that affected by mere males.[7]

Yet despite 'professional lifters' having evolved a system of hiding goods – for example, concealing rings in the heels of their shoes, or jewellery and embroidery being attached by hooks to metal garters below their knees – it was believed that it was the 'casual' shoplifter who was more of a problem for store detectives and shopkeepers. Female detectives learned that women commonly had bags tied to their waists, into which they could easily drop items, or arrange their voluminous skirts to form a 'bag' which they could fill with feathers or lace, without it being obvious. The muff, however, was the most popular way to hide stolen goods; it could be rested on a pile of handkerchiefs, for example, and while something was examined with one hand, the other would pull a couple of the handkerchiefs into her muff.[8]

Many of the casual – or more spontaneous – thieves were educated women of good social standing, who were deemed to be kleptomaniacs because of their tendency to steal. It was felt that they had the occasional, irresistible, urge to steal from shops; they were the most difficult to accuse, for if a detective made a mistake, she would be falsely accusing someone perhaps of higher social status of a criminal offence. This would still be the case well into the twentieth century. During the First World War, for example, detective Lilias Emerson was employed to patrol the Red Cross Fair being held at Westminster's Central Hall.[9] Her job was to look out for potential thieves – and so when she saw one woman take a roll of lace, secrete it in her muff, and walk away, she duly reported it to a policeman. When the case was heard at Westminster Police Court, a very aggrieved Mrs Edith Bonham Hillier, a 65-year-old Northampton woman, insisted she could not be guilty of theft because 'she held a very well-known and responsible position in Northampton [and] she was a friend of magistrates there'.[10]

It was unusual, in the early years of the twentieth century, for female detectives to target men. In 1906, when an American lady detective monitoring a shop on Sixth Avenue in New York heard an alarm clock ringing under a man's coat, she had him arrested. George Dolan was sent to trial on a charge of shoplifting; the American detective's success was reported in numerous British newspapers.[11] On this side of the Atlantic, though, it was more usual for women to be reported on as shop assistants taking on the additional role of detective when they suspected a theft, or were tipped off – such as with the case of Miss Johnson, who worked at Messrs Stagg and Mantle's. When one of her customers told her that she had lost her purse, she suspected two other women, who had been looking at hats, of having stolen it. She saw them leave the shop, and followed them to a nearby hotel, where they looked at a purse one of them was holding. She called a policeman, and Mrs Jennie West and Mrs Edith Clements were duly remanded into custody.[12]

However, this was, in some ways, an old-fashioned story, for the amateur shop assistant-turned-detective was being usurped by her professional counterpart. Even back in 1900, Slater's agency, always one to spot a new trend, had publicised how its female detectives had been 'most successful' in their involvement with the drapers' sales that had taken place over the previous few months.[13] By the same year, Minnie Johnston was working as a detective at Peter Robinson's on Oxford Street. She gave evidence at the Marlborough Street Police Court that year when Kate Carter, aged 24, was charged with stealing satin worth just over 11 shillings. Minnie stated:

On Monday afternoon she was duty at Messrs Peter Robinson's shop. She saw prisoner come in and inspect several articles; then she crossed to the silk counter, looked at a number of pieces, and then picked up the piece in question, folded it up, put it under her cape, and left her shop. [She] at once informed the constable at the door.[14]

Just as the male private detectives were engaged in working for merchants and spotting thefts of property or money, so too were the female detectives finding a niche in working in shops and businesses, spotting female shoplifters in the act. In terms of the female detectives advertising their services at around this time – such as the Mancunian woman who placed an advert in the newspaper in 1903 simply stating 'Lady Detective wants work' – it is possible that some of them were working in the expectation that it would be shops that would most need their services.[15] In 1905, it was noted that in some firms, women were directly employed as 'spies upon their own sex', and that it was a usual occurrence in America; but in Britain, although some female detectives were hired directly by tradesmen, it was common for them to be on the staff of private enquiry agencies. These agencies would receive the commission from a store and send out one of their female agents, instructing them to 'watch secretly certain ladies, and to ascertain whether shopping alone occupies so much time'.[16]

It was noted that female detectives were particularly employed by the larger 'emporiums' as the majority of their customers were also female, and so they would be less conspicuous than a male sleuth.[17] However, female detectives operating in stores were still dependent on men – primarily the policemen they had to notify to get suspected shoplifters arrested and taken to the police stations – and their work still revolved around reporting others of their gender for offending, just as they monitored them for sexual misbehaviour in divorce cases, but they were finding that their status as females was sometimes, in work, an advantage. It enabled them to undertake cases where men would be obvious or out of place; other women trusted them, and thought they would not be watched by them. They were, clearly, wrong.

In the Edwardian era, some quite creative efforts were made to stop shoplifting, including, in jewellers' shops, peepholes being cut in the moulding of ceilings, with the detective upstairs peering down through it, unseen by customers, to spot any thefts while the shop assistant was otherwise engaged.[18] In dress and women's wear shops, all the shopwalkers and counter staff were expected to keep a watch on those who came and went, but they were increasingly being joined by professional detectives, who 'assumed the guise' of either shop assistants or customers to hide their real task. When a shop assistant became suspicious of a customer, she would call the detective by a prearranged sign, and so signal the need for the detective to shadow an individual.

The detective had to walk a fine line in her job. Many shop owners and managers wanted to avoid the prosecution of female shoplifters, as they felt it was bad for business, and so, even after a detective's surveillance, they might seek to resolve matters informally. They also used a range of measures to make their shops as safe as possible. Despite this, however, it was seen as relatively easy for 'beautiful articles of value' to be stolen from the famous or large shops, and so the female detective, with her powers of surveillance, was increasingly seen as a weapon to be utilised in the battle against shop theft.[19] Cases where female store detectives had successfully caught shoplifters were praised in court and in the press, further publicising their usefulness; for example, when Mary Stadgett, a 59-year-old shoplifter appeared in court at Westminster, the magistrate complimented the two 'young women' employed by the Army and Navy Stores as detectives, who had followed Mary several times, very patiently, until they finally caught her with stolen goods. The magistrate noted that Mary would not have been committed for trial without their 'shrewdness'; the press, in reporting the case, added that 'the lady detective has been honourably recognised', the one story being used as a means of justifying the existence of a whole profession for the New Woman.[20] This case came from the very end of the Victorian era, the same month that the old queen died, and it feels as though it heralds a new age for the female detective – with increased opportunities and increased recognition.

The female detective's role in capturing shoplifters complemented her other perceived skills. It had been noted throughout the first decade of the twentieth century that not many lady detectives were involved in tracking other sorts of criminals; they were more commonly engaged by businesses to uncover acts committed by either staff or customers that would impact negatively on that business. Therefore, a woman might investigate a case where a firm suspected that another had stolen their patent, or their goods shown to rival firms who had then copied them, trying to find out if an employee had given their employer's secrets away. They might investigate bogus companies or swindlers, and uncover cases of internal fraud within a company. In short, 'any affair where a woman's wit is serviceable [is] where the lady detective goes...It is not an easy occupation, but it is an exciting one for an energetic woman.'[21] A woman was therefore seen to have the energy and intelligence, as well as the capability for studying characters and individuals, to be a useful addition to any company with concerns about its profits and property.

It is not altogether surprising, then, that by the end of the Edwardian era, the female store detective was becoming a more common sight. As one Liverpool magistrate noted:

These emporiums were entrancing even to women of advanced years, he supposed, at the same time these women must not forget that there were detectives in these big shops who were continually on the watch.[22]

Another newspaper explained succinctly why the female store detective, based at such 'emporiums', was so in demand:

It is with the great shopping firms that the lady detective generally finds her chief sphere of employment...A woman has, in dealing with the shoplifter, a thousand better opportunities than a man of watching unobserved. She can make her appearance at the same counter as the suspected lady, and make ostensible purchases which the most acute male detective would infallibly bungle over. The culprit little dreams that the lady who was so intent upon purchases at the same counter, and who seemed so absorbed in the examination of laces and other trifles, gave the signal that called to her the courteous manager, who informed her he had reason to believe she had 'made a mistake' and he must request her presence in his office.[23]

This paragraph is worth dissecting a little bit further. It shows that the female store detective was required to play a part – she had to pose as a customer, and be believed by the other shoppers. She had to look as though she was a genteel lady with money to spare, browsing the items on sale. She had to be able to look intent on choosing an item, while at the same time watching another individual, and noting their behaviour and actions. She was seen to be more capable to subtle actions that did not give her away than a male detective, who would 'bungle' a potential purchase. Although there is the underlying implication that it was only a woman who could make little purchases successfully, it also demonstrates the skillset these women needed, and the necessity of being able to act a role, and act it well. This is an important element of the detective's job that will be explored in more detail in the next chapter.

'Tonight I may be called upon to act as parlourmaid in the house of a man or woman who will figure one of these days as the co-respondent in a divorce case. Later, I may be raising a scene at a bridge table in Belgravia, and so opening the eyes of a bridge-stricken young lady to the way she is being cheated.'

'Why I Shadow People', *Pearson's Weekly*, 4 May 1911, p.759

Chapter 9

Acting the Part

Isadore Rush, in the 1890s, had tried to demonstrate how she, as an actress, could successfully portray a private detective. Conversely, the female private detective had to be something of an actress in order to be successful – more so than her male counterpart. It was relatively simple for a male detective to shadow others, and to be visible and accepted in different environments. For a female, life could be more circumscribed, and so to be if not unnoticeable, then tolerated and accepted, in a number of environments, she had to take on different roles and personas. It was not enough to pretend to be someone else – the female detective had to inhabit that role, to be believed. These women often had to play at being different characters – impoverished widows, governesses, genteel tenants of furnished rooms in lodging houses, or even society women. Given this necessity to act, it was unsurprising that several professional actresses moved into private detective work on a permanent or temporary basis. This may always have been the case – one account of Kate Warne's life states that in her early twenties, Warne also worked as an actress.[1] Although this cannot be corroborated, later in the century, there were several actresses who became private detectives, both because the jobs utilised similar skills in terms of adopting different personas and taking on varied roles – some of which resulted in the press seeing them as somehow immoral, unable to differentiate between reality and the 'fake' identities necessary to carry out both jobs successfully.[2] In addition, because being an actress for much of the nineteenth century was a job that 'fell outside the boundaries of "respectable" womanhood', women undertaking such work might also be willing to consider other non-traditional or respectable jobs for women, such as detective work.[3] By the late 1880s, this was recognised in fiction, at least, for the central character of *Mr Bazalgette's Agent*, the private detective Miriam Lea, is a former actress herself. Another actress turned private detective emerged ten years later with George Sims' fictional creation Dorcas Dene.[4]

These two careers had much in common. Firstly, both actresses and female private detectives came from all classes – both professions were egalitarian in that respect.[5] Often, actresses and female detectives were employed by men in higher-up positions – theatrical managers, agents, the proprietors of detective agencies; although there were, of course, females in these positions, men predominated. Both jobs could be insecure, consisting of short-term engagements where, when the job ended, the money stopped suddenly, too. Both jobs could both involve a fight to get the money due to them; they both involved competition in order to get work in the first place. A female detective was increasingly dependent on newspaper advertising that promoted her skillset and experience; actresses and other performers, too, advertised their availability in the press, flagging their skills in acting, singing, or dancing (often all of the above to highlight their versatility), and highlighting the productions they had previously appeared in. Reading the columns of adverts in late Victorian and Edwardian newspapers, there is an element of desperation in the competing adverts, as women vied with each other for work.[6] What established private detectives made of new entrants into their field – such as the actresses with valuable experience in adopting different roles, seeking what they might have hoped was a more stable career – can only be guessed at, but it's clear that although acting was an incredibly useful background to have, it took courage, determination, and a long-term view to make a good career out of private investigation work.

Maud West, perhaps the most famous of the early twentieth century lady detectives, was born Edith Maria Barber in south London in 1880, an illegitimate child from a working-class family. Clearly both resourceful and intelligent, some sources state that she started working as a private detective in 1905, and she was certainly established enough by 1909 to be able to afford to pay for newspaper adverts publicising her business, and to be able to use separate business premises.[7] However, Susannah Stapleton has given very plausible evidence as to Maud having previously been an actress, noting that Maud even acknowledged, late in life, the value of theatrical skills in one interview, saying, 'one has to be a good many things in this profession ... above all an actress'.[8] Maud was joined by several more high profile entertainers in the Edwardian era and teens of the twentieth century; one being Kate Easton, her main rival, and another being the more eccentric Dorothy Tempest, who would continue to take on work in the theatre whenever her private detective work slowed down.[9]

Although nothing definite is known about Maud's possible theatrical career, it being based on supposition – although powerful – slightly more is known about Kate's. Like Maud, she was from south London, but her family were slightly higher up the social scale. There was no history of either policing or theatricality in her parents – her father, William Mead Easton, was a waterman at the time of her birth in 1856, like his own father had been, and her mother, Sarah, was the daughter of an illiterate shoemaker.[10]

The younger generation of Eastons were both literate and somewhat unconventional, as well as artistic. Kate's brother William was a music professor, but more significantly, perhaps, Kate's niece Madeleine would go on to become a famous actress and playwright under the name of Madeleine Lucette, as well as being the second wife of actor J.H. Ryley.[11] Madeleine, who in adulthood was an active supporter of the women's suffrage movement, had first appeared on stage in her mid-teens; the first press reference to her is in the summer of 1876, when she would have been 16 or 17, although she may have started her career before this.[12] There was a large age gap between Kate Easton and Madeleine's mother, who was Kate's older sister, Madeleine Bradley (née Easton). The siblings were sixteen years apart in age, and as a result, Kate was far closer in age to her niece than to her sister.

Kate Easton may have started her stage career at around the same time as her niece Madeleine, or alternatively, after she saw Madeleine make a success of the stage, and then decide to move into this sphere herself. Madeleine's career can be reconstructed because her stage name is known and recorded; however, the name of Kate Easton cannot be seen in theatre reviews or adverts, suggesting either that Kate was never successful enough to merit named billing, or that she used a stage name like her niece did. What that stage name was, sadly, is not known. The census records do not help establish an approximate start of her career either, as Kate is absent from the 1881 census. However, by the time the 1891 census was taken, her father had died, and she was living with her mother in Bloomsbury – a popular location for young performers, who took rooms in the plentiful boarding houses of the area, close to the West End and Theatreland. Kate was now described as a vocalist, aged 20, but it was not uncommon for performers to knock a few years off their ages to give the impression of being young ingenues.[13]

Kate was still a 'vocalist and actress' in the 1901 census, but she may have already started combining this work with some investigative work to give herself a bit more security in her finances. A later press advert, from 1917, states that her detective agency had been established for thirteen years, which would suggest that she had started in this line of work in 1896 – but this could of course be a fiction, done to emphasise her experience and longevity.[14] She was certainly working as a detective by early 1904, the year before her mother's death, as this is when the first reference to her as a professional detective is made in the press.[15]

This first reference involved a divorce case brought by Sir Robert McConnell of Belfast, whose wife had left him three years after their marriage, and was believed to have subsequently had a child by a man she had known since before her marriage. The evidence brought against the wife, Elsie, was from two women – the woman who had attended her when she gave birth, and Kate. Kate had been employed by Sir Robert, and sent to Brighton to monitor Elsie, who was staying at Berner's Hotel in the town, as it then was. She spotted her being frequently visited by a gentleman who called her by her first name. The assignment went on for several months, as three months after her initial stay in Brighton, Kate was there again, staying at the same hotel as Elsie and able to catch her lover visiting her again. Her later evidence was clear and concise; she refused to speculate on things she had not seen, stating that although she had seen the alleged lover visiting Elsie in Brighton, she could not say whether he was staying at the same hotel or not. Elsie, meanwhile, decided not to contest the divorce case.

Kate had made the papers – albeit only in Belfast – and proved herself to be a good witness in a high-profile divorce case. The following year, her mother died, and the combination of a change in circumstances, and her previous success, prompted her to invest in her private detective work, and to make it her only full-time occupation from now on. The earliest surviving newspaper advert for her services was published in October 1905:

LADY DETECTIVE, thoroughly experienced, undertakes private and confidential inquiries. DIVORCE, COMMERCIAL, FAMILY MATTERS, NEGOTIATIONS, &C. Highest references from solicitors as to ABILITY and INTEGRITY. Male and female assistants. Consultations free. – Call or write, Miss KATE EASTON, 241 Shaftesbury Avenue (two doors from New Oxford-street), and in Paris.[16]

It was fairly common for private detectives to enhance their skills, experience and reputation with the addition of some dubious claims. Maurice Moser at best exaggerated his success with 'foreign government departments' (he had been involved with attempts to foil Fenian plots, with mixed results); Henry Slater advertised a flock of bicycling female detectives, with little evidence that they existed, and certainly not in the numbers he suggested; and several agencies claimed to have agents in 'every city in the world' (or, in the case of Henry Simmonds' agency, 'secret shadowing and inquiries in any part of the WORLD').[17] Therefore, if Kate, only a few years into any sort of detective career, claimed an office in Paris that was based largely on her imagination, she would not have been alone. It's certainly hard to believe that at this stage of her career, she would have been able to open a European outpost; however, she may have had an acting friend or contact in Paris who she had asked to become her European 'agent' if work necessitated it. Working as an actress usually meant travelling the provinces, but sometimes a woman might become lucky, or successful, enough to visit a foreign city to perform. If Kate had a former colleague or friend working abroad, it would certainly be a useful contact for a private detective to maintain.

If Kate was seeking to enhance her reputation with the public by suggesting a longevity she hadn't got in reality – claiming that she was working as a private detective by the late 1890s, when, at best, she was doing so simply to supplement her earnings singing and acting – and an office in Paris that there is no evidence she could have afforded, this would not be unheard of, nor unexpected. Given the multitude of private detectives operating by the early twentieth century, individuals had to act as their own PR people, exaggerating their skills, longevity, or successes in order to gain new clients at the expense of other operators, as the next chapter will show. It is, however, highly likely that Kate would have needed an alternative source of income whilst officially a stage performer. Many minor actors and singers, then as now, took on other forms of employment when work was quiet, and although it is possible that Kate adopted a stage name, if she did not, then references to a Kate Easton in the theatrical newspaper are few and far between, with the majority of those few relating to a different individual, and there are no references for a Kate Easton in the main theatre publication, *The Era*, outside of two in 1874.[18]

Dorothy Tempest was another performer who became a private detective; she may well have been more successful on the stage than Kate, as there are more references to her in the theatrical news sections of the newspapers, and it appears that she took on other work – private detective work, but also palmistry readings – when theatrical engagements were not forthcoming, but focused on her theatre work otherwise. The records show that this Dublin-born actress was working regularly on the provincial theatre circuit from 1895 to at least 1900, and again from 1905 to 1910, with mention of her as a private detective in the press primarily in 1903 and 1904. In November 1911, she was advertising herself as an experienced pantomime actress who was currently 'disengaged', and by 1918, at the age of 44, she was again working as a private detective and solicitor's process server (serving divorce petitions on individuals).[19] The pattern of press mentions clearly indicates that when acting jobs were not forthcoming, Dorothy worked as a private detective, showing a versatility and initiative that Kate Easton may also have had to employ. In Kate's case, however, it seems that detective work then became her longer-term mainstay, and that her acting career stopped when her detective work took off. A later detective, Annette Kerner, had again a different approach; she claimed to have been working as a singer in 1919 when she was approached to undertake counter-espionage work for the security services; a career in private detective work then followed.[20]

Two other women who, like Kate Easton, started their careers in the theatre before moving over to detective work were Margaret Cooke and Matilda Mitchell. Their backgrounds show how disparate these female detectives were, albeit united in their desire to be financially independent career women. Margaret was from a theatrical family – her father, William Braithwaite, was for much of her life an accountant or a publican, but he

76 Southampton Row – home to Kate Easton and her mother in 1891. (*Nell Darby*)

317 High Holborn – Antonia Moser's office by 1911. (*Nell Darby*)

Sussex Mansions, Maiden Lane, London: this was the office of Antonia's employer, and later partner, then competitor, Maurice Moser, in 1890. (*Nell Darby*)

Warwick Court, where Kate Easton worked in 1917. (*Nell Darby*)

Frances Power Cobbe, who argued that female detectives should have been employed to catch Jack the Ripper in 1888. (*Public domain*)

Rosalie Kennedy, nee Thompson, worked as a spiritualist before becoming a private detective. This is her passport photo from 1920, by which time she appears to have stopped her career. (*National Archives (US)*)

Allan Pinkerton (L), Abraham Lincoln (C) and Major General John A McClernand, pictured in 1862. Glaswegian Pinkerton established a detective agency in Chicago in the 1850s, and employed Kate Warne as his first female detective. (*Library of Congress (US)*)

Private detective Maud West prided herself on her ability to disguise herself – here she is c.1920, dressed as a Salvation Army officer. (*Public domain*)

The fictional private detective Loveday Brooke – pictured here in an illustration by Bernard Higham – was created by Catherine Louisa Pirkis in 1893.

Coverage of Charles Kersey's female detective training agency, which was based on London's iconic Baker Street, in The Graphic of 30 April 1927. (*Illustrated London News/Mary Evans Picture Library*)

BEATRICE LILLIE AS AN ACROBAT IN " BAGDAD DADDIES ": THE LADY DETECTIVE IN A WONDERFUL DISGUISE.

Film depictions of female detectives were often more exciting than the reality. Here, Beatrice Lillie stars as lady detective Shirley Travis – in disguise as a circus acrobat (The Sketch, 21 January 1931). (*Illustrated London News/ Mary Evans*)

The most famous detective in literature was Sherlock Holmes (shown here in an 1892 illustration by Sidney Paget) – therefore, it was perhaps inevitable that female detectives such as Maud West would be deemed 'the female Sherlock Holmes' in the press. (*Public domain*)

Prior to becoming a private detective, Kate Easton was an actress, with several actors in her family – her niece, pictured here, was the successful actress and playwright Madeline Lucette. (*Public domain*)

Some female detectives were from policing families; Patience Lawrence, for example, was brought up here, at Chipping Campden Police Station, with her father Jesse being a police constable. (*Nell Darby*)

The entrance to Great Turnstile, an alley off High Holborn in London, and home to siffleuse turned private detective Margaret Cooke – aka Mab Barton – in 1911. (*Andrew Davidson [cc]*)

Irish-born private detective Dorothy Tempest, depicted in the Penny Illustrated Paper, giving evidence during the Keiro trial in 1904. (*Courtesy of the British Library Board*)

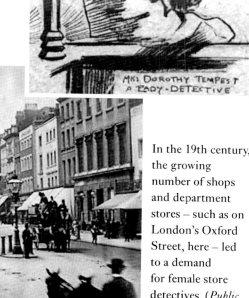

In the 19th century, the growing number of shops and department stores – such as on London's Oxford Street, here – led to a demand for female store detectives. (*Public domain*)

Agatha Christie created the female sleuth Miss Marple in the 1920s, as well as the husband-and-wife team of Tommy and Tuppence. (*Public domain*)

The former Whiteleys store in west London. Annie Betts worked as a store detective here during the First World War, alongside her other detective work. (*Fritz Jörn (public domain)*)

If women saw goods they wanted but couldn't afford in shops, they might be tempted to steal them. It was up to the female detectives to catch these shoplifters. (*Public domain*)

had previously had a good career as a comedian, under the stage name of Walter Barton.[21] Margaret, who was from Liverpool and born in 1866, similarly started off as a performer. Her full birth name was Margaret Alice Braithwaite, and she combined these initials with her father's stage name to become Mab Barton, the 'English siffleuse' – or a whistling singer. Newspapers suggest that she regularly performed between 1887 and 1893, but then stopped.

Her involvement with performing did not altogether cease, however, as she embarked on a relationship with the colourful circus proprietor Alfred Eugene Godolphin Cooke, who already had several children by two women – four boys and five girls by his first wife Helena, and then two girls by a younger woman, Emily Adams, who he would marry after Helena's death in 1890. In 1896, Margaret gave birth to a daughter, who she named Olga Mabena Alexandra Cooke, the first middle name being a tribute to her own stage name of Mab. Although both she and Olga would remain Cookes for the rest of their lives, Margaret was never married to Cooke, who died when Olga was just 4 years old. She was therefore left as a single mother, with a need to maintain her daughter; she was also used to earning her own money, and working in an industry where hours were irregular, where there was variety, and travel. One logical step for such a woman was to become a private detective, and Margaret did so, operating from the Lincolns Inn Fields area of London. She worked as such for at least three years, and probably longer; she is missing from the 1901 census so it is not possible to see whether she started in this career after Alfred Cooke's death, but she was certainly listed in the 1911 census as a private detective.[22]

That Margaret was a strong and financially astute woman who could not be taken advantage of can be seen from a court case she was involved with in 1914. The case also shows that although divorce cases may have been common in this line of work, the private detective also undertook a variety of financial work. Margaret had sued one of her clients, Marie Toulman – a widow also known as the Baroness de Wetzel – for £31 for professional services she had undertaken for the baroness. These related to the latter needing Margaret to enter into negotiations with financiers and other individuals with a view of obtaining a loan for £550. Although these individuals weren't listed, newspaper reports referred to correspondence involving an MP and 'other well-known people', with the imputation that the job had involved corresponding with famous individuals in such a way that these people would not have wanted their details becoming public. The baroness appears to have also wanted to avoid more details becoming public, and the two women negotiated and came to a deal, thus avoiding a drawn-out legal case.[23] Margaret's experience negotiating theatrical contracts, and perhaps fighting to get paid on time, or dealing with agents and theatrical managers, meant that she was not afraid to fight to get what she was owed in her new line of business, and to take a client to court if necessary.

Operating around the same time as Margaret was Matilda Emma Mitchell, seven years her junior. Matilda was from south London, the daughter of a publisher's clerk. She later claimed to have first performed at the Royal Opera House at the age of 15, but given that the census three years later listed her as a confectioner's assistant, this may be misremembering, embellishment, or a short-lived initial career that did not offer enough financial security. However, she later adopted the stage name of Ethel Chester and moved into that staple of late nineteenth and early twentieth century performing work – the pantomime.

In addition to her acting roles, which involved costumes and different identities, in an interview in 1914, she noted how she also attended fancy dress balls in Covent Garden where she had to adopt different disguises – and frequently won first prize with her imagination and talent for disguise. While at one of these balls, she was offered her first detecting job – in a divorce case. She then developed a specialism for what she called 'matrimonial misfits', discovering that 'the injured husband is a much more forgiving and merciful person than a wronged wife'.[24] Among the identities that Matilda adopted during her time as a private detective was that of a male painter, engaged on painting house windows while surreptitiously spying on the lady of the house. That she was successful in this was partly due to her height – she was tall, so was able to pass herself off as a man, despite being a 'striking blonde with commanding figure and steady blue eyes'.[25] A photograph of her in middle age suggests that although she was certainly striking, she was not typically feminine in her looks, having strong features and expression. She looks both unflappable and determined. Matilda may have had a special skill in dealing with marital cases, but financial security appears to have been better offered by a role as head of Selfridges' 'Secret Service'.[26]

In Matilda's case, she implies that her move from acting to detective work was by chance – someone saw her potential, gave her a job, and she found that she was talented in this new arena and simply went along with it. When she married Surrey cricketer Tom Hayward in 1914, when she was 41, both retired; it appears that she no longer needed to work, and that marrying later in life, she wanted to revert to a more traditional female role. It was when she had just married that she gave an interview to *The People* detailing her career to date. She commented:

> 'Am I glad that my detective days are over? Well, yes ... you must recognise that a lady detective's life is a trying and risky one.'[27]

Yet in detailing her exploits in such details, she gave the impression of having greatly enjoyed the danger and subterfuge of her detective work, and was proud of her skills in disguise, common in both her theatrical and detective careers. She may have felt her job had been risky, but that is not to mean she didn't miss it once she retired.[28]

Given the inter-relationship and overlap between the skills needed to be a competent actress, and those needed to be an equally competent private detective, it seems unlikely that the women mentioned here would have been the only ones to have gone from one to the other over the Edwardian era. A woman who wanted to become a performer enjoyed taking on different roles, adopting different personas, dressing up, and working irregular hours. She wanted to earn her own money, but not take on one of the jobs that were seen as 'feminine' to her parents. Instead, she wanted to do something more unusual or less socially acceptable, to challenge the status quo. Such a woman was resourceful, and flexible, and it is easy to see why such a woman, fed up of chasing roles or needing to supplement her income, might decide to move into a complementary job that seemed like it was made for her – the life of a lady detective. But to do so, she would need to advertise her services, just as the Victorian and Edwardian actresses paid for adverts in the press to provide the parts they played, and the experience they had. To be a successful lady detective, you had to sell yourself.

LAUNDRY.
DIVORCE OR SEPARATION?
A LADY DETECTIVE states (in confidence)
To avoid this NO WASHING should be done at
Home, but sent to the
BRADFORD LAUNDRY WORKS,
Bowland Street,
MANNINGHAM LANE, BRADFORD.

Shipley Times and Express, 27 June 1913, p.1

Chapter 10

Press and Publicity

The work of a private detective primarily involved a few certain types of cases. Divorce and family matters; financial investigations, including debt and blackmail; 'embarrassing entanglements' of one form or another – these were the cases that detectives took on. Although many clients were ordinary individuals, some of the more successful agencies took on work for newspapers, politicians, financiers and wealthy merchants. Some of the assignments were seen to require a 'woman's delicacy and tact', and female detectives eagerly advertised their 'feminine' qualities in order to take these jobs on rather than their male equivalents.[1]

One of the ways to differentiate the more ambitious, or successful, female detectives in the early years of the twentieth century from the smaller-scale operators is by looking at the classified columns of the newspapers. By the turn of the century, there were a growing number of women wanting to grow their businesses, but the three who most consistently advertised, and highlighted their skills, were Maud West, Kate Easton and Antonia Moser. As already discussed, Maud and Kate in particular were rivals, working for some time in offices opposite each other. Kate was operating by 1904; Maud and Antonia by the following year.[2]

Antonia was an interesting character, from an entirely different background to her rivals. Firstly, she was from a far wealthier background, being the daughter of a well-to-do mechanical engineer. Although like Maud and Kate, she was a born and bred Londoner, her London was very different. Born the same year as Kate, she grew up at 133 High Holborn as one of ten siblings, in an affluent, educated household. However, her family was somewhat unconventional; after her mother's death, the patriarch, Welburn Wilks Williamson, took all his younger daughters off to be baptised, and they were all given their mother's first name, with

Antonia – born Charlotte Antonia – becoming Sarah Charlotte Antonia. Although presumably meant as a gesture of love and remembrance towards his wife, it feels slightly ghoulish for the daughters, now aged between 12 and 19, to be renamed after their dead mother.[3]

These unusually close family ties were further strengthened when Antonia married her first cousin, Edward Williamson, in 1882.[4] Two children, a son and a daughter, followed, and it seemed that Antonia was destined to live a conventional female life. However, she refused to accept that fate. Instead, she told her husband that she wanted a job, and promptly went to the offices of Maurice Moser's detective agency off the Strand to ask for one. Working with the married Moser led to an affair, which Antonia was not very discreet about, even trying to put a portrait of him in her marital bedroom, to her husband's fury. It suggests that she was almost trying to sabotage a marriage she had never really wanted to be in, or had a sudden awareness that there was more to life than what her father expected of her.

Either way, her actions led to the break-up of two marriages. Moser's was particularly newsworthy, with he and his wife submitting petitions against each other; Antonia's similarly involved allegations of adultery on each side, but in her case, her husband submitted a petition for divorce on the grounds of her adultery in 1889. The final decree was issued in 1891.[5] In a competitive world, it should perhaps not be surprising that Antonia's husband employed Henry Slater to investigate his fellow detective Maurice Moser, and in his subsequent divorce case, Edward Williamson made another of Moser's female detectives, Louisa Sangster, give evidence against Antonia.[6]

Moser had been a detective with the Metropolitan Police between 1877 and 1887, and published his memoirs of a decade in the force, which were serialised in the press and subsequently published as *Stories from Scotland Yard*. He was an experienced detective and taught Antonia all the skills she needed. By the time they were divorced from their respective partners, they were operating Maurice Moser's Detective Agency together, on an equal basis. Professionally, she may have been happy, but the relationship was more complex; the couple lived together as man and wife but there are doubts about whether they actually married.[7] By 1901, they had split up, and Antonia was accusing Moser of assaulting her.[8] However, she then continued to make a living as a private detective, working initially on her own, and then aided by her daughter Margaret (who would go on to take over the business), who, rather confusingly, also took on the name of Antonia Moser for this purpose.

The name of Moser was well known, and so it is unsurprising that Antonia continued to use the name, and to set herself up as a private detective under it. Operating initially from 37 and 38 Strand, and later from her home at High Holborn, she advertised her services regularly in the newspapers over the course of the Edwardian era. Some of her adverts state: 'Moser's Detective Agency: Antonia Moser', clearly playing on the link between her and Maurice Moser, using a name that people would be more likely to associate with the ex-Scotland Yard detective than with his estranged 'wife'. Antonia needed the public awareness of that name to build her own independent career, and took her time to create a distance between her and Maurice.

Her advertisements emphasised her skills: she was prompt, could keep a secret, and was reliable. She claimed to be able to provide references from former clients, who were 'solicitors and clients of the highest repute', but this was a standard form of words used by many private detectives, and it is hard to establish how popular or successful a detective was by their newspaper adverts, as these all followed a form of hyperbole and accepted language designed to make them appear both legitimate and in demand, regardless of whether they employed one person or twenty. Maud West, advertising at the same time and often in the same columns of the same papers, similarly stated that she could provide 'references to leading solicitors'; this simply meant that both women were likely to be employed primarily on divorce suits, and it was also a strapline often used by male detectives as well.[9]

Both women, though, recognised the importance of advertising their services. Word of mouth was important, but to get their name out to a wider audience, it was vital to place regular advertisements in London newspapers, such as the *Morning Post* and the *Daily Telegraph*. The classified columns of the late nineteenth century included many such adverts, and the female detectives were competing with men who had sometimes substantial professional experience, including Maurice Moser.[10]

Since the adverts placed by Ward's detective agency in 1879 and 1880, the classified columns of the London newspapers had increasingly included references to female detectives.[11] Barclay's of 368 Strand ('opposite Savoy Hotel') boasted of their male and female detectives, their 'up-to-date' skills, the fact that the agency was 'old established' and also that it had a second office off the Avenue de l'Opera in Paris; Henry Simmonds' well-known agency on King Street, Cheapside, similarly noted that their 'male and female' detectives were able to obtain 'reliable evidence for divorce, watchings, inquiries, &c'.[12] Henry Slater had – prior to his agency ending under a black cloud in 1904 – consistently highlighted his employment not only of female detectives, but also, for a period in the mid-1890s, his use of cycling lady detectives, connecting himself to the New Woman zeitgeist, with his modern ladies chasing down evidence on their new bicycles.[13] It is clear that female detectives were a marketing strategy here – but that they were so suggests that people wanted to see and hear about them, and did not regard them as a novelty per se any more; hence the need to now put them on bicycles.

In the world of female detectives, Maud West and Kate Easton were encroaching on Antonia's business, with Easton calling herself 'THE Lady Detective' and 'London's leading woman in every branch of detective work'.[14] Kate was also able to match the male detectives' propensity for hyperbole and confidence, yet was also adept at altering her wording and descriptions to suit the market. Therefore, in 1905, she placed a modest advert in a Staffordshire paper, describing herself as 'lady detective, educated, experienced, undertakes private and confidential inquiries – strict integrity', the same year, she was stressing in the London papers that she was 'thoroughly experienced' and had an office in Paris, despite, as mentioned earlier, there being no evidence that she had one.[15]

The following year, Antonia was calling herself the 'detective expert' and boasting that she had 'agents in all cities of the world' – an unlikely claim.[16] In January 1907, she made her agency a partnership, with her daughter Margaret as partner. She had been building her own career as an independent lady detective, having gained nearly twenty years' experience in the field now. This counted for little in Edwardian London, though, where clients focused on the detectives who appeared the most successful, or who had the best advertising (or the most money to spend on advertising). In August 1908, Antonia was declared bankrupt. Accounts lodged showed that she had nearly £500 of liabilities – and no assets whatsoever.[17]

Her business did not stop, though, although Antonia stood down from it. Instead, Margaret Williamson took over, adopting both her mother's business – and her name. This makes it slightly confusing to track what happened to Antonia from this period, given that both women were being known professionally as Antonia Moser, but the primary difference was that Moser's agency continued to be based at the Strand, whilst Antonia – and/or Margaret – now used her home address – 317 High Holborn, her old marital home – as her professional address as well. She briefly tried her luck at being an estate agent, but then established herself as a cross between a detective and a citizen's advice service, advertising in the papers that she offered free advice to those needing to know 'where to go when in trouble, whether of a legal, social, or private nature'.[18] Ironically, in a classified column of October 1909, the small advert for Antonia Moser's services was right at the bottom of a column of adverts for private detectives – and the one immediately before it was for her ex-partner, Maurice Moser.[19]

What is significant about both Antonia and Maurice Moser's adverts is that they appear to be old-fashioned, as though times had not moved on since their separation. The other adverts for private detectives used slogans, quotes, capital letters and stylistic changes to emphasise their services, from Maud West's demand to the reader to 'read this!' to Pierrepont's Detectives catchy slogan: 'When blackmailed, go to Pierrepont. When watched, go to Pierrepont. When troubled, go to Pierrepont. Call, write, phone, or wire. Always there.'[20]

William Pierrepont, on Chancery Lane, also had a more unusual sales pitch: 'To Ladies. Many men say women have been their downfall. William Pierrepont does not agree. His staff of Lady Detectives has been his success. They move in all circles, from the highest to the lowest.'[21]

Pierrepont's adverts showed both that the number of private detectives had increased since the time of Moser's establishment of his agency, and that more of the traditionally male-run agencies were employing lady detectives, and recognising their value as part of their sales pitch. McGregor's agency, based on Strand, was another of the male-run agencies that advertised their 'men and lady detectives' as being part of a 'first class firm'.[22] Lady detectives were a draw in an ever competitive world, but Antonia Moser's tiny, relatively new, agency could not compete with the larger agencies run by men with a good eye for publicity and advertising.

However, this does not mean that female detectives were all alike. While Antonia Moser struggled to make a significant imprint on the detective world, the likes of Kate Easton and Maud West continued to thrive, utilising the press to gain both work and publicity of themselves. Kate Easton proved a shrewd operator during the First World War, choosing to advertise in the *Army and Navy Gazette*, next to pleas for donations to hospitals aiding soldiers with mental health issues. Her adverts, calling herself 'London's Leading Woman in every branch of Detective Work', highlighted her work in divorce and blackmail cases. It suggests that she saw war as an opportunity rather than a threat, offering the chance to exploit soldiers' fears that their wives might stray while they were away fighting – or on their return.[23]

Maud, though, was at the forefront, selling stories of her exploits to the newspapers – and their detailing of her exciting jobs, often involving dressing up as different characters (often photographed in 'disguise' as boys or old women as part of her published articles) may have combined both fact and fiction, to make her work sound as exciting and full of variety as possible.[24] She would continue to market herself and her work in as pro-active a way as possible until the early 1930s, although she was not the first to sell her exploits to the newspapers: as earlier chapters have shown, anonymous female detectives were keen to tell their stories. In reality, it is likely that divorce cases made up the bread and butter of her career, as they did so many other private detectives, but although they were often newsworthy, they did not always help the private detective publicise themselves. To do that, the astute lady detective, such as Maud, had to either write about more fantastical cases they had been involved in – or to create such cases where they did not exist. For the newspaper reader, it didn't really matter whether these stories were fact or fiction – they were simply a good yarn, and one that helped them remember an individual detective's name. And in the private detective world, some women – although by no means all, for some liked the secrecy of their work – wanted to be known as more than just the 'lady detective'.

Prisoner was a single woman ... [She stated that she] was sent to York to keep observation on a certain lady in the neighbourhood. Subsequent inquiries revealed that all her stories were false.

Durham County Advertiser, 14 March 1902, p.6

Chapter 11

Frauds and Fakes

It didn't take much to become a private detective: a newspaper advert, perhaps, or discreet publicity more locally, or a word with local police or solicitors that you were willing to work with them on cases. You needed no equipment; employers would pay your expenses; you could work from home, and all that was required was some resourcefulness, strength of mind and character, and the ability to stay in the shadows. It was, as has been seen, a career that almost anyone with a certain level of education could do, from the bored middle-class wife or the genteel but impoverished woman of uncertain status, to the ambitious working-class woman who, thanks to the Education Acts, now could read and write and perhaps wanted more from life than her mother or grandmothers had been expected to be content with.

Yet despite the relatively egalitarian nature of detective work, not all women were prepared to take on the role for real. As lady detectives became less of an oddity and more accepted by society – although the press continued to treat them as something of a novelty – some women saw the opportunity to use the profession as a means of committing crime. Men also used the profession as a cover, but in a different way; for example, in 1893, George Binet set up the National Detective Agency – a company with letterheads and an office in London, but without any detectives or jobs or real credentials. He placed adverts in provincial newspapers asking people to apply to become his regional representatives, taking on detective jobs outside of London. Many men and women, primarily from the working classes, applied, and were asked to pay to receive an 'official' accreditation as a detective, and to start being notified of jobs. Once the money was paid, no jobs, of course, resulted. A fraud case was brought at the Old Bailey, and Binet was duly jailed.[1] A similar sham agency was established by James Badger and John Compton, again in London, two years later.[2] Other men were charged at various points in the late nineteenth century with pretending to be detectives, but these were often men who had claimed to be police detectives – something women, of course, could not do. In 1902, Frederick Parkinson was sent to prison after pretending to be a Liverpool police detective and using his pseudonym to commit various thefts. He had obtained two different sets of lodgings under his fake identity – proving his police credentials with a 'kit' comprising a pair of handcuffs and a police whistle – and then robbed the bedrooms in the lodging houses. He was tracked down to Lockerbie and tried at Carlisle.[3]

The women who pretended to be private detectives, though, had less ambitious plans, and although they committed frauds or thefts, they tended to be more small-scale affairs. This was partly because of the different roles of men and women in detective work: men were, in part at least, more believable as the proprietors of their own detective agencies – it was still assumed that men would be the bosses, employing women, certainly in the nineteenth century – and so crimes such as the National Detective Agency scandal might not have succeeded for so long, or at all, if a woman had created the plan. Although the National Detective Agency case was, in places, reported to have involved a female detective, in most accounts she was an underling of the male 'detectives' (Binet and his accomplice), and in some, she was either a hired secretary, to make the agency look legitimate, or even a housekeeper employed to look after the building where they rented an office. Until the teens of the twentieth century, no women were formally represented in any English police force; so prior to the inter-war period, women were unable to pose as police officers, let alone detectives, as these roles did not exist, and those they were trying to scam would have been aware of it. Therefore, in order to commit frauds or thefts, they needed to pose as private detectives instead.

Elizabeth Archer was one of these women. She was 'a middle-aged woman of respectable appearance' and appeared in court in Manchester in October 1886, charged with theft. She had been lodging at a house there for some weeks, having told her landlord that she was a private detective who had returned from America four months earlier, and was busy 'looking up' a number of cases in Manchester.[4] Just over fifteen years later, another woman, Martha Unsworth, was also charged with an offence after pretending to be a private detective. She was actually the daughter of a highway labourer and former railway platelayer from Culcheth, some 6 miles north of Warrington.[5] Martha had, it seemed, done well for herself, getting a decent education and then a job as a school teacher – not bad for someone whose mother was a cotton winder in the local mills.

She was said to be a well-dressed young woman, creating a good impression. But then she had lost her job, found and lost a subsequent job as a servant and, said her father Isaac later, fallen in with a bad crowd.[6] Martha then obtained food and lodging in nearby Leigh, claiming falsely that she was 'a lady detective from Manchester and was working in conjunction with the Leigh police'.[7] When it was found that she was no such thing, she was investigated and charged with fraudulently obtaining food and lodging. The Leigh magistrates were lenient with Martha, however, and as she was a first offender, and had pleaded guilty, they simply bound her over to good behaviour.[8] The same year, Ada Brentwood Bowman had pleaded guilty at York Police Court to obtaining food, lodging and clothes by false pretences. Bowman appears to have been more of a cynical offender than Martha, however, she had taken on a variety of guises: pretending to be a farmer's wife in one fraud, then a governess in another, before finally posing as a private detective who was being employed by Scotland Yard to investigate, or shadow, a woman in York. None of these stories were true, and she was sent to prison for three months with hard labour.[9]

For women pretending to be lady detectives, 1902 was either a bonanza year or the press had caught up with the fact that women were committing crimes under the guise of being detectives, helping to raise renewed concerns about the profession and its image. In May this year, a 32-year-old dressmaker, Helen Mabel Juniper, appeared at the Essex Quarter Sessions, accused of stealing various items from a woman in Chelmsford, while posing as a lady detective. Helen was a quite sad character: although again from a respectable family, she had been deserted by her husband – a fact that was described by the prosecutor as being 'through no fault of her own'. She had been upset greatly by her husband's actions, and for the previous ten months, had been 'wandering about', letting nobody in her family, even her mother, know where she was.[10] Although she had no prior convictions, she had pretended to be a lady detective before, in order to get people to trust her and give her food and other items; these individuals, however, had felt sorry for her once they knew the truth, and had declined to prosecute her. Even in this latest case, the prosecutor stated that he didn't wish to press the case, and that although Helen was not obviously mentally ill, the best course for her would be to stay in a home. Helen expressed her willingness to do so, and so was bound over under the First Offenders' Act, and told to stay in the home for at least six months.[11]

There were superficial differences between Elizabeth Archer and Martha Unsworth; one was middle-aged, the other young; one was charged in the 1880s, the other in the new century. However, they had things in common. They were both described as well dressed (and Ada Brentwood Bowman, in York, was also said to be 'a stylishly-dressed young woman'), from respectable backgrounds (not necessarily middle class, as working-class households could be differentiated as either criminal or respectable; Helen Juniper was similarly described as respectable), and from the north-west of England. There is no evidence that either woman had committed a crime prior to their 'detective' offence, nor that they committed any more offences subsequently. Therefore, their posing as private detectives was a one-off, more of a spontaneous act than a pre-planned one, and not part of a regular portrayal in order to commit crime.

Why, then, did these women choose to pretend to be private detectives? Firstly, it was a way of getting lodgings without too many questions being asked, but it also involved adopting a more exciting persona, perhaps, than their reality. To pretend to be a private detective meant stirring the interest of those they came into contact with, such as landlords or the other men and women they might be sharing lodgings with. It meant they could create stories about their lives, invoke interest and admiration for their imagined feats of bravery. In this modern era, the late nineteenth century and the early twentieth, women of all ages and all backgrounds could plausibly be private detectives – it was an occupation that transcended the hitherto rigid social classes of British society. It also enabled these women, if only for a while, to escape their humdrum lives and, instead of being a labourer's daughter from Culcheth, become a lady detective, provided with food and lodging by a fascinated landlord. Just as being a real detective offered an escape, to some extent, from the unpleasant realities of individuals' lives, so too did being a sham detective offer the same escape – at least, until the police caught up with these women.

It was not unheard of, then, for women to fraudulently pose as detectives – and as time went on, this included posing as a police detective. In 1931, Daphne Freeland, a well-dressed 44-year-old 'who wore a heavily-lined leather coat', appeared at Exeter to plead guilty to three charges of fraud on various tradesman locally, plus the London & Exeter Hotels, and was sentenced to nine months in prison. She had been posing as a lady detective from Scotland Yard.[12] Three decades earlier, a married woman had posed as a private detective in order to stop people finding out her true identity. Mary Dean, née Walsh, had been unhappily married to her railway clerk husband Charles since she was 18; he had believed her to be committing adultery with a man named James Vincent Scully at Liverpool – miles away from the family home in Stoke-on-Trent. Mary was tracked down to Liverpool, where she was found to be posing as 'Miss Graham, a lady detective'. By the time Charles Dean obtained a divorce from his wife on the grounds of her adultery, her alleged lover had married someone else. As is often the case, although both Scully and Charles Dean can be found in the censuses and archives after this, Mary Dean disappears from the records following her brief moment of scandal.[13]

However, her choice of lady detective as a cover identity was a sensible one. It suggests a knowledge that single women, taking lodgings in places they did not know (and more importantly, were not known by others), needed an acceptable cover that people would not be suspicious of. Lady detectives regularly travelled on their own, taking rooms in lodging houses in order to make their acquaintance with suspected wives, or to shadow them. By posing as Miss Graham the detective, Mrs Dean hoped to provide curious neighbours with a plausible reason as to why she was furtively ensconced on her own in lodgings in Liverpool; and if James Vincent Scully came visiting, he might well be a colleague as much as a relative or lover.

Clearly, becoming a woman detective was a viable option for an increasing number of women over the course of the late nineteenth and early twentieth centuries – and when women did not want to undertake the work itself, they might be tempted to use the glamorous cover of being a lady detective in order to take advantage of individuals, and to commit frauds or thefts using that cover. The effect could have been to discredit genuine detectives, but interestingly, courts and the press did not do so. The press certainly reported it as a matter of fact, but did not use it explicitly to make a link between dishonesty or crime and the identity of a female private detective. Instead, it simply served to make the job sound more intriguing, and to make it better known: although the fact that so many crimes seem to have been ascribed to sham private detectives suggests that by the turn of the century, it was a relatively well-known and accepted career choice for both men and women.

The adoption of these fake identities, and their timing, may also be due to the increased popularity of detective literature, presenting the job as both exciting, and as a form of identity-cloaking for individuals. Take Sherlock Holmes, the most famous of all the literary private detectives, whose life is shrouded in mystery. He is a complex individual, but one who we do not see having Sunday dinner with family members, or dwelling on his childhood. His job forms a major part of his identity, distracting from the more unsavoury aspects of his personality. Did Helen Juniper, pretending to be a private detective, do so in part because it enabled her to escape her more stressful identity as a deserted wife and mother? Did it enable her to play someone else, someone more devious and strategic, who could make financial gains illegally through the adoption of this persona? Mary Dean may also have welcomed the opportunity for anonymity, or the shedding of her previous married life, provided by pretending to be a lady detective also. For these poorer but literate women, they may well have read accounts of private detectives in books and newspapers and kept them in their minds as examples of how you could escape your real life and take on different roles to live a more exciting life – and later use those memories to commit crimes and be someone different, if only for a while.

My life and home have been ruined by the accursed Spiritualism. My wife left me three years ago. Although I love her now she will not come back and make a happy home, as we easily could do only for the accursed witchcraft.

The suicide note of clerk John Ernest Carryer,
Workington Star, 25 September 1908, p.7

Chapter 12

Spiritualism and Scepticism

Rosalie Thompson was, on the surface, everything a Victorian woman should be. She was solidly middle class; educated but not intellectual; a supportive wife to her manufacturer husband, and a mother of three.[1] She lived in a tidy villa in Finchley, where, according to popular perception, she should have engaged in the life of a late nineteenth-century married woman – taking calls, meeting friends for tea, organising the servants, and, perhaps, undertaking shopping trips into the city, taking advantage of the increased consumerism of the late nineteenth century, and London's multiplicity of shops and department stores. Perhaps she did do all this; as is so often the case with women's history, the archives do not adequately record their lives because of their focus on work – the private lives, the domestic spheres, of many women are assumed rather than recorded in black and white. However, there was much more to Rosalie Thompson than simply her life as a wife and mother. In addition to her domestic roles, she was a spiritualist, actively working throughout the *fin de siècle* and into the twentieth century. On suddenly being widowed, though, she found an alternative income stream in becoming a private detective.

The move from spiritualism to detective work wasn't as odd as it might first appear, as the late Victorian era had seen a resurgence of interest in the supernatural, an interest that was reflected in many spheres, including that of detective fiction. In fact, the 1890s and the early years of the twentieth century had seen what has been termed a 'hybridisation' of ghost or supernatural fiction and detective fiction, that was a reflection of contemporary scientific work.[2] The nineteenth century as a whole was a period of scientific development and advancement; in fact, science was developing so quickly that it led to both a religious revival and a growing interest in the supernatural, as individuals struggled to reconcile science with faith.[3] By the middle of the century, there had been a mesmerism craze, where practitioners would put their subjects into a trance, claiming that they were able to 'energise' them through their own powers of magnetism. Charles Dickens was one of the many fans of mesmerism, believing himself to be an expert practitioner.[4] Those who had been mesmerised claimed all sorts of powers as a result of the Act, from being able to see the future, to curing others. Then, from the middle of the century, the spiritualism movement developed. This was a means of communicating with the dead in séances; many mediums were women, because they were seen to have more perceptive skills and sensitive natures than men, and were thus seen as more receptive to influence from spirits. Spiritualists and their followers were looking for meaning in life, for evidence of life after death; combating the reasoning of science with their own need for purpose.

Many séances were harmless, with spiritualists simply offering comfort to clients by providing them with soothing messages from loved ones in the world 'beyond'. Spiritualism was an inherent part of Victorian Gothic literature, being evident in ghost stories, for example, with their similar belief in an afterlife; but it was also key to the work of the fictional detective, such as in Wilkie Collins' *The Moonstone*, where 'it becomes clear that the same scene, perceived from a different angle and by someone else, tells a different story'.[5] Likewise, at the end of the century, Sherlock Holmes, despite his emphasis on scientific detection techniques was also adept at 'reading' people and situations, in a similar way to the spiritualists of Arthur Conan Doyle's time.[6] By the time *The Hound of the Baskervilles* was first serialised, in the first two years of the twentieth century, Conan Doyle had both become a 'passionate advocate of spiritualism' and a resurrectionist, in bringing his fictional detective back to life.[7]

There was both a desire to see spiritualists as really communicating with the dead, but also a recognition that fraud existed in this field. There was also a strong link between spiritualism and the theatre; a medium's act was theatrical by its nature, involving both performance and the adoption of a believable role – just as the role of the female detective similarly involved such theatre, as well as deception. Both spiritualism and detective work depended on human nature: the desire to understand life and death, to believe that there was something 'beyond' our realm;

and, in the case of those who employed detectives, either a cynicism about human nature or a desire to believe the best in it, and to hope that those being investigated might prove to be beyond reproach in their behaviour.

Both spiritualists and detectives were adept at disguising themselves, at 'reading' the personalities and lives of their subjects, and at projecting themselves into the lives of others. Their techniques could be imaginative, convincing, and the goal was the same – to find things out about others, in order to earn their wages. It was perhaps unsurprising that detectives – both male and female – started to be employed to take part in séances and palmistry readings, in order to detect fraud. Fake clairvoyants were prosecuted under one of two pieces of legislation – the 1735 Witchcraft Act, and the 1824 Vagrancy Act.[8] The former repealed existing laws against witchcraft; the 1542 Witchcraft Act, which had made witchcraft a capital offence, had been repealed after only five years but had been replaced by a further Act in 1562, and one more in 1604. However, the 1735 Act imposed fines or imprisonment on those who claimed to be able to use magical powers, clearly targeting fortune-tellers. The 1824 Vagrancy Act in turn made fortune-telling, astrology and spiritualism punishable offences.[9] It was only in 1951, with the passing of the Fraudulent Mediums Act that the Witchcraft Act was repealed, with it also replacing 'certain provisions' of section 4 of the Vagrancy Act, with this new Act stating that those who 'fraudulently purport to act as spiritualistic mediums or to exercise powers of telepathy, clairvoyance or other similar powers' were guilty of an offence if they had acted 'for reward ... if any money is paid'.[10]

It was not a given that trials would result in a conviction, and in some cases, prosecutions were brought only for charges to be dismissed. Prosecuting spiritualists and fortune-tellers was not a straightforward matter, due to conflict about what constituted an offence under the two old acts, and it therefore isn't a surprise that many charges brought before the court ended up dismissed. However, in August 1904, three individuals – a man and his wife, together with a second man – were charged under the Witchcraft Act, and brought before the Marlborough Street Police Court. The first two defendants were Charles Yates Stephenson and his wife, Martha, and the other man was Charles Tricker. They performed for money as palmists and clairvoyants, with Martha using a crystal ball. Tricker used the stage name 'Yoga', while the Stephensons were well known under the pseudonyms of Keiro and Madame Keiro.[11] An advertisement placed in the *Globe* newspaper by the Keiros, just a month after their prosecution, stated: 'Keiro, the world-renowned palmist, and Madame Keiro, the world-renowned clairvoyant, will give free readings to customers.' This may have been their attempt to 'cover' themselves in the case of any police action, by arguing that they did not charge for their services, and were therefore not breaking the law – but they certainly did charge, despite what their advert alleged.[12]

The charge against them was that they pretended to tell the future in order to obtain money. Keiro charged a guinea to make a prediction, with his predictions taking differing amounts of time, depending on when his next customer was due. The majority of his and his wife's customers were other women. One, an unmarried young woman, sat before Keiro as he held a crystal in his hand; she held her hand open and he told her that her lifeline showed that she would only live until she was 45. However, she would marry in two years' time, and have a son. 'Mrs Keiro' would, he said, for an additional fee, elaborate on the prediction.[13]

The significant part of this court case was that a female detective gave evidence during proceedings, making particular news for having fainted during cross-examination. She was not named, nor her address given, as she was concerned about losing the anonymity she saw as vital to her job; she was instead described as wearing a 'crushed strawberry costume and a black hat'. She had been working as a private detective for five years, was 'not ignorant', and did not believe in witchcraft or sorcery. The situation was complicated as it was not clear whether the lady detective had been investigating the Keiros for fraud, or simply visiting them for a reading; although she stated that she was angry at Keiro's prediction of 'an illness, in all probability diphtheria, in five years', she also admitted to having had 'hard times' as a detective, and to have been 'deceived' by the Stephensons. It appears likely that this lady detective was struggling in her chosen profession, being not quite strong or resilient enough, and, in a moment of weakness, had visited the clairvoyants. When she realised that their predictions were nonsensical, she then helped to prosecute them.[14]

Yet what she didn't know was that other lady detectives had been employed specifically to prove the fraudulent nature of the Stephensons' business. One of these was the former actress Dorothy Tempest, encountered previously, and another was Annie Betts, then aged 28. Annie was a cab driver's daughter, and had been born and bred in Pimlico. Her father, Henry Lange, had died in 1899, and, as one of twelve children, the youngest of whom was just 4 years old when Henry died, she and her sisters had to find employment to help support her widowed mother. By the time of the Keiro case, she had also been working as a detective for at least three years, and, unusually for a woman in this career, had proudly detailed her occupation as 'lady detective' on her marriage certificate the year before.[15] Annie had gone to the Stephensons' home at 124 Regent Street and, on asking for a palm reading, had been told the fee (10s 6d) and asked to fill in a form, which Charles Stephenson told her was 'for his protection'. 'Madame Keiro' then took Betts for a combined clairvoyant and palmistry reading, and described Mrs Betts' husband to her: 'I see a man of medium height, blue or grey eyes, high forehead, light brown hair ... He's your husband, isn't he?' Annie said yes, although her husband did not look like this at all. Madame Keiro then stated that Mr Betts went to the City every day, and worked near the Mansion House as an engineer. None of these facts were true.

She was told she had a relative in Australia (she didn't, although she had one in Russia); that she would have a baby in eighteen months, and eventually would have 'five or six' children, one of whom would be 'a genius'. Annie had no children at this point, and would only ever have one, a daughter, during her life.[16] When she then said that Mrs Betts 'could be thoroughly trusted with money and would deceive no one', Mrs Betts admitted in court that she had blushed a little, embarrassed that she was, in fact, deceiving Madame Keiro.[17] Madame Keiro herself, however, continued to deceive audiences for some time to come, and in 1917, was sentenced to two months in prison after being found guilty of fortune-telling.[18]

Throughout the second half of the nineteenth century, there had been numerous prosecutions involving mediums, spiritualists and palmists. Women were frequently involved in court – if not as the accused, then as witnesses, victims, and, as the twentieth century dawned, professional private detectives, paid to investigate these spiritualists.[19] Into this world came Rosalie Thompson, who was a poacher turned gamekeeper: or rather, in her case, a spiritualist turned private detective.

She had been born Rosalie Middleton near Sutton Coldfield, east of Birmingham, in 1868.[20] An architect's daughter, she grew up into an educated middle-class family, although her father had been made bankrupt when she was just a year old.[21] In the winter of 1886, aged only 18, Rosalie married Edmond Thompson, then a commercial traveller, and seven years her senior. They initially lived in Harborne, now one of Birmingham's suburbs, before relocating to north London, when Edmond set up business in the city as an isinglass and glucose manufacturer.[22] Rosalie, however, was not content with domestic life while her husband worked, and instead took up spiritualist work, juggling this with her home responsibilities, which included being the mother of three children.[23] The family moved to a house named La Turbie, on the Seymour Road in the smart area of Finchley's Church End, and with a view out over the new Victoria Park.[24] The house had gardens that required the use of a Green's lawn mower; and the family kept chickens there too.[25] It was at La Turbie that, on 25 January 1907, Edmond died prematurely, at the age of 45.[26] Rosalie was left a widow at just 39 years old.

Rosalie had married well, and it is hard to believe that on being widowed, economic necessity required her to find work as a detective. The notice placed in the local press after Edmond's will had been proved, asking those with claims against his estate to come forward was not out of the ordinary – it was a usual form of wording designed to ensure that there were no individuals or businesses with claims against Edmond's business as an isinglass and glucose merchant, giving them a month to detail claims against the estate.[27] In addition, when probate was granted to Rosalie on 9 March 1907, Edmond's effects were stated to be worth £25,000 – a considerable sum.[28]

It seems more likely, given her spiritualist work, much of it conducted during her marriage, that this was a woman who wanted to work, as opposed to needing to. Spiritualism, detective work, acting and suffragist work – all areas studied in this book – had a similar basis in late Victorian society: as Louisa Hadley has described it, 'nineteenth-century spiritualism challenged Victorian ideologies of gender by providing a space in which women could earn a living'.[29] This work not only offered women the chance to earn a living, but the chance to take on different roles, to challenge themselves both physically and mentally, and to assemble for themselves an identity that was not 'just' that of mother, wife or daughter. It extended their horizons beyond the normal work available for women from different classes – beyond domestic service or teaching. Spiritualism reflected the Victorians' obsession with the dead; detective work, though, emphasised the living.[30] Rosalie had gained a rewarding occupation during her marriage, but it could be that, on being widowed, she found that detective work offered a more reliable income, whilst still involving her skills at 'reading' people. Yet the timing cannot be a coincidence for certainly, within a year of being widowed, Rosalie had found her independence again, and was appearing in the press and the courts as a twentieth-century lady detective.

The first case in the press where Rosalie was named as a detective was a divorce case heard in November 1908, where a Covent Garden fruit broker, John William Dennis – known as Jack, and then aged 42 – asked for a divorce from his wife Rose, alleging that she had committed adultery with a Herne Bay vet, George Hastings Butcher.[31] Dennis accused Rose of extravagance and drug taking, and after receiving 'information' in October 1903, he made inquiries at a Birmingham hotel. As a result of the information he found out, he stopped living with Rose. She sought a reconciliation, and wrote to her husband apologising for her behaviour, arguing that she had become 'infuriated' with him, and had been foolish, but still loved him. He forgave her, but they remained separated, with Rose receiving an allowance of £312 a year. Jack remained suspicious of her despite his stated forgiveness, and when Rose went to a hydropathic retreat at Herne Bay, he heard rumours as to her behaviour.

It was at this point that Jack hired Rosalie Thompson, lady detective, to watch Rose Dennis. Rosalie posed as a journalist, staying at the same retreat as Rose, and made efforts to draw her into conversation – she stated in court that she 'established friendly relations with Mrs Dennis and became her confidante'. From this, she found out that 'Mrs Dennis was carrying on an intrigue with Mr Butcher'. She told Rosalie that she had been regularly meeting him, and let him into her room through a window in the garden. Indeed, Rosalie spotted Butcher several times clambering in through the same window. Butcher referred to Rose as 'my own darling girlie' – what he called his own wife, Florence, who wrote to Rose asking her 'as a woman, one to another' to stop 'encouraging' her husband, is unknown.[32] What is known, however, is that Jack Dennis successfully gained a divorce from Rose, and soon after announced that he was to marry widow Betsy Keith of Marylebone; it was, perhaps, this new relationship that had finally induced him to employ Rosalie and find evidence of his first wife's behaviour, years after she had first aroused his suspicions.[33]

In July 1909, Rosalie appeared as a witness in a case at the Divorce Division of the High Court of Justice – another case which showed that, like many other women, she was often engaged to find evidence of adultery to be used in divorce cases. This particular case was brought by Harold Walter, a South Hampstead goldsmith, who wanted a divorce from his wife, Alice Elizabeth. They lived at Lancaster Gate, where a friend, Hans Bergmann, regularly visited them. In December 1908, Alice Walter complained of being ill, and 'insisted' on going to Paris to recuperate, despite her husband trying to make her go instead either to the English seaside or to her mother's house. She got her way, and went to Paris; but on 4 January 1909, they separated, initially on 'affectionate' terms. They continued to communicate by letter, and it was when Alice made the mistake of telling her husband that Hans Bergmann was travelling to Paris to visit her that Harold got angry. He hired a detective to watch his wife, and the evidence found was enough for him to bring a petition for divorce. It was, of course, Rosalie Thompson who had been hired to watch Alice in Paris. She gave evidence stating that she deliberately stayed at the same hotel as Alice, and managed to get into conversation with her. Alice told her new friend that she was 'expecting her half-brother' to visit her – and Rosalie saw Bergmann visit her every day from 19 January to 22 January, reporting that they were 'together as lovers'. Alice offered no defence, and the divorce was granted.[34]

By 1911, Rosalie was being described in the English press as 'Rosalie Thompson, the lady detective' (although, of course, other women proudly described themselves as the same, as the previous chapter showed). In the 1911 census, she gave more details, noting that she was a private detective, employed at that time by Walsh and Stockley, and living in a Marylebone flat with her son Victor.[35] Like many of her fellow female detectives, Rosalie worked on divorce cases, but she also got the opportunity both to undertake other work, and to travel. In one case, in 1911, she was employed as part of an arson case. Isabel Scruton, a

15-year-old nursery maid, was charged with setting fire to her dressing-table cover, as a means of burning down the house of her employer in Harrogate. There had been previous attempts to set fire to the house, and these were seen as so mysterious that Rosalie had been employed to find out what was going on. As one paper put it, though, 'the introduction of a lady detective, still disguised in the uniform of a nurse, into the case, gave it a melodramatic turn'.[36] As this suggests, Rosalie had been 'introduced' into the household as a nurse, complete with full uniform. The previous Monday, a cupboard holding a hot water cistern had been found aflame. The following day, a fire was set in a spare room, ruining the furniture although, luckily, not the house. Sometime between that day, Tuesday, and Friday, Rosalie had been employed and come into the house as a nurse – hired on the grounds that she was 'a lady detective from London with seventeen years' experience of detective work' behind her.[37]

In the event, not much detective work was required by Rosalie, for on the Saturday the maid was seen by a parlourmaid, Kate Robinson, in her nightdress, crying, 'I've set my room on fire; my room is on fire!' Matches were found under her pillow, with burnt ones on the floor by the bed and in the fireplace. Rosalie was then called to give evidence, starting by saying 'she was in Mr Heaven's house for a purpose'. She stated that about midnight on the Thursday, she had retired to her room, where she sat up until after 2am. At that point, she heard a thump – as though a chair had fallen – overhead, from the room above hers. She continued:

> 'I then heard a scream and a voice say, "Oh my God, Isabel has set the house on fire." I ran upstairs to find out what it was all about, and found Scruton in Robinson's bedroom. On passing Scruton's own room, I saw the tablecover on fire. I did not touch the fire, but went to catch the culprit. In Robinson's bedroom, I saw the girl Evelyn [Jefferson, a between-maid] on the bed and Scruton standing in the room. Scruton said, "I should not have done it, but I heard two horrid men's voices say, "Lie down".'

Rosalie believed the girl was 'insane', and, displaying compassion towards her, she took her by the arm and led her to her own room, staying with her a while to calm her down. She then went upstairs to Scruton's bedroom – not to go through her things for evidence, but to fetch her some warm clothing. However, while there, she realised that this was a good opportunity to look through Scruton's belongings. She found that all her clothes were locked up in her trunk, except for one print dress. Rosalie later told police that she felt the girl had the idea of setting her bedroom on fire, and with presence of mind, had then packed her box 'so as to make her escape when she had done it'. She believed that Scruton, once she had started the fire, had 'come to' – the shock of her actions had brought her to her senses. Interestingly, Rosalie then commented, 'I have had a great deal of experience of people of abnormal mind, and also of dual personalities.' It was determined that Scruton had set the room on fire, but it was likely to have been the result of somnambulism or a disturbed mind, rather than a conscious act. It could not, then, have been a malicious act – in other words, arson – and the girl was dismissed with no further action taken.[38]

It's difficult to ascertain with any certainty for how long Rosalie Thompson worked as either a spiritualist or a detective. In the latter case, she was certainly active from 1908 to 1911, and she appears to have enjoyed the subterfuge of being a detective, along with appearances in court. Both her jobs involved taking on different roles and performing – whether to audiences, to households, or to police and juries – and both offered a different life (or lives) to the one she had been brought up into. Most importantly, however, were the facts that her work offered her financial independence and intellectual stimulation. She also appears to have been fascinated by individual psychology, which is evident both in her manipulation of her paying audience in her spiritualist work, and in her watching and detailing of Scruton's motivations and actions. It is significant that the late nineteenth century had witnessed the birth of modern psychology.[39] As the twentieth century dawned, ways of understanding criminal behaviour were also being developed and dwelt on.[40] In this sense, Rosalie was reflecting this growing interest in rationalising and contextualising behaviour by understanding the psychology behind it, and the impact of mental health issues. Although Rosalie was a professional, and did not obviously display a 'maternal' sympathy towards those she was studying, it is clear that she was interested in their motivations, and that her detective work therefore gave her the opportunity to use her intellectual ability, analysing and reporting on the individuals before her.

What is significant, looking at Rosalie's case, is that the 'craze' for spiritualism and palm-reading at the end of the nineteenth century – the desire to 'make sense' of the world by investigating the possibility of life after death – was linked to the acting world. Spiritualists 'acted' a part; depending on their act, they became a character, producing voices, sound effects, mysterious phenomena such as ectoplasm or moving objects. They might be frauds, but they were often very clever frauds, keeping their paying audience captivated, and coming back for more. In this sense, they were actors or performers; and, given that professional actresses could become successful private detectives because of their skill in adopting different characters, then it is perhaps logical that spiritualists such as Rosalie found that their skills were useful in the detective arena, too.

The advocates of Women's Suffrage base their claim on a number of different arguments; but probably the working woman, of whatever class, puts forward the strongest claim of all for enfranchisement, not only from a personal point of view, but from that of the entire community.

Antonia Moser, in *Votes for Women*, 8 August 1913, p.650

Chapter 13

Suffragist Agents

It has already been shown how several professional performers turned at various points in their careers to private detection. It sometimes, although not always, offered more stability and job security; but both careers offered the opportunity of independence, variety, and travel. This independence – to have a career, to earn one's own money, and not to have to depend on a spouse or father for income and a roof over one's head – makes it easy to understand why both actresses and private detectives may have been supporters of the women's suffrage movement. Over 900 actresses were members of the Actresses' Franchise League, established in 1908; by 1913, both actresses and private detectives may have experienced gender inequality or expectations that they knew were not for them.[1] With both professions including strong, single women earning their own living, it is clear that they were politically and economically aware, and that they had ample cause to resent the limitations placed on them by prohibitive legislation and a patriarchal society.

The suffragist movement had its roots in the late eighteenth century advocating of equal rights by political reformers, but the movement really started to increase in the mid to late nineteenth century, as the male franchise was gradually extended. Debates on female suffrage in parliament began in the 1860s and continued annually throughout the 1870s and early 1880s.[2] In 1897, the National Union of Women's Suffrage Societies, led by Millicent Garrett Fawcett, was formed, becoming an influential organisation.[3] In 1903, the Women's Social and Political Union (WSPU) had been formed in Manchester by Emmeline Pankhurst, and became increasingly militant from 1905.[4] The Women's Freedom League was subsequently established in 1907, by a group of women disenchanted with the leadership and decision-making of the Women's Social and Political Union. Initially comprising seventy or so members drawn from the WSPU, it rapidly grew in terms of members and local branches. It started to produce its own newspaper, *The Vote*, which was written by its members. This was a vital part of the League's communications with the public and politicians, as well as with its members and supporters, highlighting campaigns and protests. It was a militant organisation, with members taking part in demonstrations and on occasion being sent to prison; however, unlike the WSPU, the Women's Freedom League was resolutely non-violent, and it and the WSPU differed in their views about violent actions such as arson or vandalism.[5]

Antonia Moser's last advertisement was in 1910, when she was no longer working as a private detective. Her interests had been taking her in another direction, leading her to offer an advisory service for women; given her independence of mind, her continuing business interests and her awareness of how the legal and political systems could be weighted against a married woman, it is not surprising that as the second decade of the twentieth century dawned, she had become increasingly politically aware, with this manifesting itself in an adherence to the suffragist cause.

By 1911, Antonia was contributing money to the suffragist cause, donating what she could afford to the Women's Freedom League national fund. Although she was a minor donor – her contributions usually being 2s 6d – she was committed to the League, and was also a keen reader of *The Vote*. Over the course of the next three years, she contributed letters to *The Vote* and *The Suffragette* – Christabel Pankhurst's newspaper, which started in 1912 – as well as to other non-suffragist publications such as *Globe* and the *Pall Mall Gazette*, setting out her political views and expressing her support for women's political emancipation.[6]

In December 1911, for example, a letter from Antonia was published in *The Vote*, in which she agreed with a suggestion that men should be allowed to join the Women's Freedom League. She argued that she had no issue with men as individuals, and that a 'man of thought and moral life' would agree with women that a system that 'places the woman on a lower plane of life than the man, and that accords to her a less wage for equal work, and that refuses recognition of the glorious battle cry, "No taxation without representation"' was an unfair one. She made a clear link between this unfair system and the issues that faced women, specifically, as a result:

The moral man stands aghast at the spectacle of a Member of Parliament whose 'head is bowed in shame' because a Prime Minister meets with an unfavourable reception at a public meeting, but who turns his head aside at the pleading widow trying to support a family of little children on a starvation wage. The moral man viewing the streets crowded with young women forced into a life of vice because they are unable to obtain a living wage to honest labour, reading of the attempt to prevent by Act of Parliament women earning their own and children's bread – then, indeed, he bows his head with honest shame.[7]

Antonia believed that women needed men to co-operate and help with their attempts to gain the vote and to redress the gendered balance of poverty and vice – that only by men and women fighting together for the same cause, could the suffragist aims be met and the battle won. Her letter is striking in the anger and frustration that seeps through in every word: in its ability to draw emotive pictures of life in the capital for women without wealth or family. Her disdain of male politicians turning their back on the problems of twentieth century life is also clear.

The claustrophobic middle-class background that Antonia was from had clear disadvantages, and she had cast that background off to help others. Already unconventional in terms of a middle-class woman – for example, by seeking a job when she had no financial need to, having an affair with her employer, setting up her own detective agency and using her former lover's name and reputation to gain publicity – Antonia continued to strike out, becoming an outspoken critic of the convention that meant that many women and poorer individuals from society were not able to have a say in how their country was run. She continued her association with the Women's Freedom League, and would be listed as one of their donors in 1913.[8]

Back in 1908, *Votes for Women* had discussed a speech given by writer Evelyn Sharpe coinciding with the start of the Actresses' Franchise League. She had given an 'eminently practical speech' where she had 'pointed out the effect that political enfranchisement would have on women's work and wages. Working women would never be able to improve their industrial position until they could back their Unions by a Parliamentary vote.'[9] This was an issue that Antonia was particularly interested in. In 1913, a letter entitled 'Women and the Vote' was published in the *Globe* newspaper, in which Antonia replied to an earlier letter, written by a man, noting:

> I would point out that the average woman knows just about as much as the average man of political and public questions. The woman's demand for the vote is based on the constitutional claim that taxation and representation are identical. At present an intelligent rate-paying woman, with large business interests, is ranked below a practically illiterate man.[10]

This was something that clearly rankled with her. She was certainly intelligent and rate-paying; and although her business interests could not be deemed to be 'large', she had experience of running her own business, certainly, and was clearly an able individual. However, her divorce had taught her the unfairness of a system that demanded more from women than from men, yet still rated men as superior, regardless of their background. She saw herself as equal to, if not superior to some, men, and demanded to be recognised as equal. She compared the vote-less woman to a woman with a disability – she had no power, and was not listened to, or ignored, compared to the able-bodied – the man. As Antonia concluded, 'logically speaking, this is neither just nor right'.[11]

Not everyone in the private detective world was as vocal as Antonia when it came to women's suffrage – and it shouldn't be assumed that all female detectives felt the same as she did. Maud West, for example, may have been commissioned to investigate property damage caused by suffragettes, to protect houses seen as being at risk of such damage, and to investigate household staff suspected of supporting suffrage.[12] In her case, the need to earn money was perhaps more important that making a political statement. Others working at this time were more supportive.

In 1911, suffragists held a boycott of the decennial census, refusing to be counted by the government. The campaign was instigated by the Women's Freedom League, which encouraged women to spoil their census forms. Rather than input their details, they wrote messages on them, such as 'I don't count so I won't be counted', or 'no persons here, only women'.[13] Others moved round different addresses during census night in order to confuse the census enumerators or obfuscate their real details. Census enumerators would attempt to fill in the gaps, or missing details, on such forms, or note where a female resident had refused to provide her information.

Matilda Mitchell didn't take part in the boycott, simply recording her details proudly as 'lady detective' on the census, which listed her at her parents' home in Wimbledon on the night of 2 April 1911.[14] Kate Easton, however, took part. The census return for Warwick Mansions, 15 Warwick Court, London, records the presence of Kate Easton, single, private enquiry agent – but her age is given as 'about 45' and no birthplace is recorded. The entry, though, is not in Kate's handwriting, but that of the registrar, who has noted at the bottom, 'NB Information refused by Miss Easton'. Kate Easton's niece, Madeleine Lucette, incidentally, was also a supporter of the suffrage cause.[15]

In-between Kate and Matilda sat Margaret Cooke, the former siffleuse and single mother, who provided her (not wholly correct) details on the census – '40, widow, private enquiry agent, born Liverpool'. However, a notation at the bottom, which looks to be in her handwriting, although in pencil, states 'Suffragette' with a big circle round it. Next to it, a perhaps mocking enumerator has scrawled 'but answered questions'. Margaret was willing to record herself and her daughter, but wanted to make clear that she still supported the suffrage cause.[16]

Antonia Moser's former colleague and lover, Maurice Moser, died at Boulogne in 1913.[17] Two months after his death, a letter she had written appeared in the *Pall Mall Gazette*, its contents suggesting that she had been reassessing her life, and the lives of other women, in the aftermath of his demise. In this letter, Antonia noted:

It is difficult to break away from tradition, but the unprejudiced mind wonders why the little girl of the working class home has to mother the family when the real mother is out at work, to nurse a baby as big as herself, to clean down house and children, cook the food, and generally act the housekeeper, whilst the small boy is allowed his manly freedom to fish for sticklebacks, enjoy the freedom of the road, and generally employ his time in any and every way that suits his audacious little self.[18]

In the letter, Antonia listed the chores that a mother was expected to do each day, in addition to the paid work she had to do 'to augment the family income'. Her domestic chores had to take place both before work in the early morning, and on returning home in the evening, and included washing, cooking, ironing, and mending, in addition to planning meals and buying food to cook for her husband and children. The wife was left to do the bulk of household tasks, and in spending so much time cooking for others, she might only get a 'cup of tea and a bit of bread and butter' for herself. Girls were brought up to follow their mothers' example, whereas boys were 'waited upon' by the women in their families, and left 'unable to clean their own boots or brush their own clothes'. As a result of men being looked after by women, and not learning how to do things themselves, Antonia noted:

They are lacking in resource, are deficient in a sense of honour, and as men, they grow up to be worthless adventurers and triflers with women's affections.[19]

Was Antonia writing about her own experience with men here? She had firstly married a 20-year-old with little life experience, who followed his uncle and grandfather into their business. He had proved a 'worthless' man in having a relationship with her younger sister, Ada. She had then embarked on a passionate relationship with the older, experienced, Maurice Moser; but he was something of an adventurer, and had proved a violent, unpredictable partner. If she was angry, she had every reason to be so, and her sense of 'cant and hypocrisy' towards the roles of men and women was reflected here. She argued that women gaining the vote was a means of 'reclaiming the manhood of the country', and it is clear that her own experiences with men had led her to believe that this was something that urgently needed addressing.

Antonia's background was very different to many other private detectives. She had been expected to be a dutiful daughter, wife, and mother. She had been named after her dead mother, and married off to her first cousin; her family had money, so she had never been expected to need to work. Yet she had rebelled, and established her own career as a private detective as a result. Her fight to do so had led to a keen awareness of the issues facing women, and the need both for them to be able to have a career of their own, and for men to look after themselves. Kate Easton, however, from lower down the social ladder but with an ambitious family where music and performing were seen as valid ways to be independent and earn a living, had seen from a fairly young age that women could have a different way of life – and that she didn't need to conform. In 1907, she asserted that 'I have always done a man's work, and I always will.'[20]

In June 1914, a tragic event took place that preoccupied Antonia, and became a source of anger to her. It was an event that she investigated keenly, as befitted a former private detective. A suffragette named Joan Guthrie, who was also known as Laura Gray, died at the age of 24. She had killed herself, using a poison, veronal. From a young age, she had been interested in socialism, and had expressed her desire to 'dedicate her life and fortune to help her unfortunate sisters'. At 18, she had become actively involved in the suffragist movement, and had quickly become more militant in her actions, being convicted of militant tactics twice, and going on hunger strikes. She had tried to make a living as an actress, before her family installed her in a flat in Jermyn Street and gave her an annual allowance of £100.

Joan was said to be a regular user of drugs, due to suffering from neuralgia, and had been taking veronal – a barbiturate used most commonly as a sleeping draught, but also to treat mental illness – for several months before her death. On Monday, 8 June 1914, Joan Guthrie was found unconscious on the floor of her flat. A letter to her mother was found nearby, saying goodbye, and admitting to her use of veronal. Joan died; at her inquest, the coroner criticised the WSPU for sending her a letter and a medal 'for valour', with both being 'in recognition of her hunger striking'. He stated that the letter was 'calculated to upset the stability of a young girl's mind', and that Joan had been 'lost to all shame and decency, and her degradation was complete'.[21]

Antonia had known Joan, for the latter had sought her help professionally – perhaps on reading one of Antonia's newspaper adverts highlighting her 'free advice', or through their shared passion for the suffragist movement. Antonia now read the accounts of Joan's death, and the scornful comments of the coroner, and was infuriated. She wrote letters to several newspapers attempting to set the record straight about the suffragist cause, which she recognised would be damaged by the coroner's views. She was used to seeing her letters in print, and was frustrated when none of the publications she sent her letters to would agree to publish them. Now, she sent her letter to *The Suffragette*, which alleged that the mainstream press had 'suppressed' her views, and duly republished Antonia's account.

In it, she first emphasised that Joan's untimely death was nothing to do with the WSPU, its ethos or its teaching. Joan had not been swayed by their medal and commendation: instead, she had continued to live her own life – one that Antonia stressed was 'to me, a perfectly moral and upright life'. Antonia then proffered her own views about Joan's motivations, stating that eighteen months earlier, Joan had approached Antonia for advice about a man who had 'obtained an improper influence over her'. This was a girl who had been weakened in prison from force feeding, which had led to her already delicate system becoming even more delicate. This, combined with the man's subsequent desertion of her, had, Antonia stated, led to her taking drugs.

Antonia's anger was directed not only at the press coverage of Joan's suicide, but at the availability of drugs such as veronal, which could be easily purchased without a prescription or doctor's certificate.[22] Her letter was not published by any of the mainstream newspapers perhaps because the story it told was not as newsworthy, or dramatic, as one that brought the WSPU into disrepute. The male-run establishment newspapers had a line they wanted to take, and the downfall of a well-to-do woman, caused by a militant female-led organisation, was a better story for their purposes than one of a woman weakened mentally and physically by prison treatment, and by a deserting lover.

While Antonia continued to write letters and follow politics from her base at Southampton House, in Europe, tensions were building. Conflict in the Balkans was followed by the assassination of Austrian Archduke

Franz Ferdinand and his wife Sophie in Sarajevo on 28 June 1914 – an event described by one British newspaper as 'another tragedy added to the tragic history of the hapless House of Hapsburg'.[23] A month later, Austria-Hungary declared war on Serbia, suspected of involvement in the assassination plot. Germany declared war on Russia, and then on France; then Belgium refused to let German troops use its borders to cross into France. Finally, on 11pm on 4 August 1914, the British government declared war on Germany after it failed to make an assurance that Belgium's neutrality would be respected.[24]

'Oh! Don't you remember me, Ellen?' asked the lady detective; 'I had you the first time you were ever caught.'

Western Gazette, 28 January 1915, p.8

Chapter 14

War and Peace

There is often an assumption that war changes everything: it rends the fabric of society open, disrupting anything and everything. Yet although conflict is always in the background, life continues, often with all its inanities and routines. It could be argued, in fact, that life must continue as much as before as possible, in order to maintain social cohesion and order. In the winter of 1914, Britain was at war, but the seriousness and uncertainty of conflict over the next four years did not end the career of the female detective, or the desire on the part of the population for gossip, scandal, and tales of detectives' deeds. In fact, perhaps the war even increased people's desire for gossip, with some individuals, at least, wanting to avoid serious news and have a bit of entertainment to take their minds off what was going on internationally.

When what became known as the Slingsby Suit occurred, the public duly lapped up stories about it in the press; and the female detective became involved, and became news too. The case revolved around a four-year-old boy, Charles Eugene Edward Slingsby. Ostensibly the son of Charles Henry Reynard Slingsby of Scriven Park, Knaresborough, and his wife – American widow Dorothy Morgan Warner – he was heir to the Slingsby estates in Yorkshire. His parents had been married for ten years by the time he was born in 1910.[1] In 1914, Charles Slingsby Senior's two brothers alleged that little Charles was actually the illegitimate son of one Lilian Anderson, who had given birth to him in San Francisco. She was unable, or unwilling, to take care of him, and a go-between arranged for Mrs Slingsby to adopt him, and 'pass him off' as her own child.[2] The case duly went to court.

The Slingsby Suit had already occupied the mind of Judge Bargrave Deane for seven days when he heard what was deemed to be 'extraordinary evidence' regarding a 'woman detective'.[3] This female detective had been employed to investigate whether Charles Slingsby was really Anderson's child. She had spent two weeks 'bothering' an American nurse named Hattie Blain, apparently because Dorothy Slingsby had stated that her baby had been born at Blain's house – the two American women had been friends for twenty years. First, this sleuth offered Hattie money to testify against Mrs Slingsby, and when this failed, she tried a different method. The unnamed lady detective had done her homework, and discovered that Hattie had been performing illegal abortions from her home. She tried to blackmail her, knowing that Hattie couldn't afford to have her business uncovered, and stating that if Hattie did not testify that the baby was not a Slingsby, she would expose her. She told Hattie:

'I know Mrs Slingsby's whole history. She is nothing but an adventuress. There is your price. You had better tell the truth.'

Although Hattie duly gave evidence against Dorothy Slingsby, it was later decided that Charles was a legitimate Slingsby, and the case settled. It appears to have been simply an attempt by other family members to ensure they inherited the family estate.[4]

The case was fascinating not just because of the complex family relationships it exposed, and the underlying snobbery towards a woman of American birth, as Mrs Slingsby was, but also because of the apparent lack of solidarity between women. Hattie was willing to give evidence against her friend of twenty years; the female detective – whose name was less important than her gender and job – was allegedly willing to blackmail a woman for helping others obtain abortions. This was a modern world where it was survival of the fittest; there was little sisterhood evident in this case.[5]

The Slingsby Suit also highlighted a further use of female detectives in trying to obtain information from other women in issues around legitimacy. This was, however, similar to divorce cases: the emphasis was on women's sexual behaviour, their perceived morality and 'betrayal' of men. Female detectives were used along with male, but the role of the women detectives was clear – they were seen to be more likely to gain the trust of the women they needed to question, and to obtain valuable information from them. Yet it also seems that these female detectives were not perceived to act in a suitably 'feminine' way – they were willing to extort, to blackmail, to use money to get the results their clients required.[6] This would have reinforced some perceptions of the private detective being unscrupulous and even unprofessional – perceptions that linger today.

In recognition of these perceptions, a year before the war started, in 1913, a retired Met police detective named Harry Smale had met with a group of London private inquiry agents to form the British Detectives Association. The Association aimed to both promote and protect its members, to stamp out abuses, to improve methods of private detection and to stop fraudsters from operating. In short, to 'make it a clean profession by our example and endeavour to purge it of undesirables'.[7] However, the agency had limited results or publicity until the 1930s, and in reality, the life and work of the private detective in Britain, both male and female, continued in a similar vein as before, notwithstanding this new organisation's creation.[8]

Therefore, throughout the First World War, female detectives continued to go to work, their lives disrupted less than those men who had to head to mainland Europe to fight. They perhaps benefited, in fact, from the absence of some men who at home worked as private detectives or police officers – their absence creating more work opportunities for the women left behind. Although there were plenty of opportunities for women to get involved in the war effort, the likes of Kate Easton and Maud West continued to work hard in their businesses, and in fact may have made the most of war, with Kate, as we have seen, using the opportunity to advertise in different publications, targeting servicemen who may have been afraid of their wives having affairs while they were away. Although this seems a cynical, hard-headed approach, Kate was solely responsible for her own economic survival, and to utilise all the opportunities that came her way made sense.

Although Kate's life may have continued along similar lines as before, for one other private detective, at least, the war would be life-changing. Rose Hannah Pattine Joyce St Cass Graham, a Scottish-born private detective who again had theatrical connections (she was a former theatre usher, the wife of a theatrical props maker, and the mother of a music hall artiste), had been working as a private detective in Sheffield back in 1911. Rose appears to have separated from her husband – they were living in different locations in Sheffield – but had two of her three children still living with her, who she needed to support. Her youngest child, Robert, was at this time 14 and still at school.[9] He later joined the Royal Navy as an Able Seaman, and during the war went off to see action on HMS *Defence*. On 31 May 1916, aged 19, he was killed in an explosion on board the ship. For his grieving mother, by this point living in Manchester, there was no sense of closure in a funeral, for Robert's body could not be recovered for burial.[10]

A new opportunity opened up for some other female detectives during the war: theft continued to be an issue during wartime, and women appeared in courtrooms across the country charged with stealing. Some thefts were the result of economic deprivation either caused by, or exacerbated by, the war. In York in December 1916, for example, one widow was convicted of stealing 11*s* 6*d*, 'the property of the Minister of Munitions' (David Lloyd George), but was bound over to good behaviour rather than being sent to prison, after it was found that she was poor and was struggling to feed several children.

Munitions factories were set up in the First World War to make armaments and equipment to be sent to troops on the frontline. In 1915, production levels at these factories needed to be increased, and so an appeal was made to encourage women to register for war work. Thousands did so, and many were employed in the increasing number of munitions factories, becoming known as 'munitionettes'.[11] The work was tiring and sometimes dangerous, but there were also instances where female solidarity failed, and women accused their colleagues of stealing their property. A married woman, Annie Robinson, from Pontefract, who worked at a munitions factory, pleaded guilty to stealing a pair of boots from a munitions worker and was fined 40 shillings. Thefts from and by workers in these munitions factories led to some employing their own female detectives.

These women were not pretending to be ordinary workers – instead, their role appears to have been well known and understood. Mrs Mary Perkins was employed as a detective for a munitions factory in Harrogate; when a worker, Florence Inman, suspected that her boots had been stolen after she had placed them under her coat in the factory's shifting room, she went straight to Mary Perkins to report it. Mary Perkins spotted another worker, Mary Rhodes, taking a small bag away, with the shoes sticking out of them; when the latter saw the detective watching her, she dropped the bag and ran back into the factory in her stockinged feet. Mrs Perkins' evidence saw Mary charged with theft.[12] Mary Perkins was herself an interesting character; she was the wife of George Perkins, the chief warder of Armley Gaol. After thirty years' prison service across England, George had died in July 1916, and now his newly widowed spouse was dealing with her grief by tracking down thefts in a munitions factory – her own war effort. A month before Mrs Perkins caught Mary Rhodes with the stolen shoes, she had received the King's Medal for meritorious service on behalf of her late husband.[13]

In Bristol, meanwhile, female detective Patience Lawrence – who had grown up at Chipping Campden Police Station in Gloucestershire, learning skills from her father, a police constable – was undertaking a range of investigative tasks, for different employers. One of her regular jobs was to go undercover at bazaars to detect thieves. In April 1916, she spotted a woman put a leather case into her bag before leaving. Patience followed her out, took her, and 'gave her into the custody of a policeman'. In court, the thief was bound over to good behaviour, and Patience was complimented on her professional skills.[14] However, Patience does not appear to have been a permanent store detective, but rather worked on a variety of cases; for example, during the First World War, she was also working on fortune-telling cases.[15]

The war may have caused changes in society, and given women new work opportunities in the absence of men, but for the private detectives, there was continuity in terms of some of their work. Individuals still petitioned for divorce; others continued to steal. War did not see private detectives' work dry up, and in some cases, it offered the opportunity to make money from it, as can be seen in Kate Easton's attempts to target the armed forces, and to perhaps encourage them to wonder if their wives, back home, were being altogether faithful to them.

As some of Patience Lawrence's cases, for example, suggest, there were many opportunities being offered to female detectives by the big stores and shops, not just in the metropolis, but in other cities. By 1913, Selfridges had its own, rather grandly named, secret service department, and, as mentioned earlier, Matilda Mitchell was its superintendent prior to the war. Another woman, Ada Alice Humphries, was also employed there as a lady detective.[16] These store detectives were seen as equal to the other 'lady detectives' who ran their own agencies, or who were largely employed on divorce cases. It's possible that they also represented a more 'acceptable' face of female detective work during the war period and immediately post-war, and in some cases, they were described in slightly patronising terms.

By this period, it was acceptable to refer to a lady detective as a 'female Sherlock Holmes', both capitalising on the continued popularity of Conan Doyle's creation, and ascribing to these women ingenuity and brains, but they were seen in the same newspaper articles as undertaking 'smart work' (as though this was not to be expected) and being 'little lady detectives'. This was how Blanch Bolton, a store detective for Debenhams in the West End, was described in 1919 after catching the 'stylish-dressed Russian lady' Marie Epstern Levinskaya stealing a lady's cloak worth over £8 from the store.[17] She had been aided by another of the store's detectives, a Miss Garrod. These store detectives benefited from regular wages, work and hours, representing a compromise between a 'normal' job and the flexibility (but accompanying uncertainty) of agency work or self-employment.

Therefore, it's not surprising that some private detectives became store detectives, or combined work on shoplifting cases with other types of detective work. Annie Betts – who, as a newly married woman a decade earlier had worked on the Keiro case – was, by the start of the war, employed by a detective agency run by former Scotland Yard detective Joseph Walker Madigan and his colleague William Brewster Kemp. However, she is also mentioned in the press as a detective based at Whiteleys store in Bayswater during 1914 and 1915.[18] She may have combined two jobs – one for the store, and one with the agency – or perhaps the agency gained her steady employment with Whiteleys and other stores, and took commission. She certainly took on other work, as, in a 1916 trial reminiscent of the Keiro case, she gave evidence regarding an alleged psychic and fortune teller.[19] However, whilst at Madigan and Kemp's in 1914, a month before the war started, she was tasked with posing as a customer at a sale held at John Barker & Co.'s on High Street, Kensington, with the aim of 'bringing shoplifters to justice'. When she saw anyone she regarded as suspicious, she had to watch them – and, of course, she successfully reported seeing two women steal a roll of silk and some silk scarves, hiding them under their voluminous coats. When she had taken hold of one of the women, 68-year-old machinist Hannah Kelly, Kelly had turned to her and said, 'Take your hands off me – you ought to be a man.'[20] Although the newspapers were accepting of lady detectives, it seems that some of their own gender could be less so.

'I may say that I am not by any means an ordinary detective; I am not a woman who is at the beck and call of a private inquiry agent who pays me so much weekly for my services, because that is not my way of doing business.'

'Adventures of a Lady Detective', *Ally Sloper's Half Holiday*, 7 July 1923, p.6

Chapter 15

Roaring into the Post-war Era

The 1920s heralded another new era for women: the war had ended, women over 30 now had the vote, and – crucially for those women who wanted to police their community or detect crime, but wanted a regular income and hours – becoming a policewoman was now an option. Attempts had been made since the end of the Edwardian era for women to be more formally employed by the police, and in Bath, for example, a Voluntary Women's Force had been in operation since 1912. However, it took the First World War for real change to take place, with so many working men heading off to fight. By the end of the war, various women's patrols had been established, and the first female police constable had been sworn in – Edith Smith, in Grantham, Lincolnshire.[1] Interestingly, part of Smith's job involved monitoring the morality of wives while their husbands were serving their country. This monitoring of wives' behaviour had, of course, been a key part of the female private detective's role for more than half a century.[2]

Shortly after the signing of the Armistice, on 22 November 1918, the Metropolitan Police Commissioner, Sir Nevil Macready, announced that the Met would introduce female police officers to its ranks – the Women Patrols – and twenty-one female officers duly started work in February 1919.[3] Outside of London, women also became police officers. In Bristol, for example, 'lady clerks' had been employed in the administration department of the Bristol City Police (later the Bristol Constabulary) since 1915, and female police officers joined the following year.[4] Women were not necessarily employed on the same basis as men; for example, the women initially employed by the Met had no powers of arrest, and were employed on a yearly 'experimental' basis.[5] However, the employment of women by the police was no longer a secretive act, nor one that was ad hoc and done on a case-by-case, informal, basis. Women who wanted to fight crime, or to sleuth, now had the opportunity to do so as a paid member of the police, and no longer had to be private detectives to do so. Patience Lawrence, in Bristol, may have been one of these women; a 1923 article about a case at Bristol Police Court refers to a deposition made by 'Patience Lawrence, policewoman'.[6]

Yet this was not the end for the female private detective, despite the apparent overlap between the role of policewoman as undertaken by Edith Smith, and that of the independent detective. A prime example of a 'hybrid' detective was Annette Kerner, who claimed – and it is important to stress this, as, like Maud West, she perhaps exaggerated her career in order to get work and be known – to have started work as a private detective back in 1919, working undercover for the Metropolitan Police, and monitoring the glamorous nightclubs inhabited by the flappers of the era.[7] Although still regarded as something unusual – given both the dominance of male detectives, and the tendency of women to work as detectives on a shorter-term basis, or on a more discreet basis – women continued to work in this field. Key to this, perhaps, was the freedom that working for themselves or for one of the established detective agencies gave. It was more flexible than employment with the police; it enabled personal as well as financial independence (although some would have earned only a small amount in their careers); and it also offered the chance to use methods that might not be acceptable in the police. Added to this was the start of the Golden Age of detective fiction, with books that suggested that those working for themselves to solve mysteries were more exciting, more exotic, creatures than the sturdy, methodical police detectives depicted in stories and newspaper articles.

In 1920, Agatha Christie published her first book – and the first featuring Belgian detective Hercule Poirot – *The Mysterious Affair at Styles*, and seven years later, the formidably intelligent female sleuth Miss Marple first appeared in a short story. Although Marple would not feature in a novel until 1930, Christie's works not only offered readers gripping stories of murders, mysteries, and detective work, they would also present a mainstream depiction of a woman solving crimes, proving more than a match for nefarious men and women. She was older, single, but not to be messed with. Christie published a book every year of the 1920s, tapping into the public desire for suspense and intrigue.[8] Her short stories were also published in newspapers during this decade, including 'Tommy and Tuppence', who had first appeared in print in 1922, and who were a married couple who went on various adventures (including chasing German spies). In a tale published in *The Sketch* in 1924, they decided to take over a private detective agency after its male owner is imprisoned for being 'rather indiscreet'. In this story, Christie draws attention to the gendered attitudes towards private inquiry work: the couple's 'chief', Mr Carter, fancies that Tuppence – who he refers to as 'Mrs Tommy' – might 'amuse' herself by 'trying her hand' at 'a little detective work'. Tuppence, meanwhile, imagines that this line of work will involve tracking murderers and finding missing family jewels, and has to be reminded by her husband that more mundane divorce cases are the main way in which private detectives earn their living.[9] Even into the 1920s, the belief remained in some quarters that women were merely 'playing' at being detectives, and had a romanticised view of what the job entailed.

Sherlock Holmes, the Victorian eccentric, remained popular throughout the 1920s, and also featured in numerous silent films, with *The Return of Sherlock Holmes* becoming the first Sherlock film with sound in 1929. Meanwhile, in the press, *Ally Sloper's Half-Holiday* published a regular series, 'Adventures of a Lady Detective', that purported to tell the stories of a real female sleuth's work. This series started on Saturday, 7 July 1923, with 'The Leaf of the Ivory Card-Case', and was prefaced with the sleuth's insistence that she was not the usual lady detective, employed by a (male) private inquiry agent who paid her a weekly amount for her services. This would be, the imputation was, the lower-class type of lady detective, whereas this lady was 'the daughter of a poor baronet, my mother was the child of a well-known archdeacon'.[10] It appears that there was now a sufficient number of lady detectives to be able to differentiate them by class; however, it has to be remembered that this series was the natural successor to the 1860s fictional tales of lady detectives, where the heroine is a respectable lady drawn into dangerous work by her lack of finances, but who always remembers to maintain her sense of morality and respectability. In the case of the *Ally Sloper* detective, she also maintains her gender identity, noting that although she had become 'fairly well known' as a feature writer – writing about her detective exploits – it had only been 'in an amateur way – that is, for ladies' papers only'.[11] The inference is made that just as writing for women's publications is 'amateur', so too is being a female detective. It is the men's roles that are the professional ones.

Yet such views were becoming old-fashioned, and perhaps represented a complexity of feeling amongst the British public about a rapidly changing society, reflecting views on what women's roles should be post-war. Although women who had taken on 'men's work' during the war were expected to stop in peacetime and let the returning fighters take up their prior employment again, many women did not want to. They had experienced financial independence and proved what they could do in the workplace, and it could not be expected that they would all become subservient domestic goddesses again now that they had experienced a different life. If the end of the teens brought with it the ability to vote for some women, and the opening up of public offices, then the 1920s would bring other changes, including the vote for all women over 21. Modern detective fiction made such work increasingly acceptable, albeit still attracting curiosity, and in the private detective world, women would become more open about their jobs and identities, while the industry became increasingly professionalised.

This perceived professionalisation was driven, at least in part, by men seeking to publicise themselves by their involvement with the world of lady detectives. Just as Henry Slater, two decades or so earlier, had realised that he could gain more publicity by associating himself with the modern lady detectives, so too did these more modern men. Charles Henry Kersey was the Henry Slater of the 1920s, in this sense at least. Charles was born in 1877 and joined the Metropolitan Police at the age of 22. After twenty-five years' service, in May 1925, at the age of 47, he retired. Armed with his police pension of over £181, he could have relaxed a bit, but he was still fairly young, and so, like several other Met retirees, he became a private detective. As a police sergeant, he had been in D Division, based in Marylebone, and as a private detective, he stayed there, combining the continued interest in female detectives with the popularity of Sherlock Holmes, by opening up his own College for Feminine Undergraduates of Crime Investigation. This was, fundamentally, a training school for female private detectives, based, inevitably, on Baker Street in London, but at number 130, not 221B.

In a series of photo portraits in 1927, published in *The Graphic*, Kersey demonstrated various elements of detective work to his young, female students. These included showing them how to do the 'copper's clinch' to apprehend individuals, how to disguise themselves as men, learning about how to spot shoplifters and, in what we would call a prime example of 'mansplaining', how to put on make-up.[12] Unfortunately for Kersey, who was presumably seeking publicity for himself as well as his female detectives' college, *The Graphic* misspelled his name, calling him G.H. Kersey instead of C.H. The former policeman presented a paternal air in the photographs; he was 50 at the time, and tall – 6 feet 3 inches. He also had a wife incarcerated in the Manor House asylum in Salisbury; he stated that she was mentally imbalanced and there was no hope of her recovery.[13] Therefore, perhaps lonely and wanting to have a purpose in life post-retirement, he gave these younger women advice and training based on his own long police career, and the opportunity to earn their own living. On a more practical side, though, it was also a way of taking advantage of the popularity of detective fiction and of the 1920s' woman seeking more exciting, challenging jobs in a modern era. The impression given by the photo portraits is that of an older man making money and getting publicity by engaging women in something novel: they make the photos newsworthy and attractive, but it is ultimately the man who benefits most.

Benjamin Welton, writing of the private detective industry in America during this decade, notes that such detectives were 'becoming affordable to the increasingly prosperous American middle class of the Jazz Age' although marital complaints and will disputes were the 'meat and potatoes' of their work, in contrast to the often more exciting cases worked on by the fictional Golden Age detectives.[14] Similarly, in Britain, there was a sense of prosperity and freedom after the war that meant a willingness to spend on the services of private detectives, as well as perhaps a decisiveness about seeking divorces, and the evidence needed to procure them – and a confidence on the part of the private detectives that work would be plentiful.

Although divorce continued to be a primary source of work and income for the private detective, other matters also occupied them now: they searched for dead or lost friends, and located birth certificates for individuals. Successful agencies depended on having networks of detectives in different parts of the UK or even worldwide, in order to be able to track down individuals or documents for those who were trying to contact people from outside of their local area. In 1920, a Mrs Schowb [sic], who was working as a private detective, gave evidence in a case where seven individuals were charged with melting down sovereigns into bars and disposing of them via merchants in Hatton Garden. Two of the seven suspects were a married couple named Stevens, who were staying at the Cosmo Hotel. Mrs Schowb had been employed to 'keep observations' in the hotel, follow the suspects – six men and a woman – and testified that she had seen them filling bags with bar-shaped parcels in the hotel's reading room, and then carrying the bags, now far heavier, away. Mrs Schowb had to stay at the hotel for at least a week, from 25 November to 2 December 1919, and noted 'almost daily' visits by other suspects to the hotel with empty bags that were then filled.[15] Meanwhile, experienced lady detectives continued to find regular work. Annie Betts, for example, had been working since the start of the twentieth century, when she was in her early twenties. She had a long and understated career that lasted at least until 1928. The 1920s saw her work, as far as can be discerned, purely as a store detective for Messrs Bourne and Hollingworth on London's Oxford Street, where she spent the decade bringing shoplifters to justice.[16]

Although detective work involved the basic skills that the likes of Mrs Schowb and Annie Betts demonstrated – sitting, watching, following, noting – technology by now also aided detectives in their jobs. Technology both enabled clients and potential clients to get in touch quickly, detectives to find out information without leaving their offices, and to report back to their clients. It is therefore unsurprising that the likes of Kate Easton and Maud West had telegraphy addresses and telephone lines to help them with their work. Kate's telegraphy address was 'Inquirendo' – meaning 'the authority to conduct an inquiry' – whilst Maud was 'Estamundo', a corruption of *en este mundo* ('in this world', although Maud may have meant to have *en el mundo* – 'across the world' – which would fit better with the common private detectives' boasts of having agents in cities across the world). Kate had a telephone number – Gerrard 6707 – by 1908, with Maud's 1911 number being

Gerrard 8561.[17] These both enabled faster communications with clients and their agents, but also meant they could try and position themselves at the forefront of the private detective world. From the Victorian era onwards, you had to be seen to be technologically superior, to have the latest gadgets and gizmos, which both showed your superior investigative powers, but also your success, for these things cost money. To advertise the technology you utilised showed that you were already successful and making money in your field, and those who could afford you would be drawn to your advert above those of smaller operators (or those perceived to be smaller).

These women were still in a minority of private detectives, operating from their own offices, and being their own employer, as far as archival evidence can suggest. The London private detectives are the best documented, due partly because they dealt with divorce cases and were able to appear with relative ease in the divorce court of the metropolis. They were also competing with many others, and so relied more on press advertising to get their names out there, and to sell their services in the same classified ad columns as their competitors. However, the 1920s saw more provincial detective agencies operating, and some of these – albeit not all – stressed that both men and women were employed as equals to take on cases.

Wallace Reid's Detective Agency in Chiswick made clear that both its male and female staff would take on 'any detective work', including finding evidence in divorce cases, and tracing 'lost friends'.[18] Dale's Private Detective Society, with offices in Bristol and Cardiff, stated 'lady or gentleman detective supplied at short notice' to work on divorce, desertion, and blackmail cases, whilst another agency in Gloucestershire stressed the reliability of its lady and gentleman detectives. Martin's agency in Manchester similarly emphasised its 'expert staff of male and females ready at a moment's notice', as did Dicks' Detective Agency, based in Brighton but with a second office in Glasgow ('our operatives, male and female, are all fully qualified and trained specialists').[19] The continuing number of divorces being granted in the courts meant that women were still needed to undertake this type of work in particular – there was undercover work that only women were seen to be able to do, in getting information from wives – and so it is no wonder that an Ilford-based agency noted in an advert that 'private detectives (either sex) are always in demand'.[20]

Other agencies that did not specify women – such as the Glaswegian agencies Macdonald's and Stewart's, and the Wynnecliff Private Detective Agency in Sparkhill, Birmingham – were run by men, but it is not clear whether they were one-man operations, or all-men agencies.[21] Stewart's claimed to be 'Scotland's premier agency for all classes of investigation', and in light of this claim, it would be unusual for it not to employ any women.[22] However, some agencies tended to focus on the individual who ran it, and preferred not to go into details about who else it employed. In some cases, this was to disguise the size of the organisation – private detective agencies could be operated on a 'smoke and mirrors' basis, press adverts giving the impression of a large organisation when, in fact, it might only have a couple of operators – or even only one.

In the theatres and picture-houses, however, the lady detective continued to strike a glamorous and exciting figure. In 1928, for example, *For Men Only* was released in cinemas, focusing on a lady detective – played by German actress Dary Holm – arriving in Switzerland to shadow a suspected forger. He manages to convince her (falsely) that he is innocent, before telling her that vigorous work such as hers is 'for men only'. Even contemporary reviews of this film criticised it for soon relegating its fascinating female lead to a 'back seat' in favour of a focus on the athleticism of its male star – Dary Holm's real-life husband, Harry Piel.[23]

Meanwhile, in theatrical productions that year, Edna Davis was playing a lady detective in *The Wrecker* at the New Theatre in London, while Elsie Randolph played lady detective Joy Dean in *That's A Good Girl* at the London Hippodrome.[24] To go with the toe-curlingly awful title of the latter, the detective in it is known as 'Snoopy', which manages to be both twee and patronising.[25] As with older fictional stories of the female detective, in this musical comedy, 'Snoopy' starts by investigating criminality, but ends by finding love – or, as *The Times* put it, she follows her suspect from London to the Riviera for 'reasons that get farther and farther from criminality and closer and closer to connubiality'.[26]

In reality, and as stressed throughout this book, private detectives did not go into the career seeking romantic love, but rather independence and to earn money; where the likes of Snoopy reflected the tales told by real detectives such as Maud West was in the emphasis on their powers of disguise (publicity photographs of the stage comedy showed Elsie Randolph, as Snoopy, disguising herself as a Dutch post office messenger girl, for example). Given that this was part of Maud's own attempts to publicise herself as a creative individual who frequently dressed up as elderly women or young men, and that this was unlikely to have been a regular occurrence given the usual nature of private detective work, both fact and fictional representations of the female detective may have over-exaggerated this aspect of their work.

The public undoubtedly liked hearing about the lady detective's work, and whereas in previous decades, these women had often been anonymous, and usually only heard of when giving evidence in court (often still without their names being recorded in the press), now, they were emerging from the shadows, as their work became more acceptable. Maud West, who was never slow to provide her name, spent the latter part of the decade selling stories of her work to publications such as *The Sunday Post*. She recognised the value of putting her name out there, to ensure that newspaper readers associated her name with 'lady detective' rather than the name of one of her competitors. Kate Easton was no longer her main rival, as Kate appears to have retired from the business by the 1920s (her adverts in the *Army & Navy Gazette* in 1917 are the last professional press references to her), and Dorothy Tempest died in 1928.[27] Meanwhile, Rosalie Thompson had remarried in 1920 and settled in South Africa.[28] However, there were others nipping at her feet, many of them younger than the Victorian Maud.

She could build on her age and maturity by stressing her years of experience in the field, but she also needed to come across as still young and active enough to track down miscreants, and to be 'modern'. In one story she appeared in in 1926, therefore, she highlighted her skill with a gun; she had been asked to attend a séance and shoot at whatever ghostly figures appeared there claiming to be from the spirit world. She insisted, 'I shall not shoot to kill, but my shot will be accurate enough to prove the point at issue. I can shoot straight. I have proved that on more than one occasion during many years of detective work in all parts of the world.'[29] Maud was striving here not only to compete with other female detectives, but with her male competitors as well. Although her gender had long made her newsworthy, in this article, she started by stressing her more male-associated qualities: her skills with a gun, her years of work, the 'excitement and adventure' she had packed into her life. Even the photograph used to illustrate this feature was of Maud dressed as a man: disconcertingly, as Charlie Chaplin.

However, Maud was still happy to also emphasise her more feminine skills. She was described as being 'an accomplished actress' – not surprising, seeing as she probably had been one previously – and this was seen as a vital part of her job, as was her ability to move happily among the social classes:

> One day she is engaged in the menial task of a charwoman and the next living the life of a millionairess in one of London's most fashionable hotels. She is just as much at home as the associate of the smart set in Bohemia as she is when called upon to live in the meanest hovel in the East End.[30]

Interestingly, Maud admitted to not enjoying portraying charwomen or chambermaids as part of her job, whereas the experience of staying at a fashionable West End hotel and pretending to be a rich woman with a maid was 'the most enjoyable experience'. Although she highlighted her gun skills ('one of the best lady shots in the country') and how skilled she was in preparing for any emergency, it was the experience of being a rich woman whose every whim was catered for that she particularly enjoyed. It was, perhaps, the role that she had never experienced growing up, and reflected the harsher reality of her background. It was rare that she got to play a 'lady', and so she particularly enjoyed doing so.

It is a curious thing, by the way, that ladies are so extraordinarily good at the technique of violent crime. Miss Dorothy Sayers and Mrs Agatha Christie can wield a blunt instrument with any man, or plan an alibi, or bamboozle a policeman. But so far as my limited experience goes, the lady detective has not made any great mark in the fiction itself. But she will come, she will come.

The Bystander, 4 March 1936, p.18

Chapter 16

The Dirty Thirties

The 1920s had seen the dawn of the Golden Age of detective fiction, but it was also the end of the Golden Age of female detectives. As the 1930s got underway, the world of these women was changing – women were increasingly working as police officers, and the old-school female detectives were starting to die off, both literally and metaphorically. Antonia Moser was dead; Dorothy Tempest was dead; and Kate Easton, one of the great London detectives, died of a broken femur in 1931. Maud West, though, bucked any trend of decline by becoming more omnipresent in the 1930s' press, selling her ever more dramatic stories, increasingly accompanied by creative photographs depicting this mature, experienced woman in various disguises. Alongside this, though, came an attempt to portray herself as a more serious professional: a surviving image in Manchester Archives shows her ostensibly in her detective's office (familiar to anyone who has watched the detective movies of the 1930s, or even *His Girl Friday* – her office bears a resemblance to Hildy's newspaper office in that film), with her magnifying glass, examining a document. Here, she is not in an outlandish disguise, but presents herself as closer to her 'real' look: a middle-aged woman with sensible hairstyle and clothing, working from a physical office rather than out on the streets. In this photograph, she is confident in her own personality and character to present herself as she is: the winner in the fight for supremacy in the rankings of 'THE lady detective'.

There is a sense, though, that Maud may have recognised that her world was coming to a close – that she was the last in the line of maverick female private detectives. Although there was still interest in the lives and work of the female detectives, and they continued to be represented in fictional works including plays throughout this decade, there was a feeling of change in the air. The 1930s started with the *Bristol Evening*

News advertising its serialised 'memories of a lady detective', with the key word being 'memories'; such detective exploits were from the past, tinged with nostalgia. Even the phrase 'lady detective' was declining in use during the 1920s, with there being far fewer mentions of it into the 1930s. Private detectives were becoming private investigators: a small change in terminology, but one that made less distinction between the genders. Indeed, the world of private detectives, regardless of gender, was evolving, as attempts were made during this decade to regulate the industry, making it, perhaps, less individualistic and less interesting as a result. Behind one of the attempts to regulate and control the industry was the formerly sidelined British Detectives Association, although its founder would also be dead by the end of the decade.

The British Detectives Association had launched back in 1913 with little fanfare, its foundation perhaps eclipsed by wider conflict and news that culminated with the start of war the following year. Its aims were laudable, but it is doubtful how much impact it had in the teens and 1920s. However, the 1930s saw concerns being increasingly raised about the unregulated private detective industry, which saw anyone able to establish themselves as a private detective, with no licensing or oversight. There had, of course, always been unscrupulous practitioners – the National Detective Agency fraud of the 1890s, the Slater's Agency court case of 1904, and the one-man British Detectives Association fraud in 1912 proving that was the case – but other operators had worked professionally and successfully up to this point.[1]

The 1930s, though, saw the British Detectives Association making more of a splash, and its efforts to professionalise its industry started to rally Members of Parliament to its cause. In September 1933, the British Detectives Association promoted a private bill, to which it claimed over 200 MPs had promised their support, that aimed to 'get rid' of fraudulent private inquiry agents from their profession.[2] The BDA claimed that there had been an 'alarming' increase in recent years of individuals establishing themselves as private detectives with the sole aim of extorting money from clients through blackmail. This had been an allegation made against private detectives for years, for during their work, they learned about secrets in people's lives that they did not want making public.

Although many detectives were professional and only used the information they gained for the purposes of the job they had been employed to do, some others did use the information in other ways. However, this was not always a black and white situation. The fact that several detectives had to resort, on occasion, to taking clients to court in order to get the wages owed to them suggests that these clients could be as slippery as some detectives; and if a detective was frustrated with being owed money, perhaps they might resort to threats or blackmail attempts in order to get paid ('Pay me, or I will tell everybody what I have learned about you or your spouse'). However, others were less scrupulous, and used the cover or identity of private detective to deliberately commit fraud, as the various cases of sham male and female detectives in the 1890s and into the Edwardian era detailed earlier had shown.

The status in 1933 was still that anybody could become a private detective and carry out confidential inquiries, and there was nothing to stop them then using that information to commit blackmail. The British Detectives Association wanted to make it mandatory for all detective agencies to be registered with a central authority, which would have the power to strike them off their register if there were any concerns about their operation, or if they were found guilty of malpractice. Only agencies with proven experience would be allowed to register. The association had decided these measures were needed because, as an official stated,

> Reputable private detective agencies are suffering heavily from the frauds of their bogus competitors, and it is necessary that the confidential nature of their business should be protected from these elements.[3]

The British Detectives Association's aims were laudable, in that they recognised a continuing problem with how private detectives were perceived by the public, not helped by the fraudsters who took advantage of the job. This reputational damage impacted on its members and the wider community, and by seeking to introduce a parliamentary bill after the summer vacation that year, they sought to both improve the reputation of the industry, and to publicise themselves in the process. The BDA expressed a wish to make it so that the public was 'assured' that any registered private detective they used had a certain level of competence – and professionalism – whereas at present, anyone could say they were a private detective, even if they had no knowledge or experience at all. Interestingly, the fraudulent detectives were seen as exclusively male – one newspaper sub-head read 'clearing out men who blackmail clients' – and reading the accounts of the proposed bill, it feels as though female detectives were being whitewashed out of the history of private detection; this was a male-run organisation proposing a private bill aimed at removing unscrupulous men.[4] This does not mean that women were perceived as being scrupulous and law-abiding detectives, but rather, that they were not considered part of the problem, or part of the solution, either. They simply didn't register on the British Detectives Association's consciousness.

This is possibly because, to parts of the media and the public, the female detective was now more associated with the store detective, or the police detective. She was less commonly thought of in terms of a private investigator, and remained a minority in this field. Now, the newspapers contained columns by 'lady detectives' who were professional store detectives. *The Dundee Evening Telegraph*'s 1930 feature 'Shoppers as I See Them: By a Lady Detective' noted that 'in London, most of the big stores employ lady detectives to watch their interests' as though this was a distinct, new, phenomenon, when of course female detectives had been employed by stores since the nineteenth century. The Dundee paper employed a store detective with 'over 20 years' experience in one of London's leading West End stores' to write a piece about her work. She, and women like her, were seen as intelligent and experts in psychology – although this female detective preferred to describe herself as 'a watch dog'.[5]

The lady detective, in the sense of a private investigator, was more of an exotic, fictional, creature in the 1930s than a widely understood reality. In 1931, Beatrice Lillie starred as 'lady tec' Shirley Travis in the film *Are You There?* This was described as a musical farce where, inevitably, much was made of the character's ability to take on various disguises, all put on as part of an attempt to free a duke's son from his seductress, a 'blonde vamp'. It being a farce, the disguises are over-the-top, with Shirley becoming a huntswoman, a nurse, and even an acrobat. This is a feisty individual who operates a gun and puts the seductress through a violent massage in order to torture her; but, of course, the denouement sees the duke fall in love with this unusual woman.[6]

In these cases, the 1930s suggests a new conservatism or regression to an earlier age: a desire to see women who sought to make a living as private detectives as objects of humour, transgressing gender stereotypes in absurd ways. Where they were acceptable was in working in shops, catching other women stealing – a more suitable, feminised, setting that did not threaten men's positions. Yet women were continuing to work as private detectives, women from different backgrounds and of differing marital statuses. The 1939 Register, taken shortly after the start of the Second World War, lists several of them. Barbara Chadburn, the newly married wife of a Met Police detective, and in her twenties, was working as a private detective and living in Mitcham, then in Surrey. In Westminster, Agnes Figg, a single woman in her early fifties, who was lodging with a retired lieutenant commander of the Royal Navy, was similarly working as a private detective, and stated that she was working for the government. Dorothy Rowella Hunt, aged 44 and single, was a private detective living near Agnes Figg, and the next door neighbour of female journalist and editor Vera Allen Anstey. In Guildford, Isabel Lovatt, a widow in her early sixties, was similarly a private detective.[7]

Meanwhile, in Sheffield, Mary Holme, aged 23, was also working as a private detective. Relatively unusually, her husband of one year, William, was also in the same profession, so they were a sleuthing couple. Unfortunately, having a shared interest and job did not equate to a happy marriage, and eight years after Mary had married William, she married her next husband.[8] These were all seemingly ordinary women, choosing to work in this field for various reasons. Only one of them – 26-year-old Anastasia Gardiner – though, appears to have been living in a boarding house in Hampstead with a student of Egyptology, a shorthand typist, and a film extra.[9]

The existence of these women shows that they were very much still part of the detective world, but that the media, professional organisations and parts of the public preferred to ignore them than recognise their skills and work. As they continued to work, attempts to professionalise the industry continued in the background. The British Detectives Association had a long, frustrating, and ultimately unsuccessful campaign to introduce legislation. Two years after their attempts started, in 1935, the Conservative politician Dr William O'Donovan stated that he was to introduce a private member's bill to 'control' the private detective, and the Home Office was also considering proposals to register private detectives.[10] The plans to introduce a bill would again come to nothing, as O'Donovan lost his parliamentary seat in November that year. However, in a report on these moves, the *Lancashire Evening Post* did recognise the involvement of women in the industry, and its report made clear that although women may have been marginalised by the likes of the British Detectives Association, they formed a significant minority of private detectives, in London at least. Its reporter stated that it was only in the 'last 40 years that private detectives have become a numerous body' – echoing the evidence here that the 1890s were a Golden Age in terms of private detective agencies – but that 'in the course of a walk through the West End I saw no fewer than 11 nameplates of women who have joined this profession', over one-fifth of the estimated fifty firms of private detectives in the capital.[11]

Women were faced with continuing competition, however, in the shape of former police detectives. These were men who were forced to retire at the age of 50, when they were still often active and wanting to continue working. Armed with their police pensions, the lure of private detective work was clear for them: it enabled them to earn more money, but also to utilise their police investigative skills while working for themselves. This had long been the case, but even in the 1930s, it was noted that 'a growing proportion of private detectives consists of ex-Scotland Yard men ... these men find in private detective work a suitable outlet for their energies, and there are several who, though they left the public service long ago, have never given up detective work.'[12] Although women were now able to join the police, they did not have the long history of working there in the same capacity as men, and so had a disadvantage in terms of both prior work experience and reputation amongst the public. They had to work that bit harder to gain future clients' trust, and to promote themselves, and in this context, it is clear why the likes of Maud West so assiduously worked to sell stories about their lives, work, and skills to the national press during the 1930s.

Before the new BBC1 drama Chandler and Co came along, Catherine Russell thought private detectives were a thing of the past. She was wrong. 'I thought, "Surely this sort of thing doesn't go on anymore", but all you've got to do is open the Yellow Pages – it's chockful of private investigators. We met a real female private detective ... and there's no way I could do what she does – I'd be too frightened of being spotted.'

Staffordshire Sentinel, 9 July 1994, p.19

Chapter 17

From Licences to Dog Leads

Although the 1930s appeared to herald a new age for private detectives, in terms of efforts being made to professionalise the industry, in truth, the situation rumbled on unchanged. Some twenty years after the British Detectives Association tried to bring forward a private bill to register all private detectives, it was still attempting to distinguish between qualified and unqualified agents, stating that it was 'disturbed by the apparent ease with which unqualified and unscrupulous men and women may take up private investigation ... there is, as yet, nothing to stop an ex "gaol bird" or blackmailer becoming or posing as a private investigator'.[1] The British Detectives Association even reported a case of a private detective 'who does fortune-telling as a sideline', which the likes of Dorothy Tempest had also done decades earlier.[2]

The 1940s saw the British Detectives Association increase its visibility, with male detectives such as Cunliffe's Detective Service in Blackpool and Preston, and the Lytham-based Hughes Detective Agency, advertising their services, and highlighting that they were members of the association.[3] Such membership was designed to make the private detective appear more professional, in the absence of other licensing or registration requirements. Private detectives, both male and female, continued to work on divorce cases, trace missing persons, and make confidential inquiries into the status of individuals and their occupation or trade. There was now an increase in other types of work, such as adoption cases, insurance cases and accident investigations.[4]

The Second World War may have temporarily reduced the number of private detectives operating in Britain to some extent, but given that many detectives were either retired police detectives or women, and that there was still a market for their services (as Kate Easton had shown during the First World War), the industry did not cease. In fact, there was a steady number of cases being dealt with by private detectives during wartime, and they continued advertising in the press, although the numbers of articles and adverts relating to private detectives decreased slightly in the latter half of the war. Missing persons were one focus of detectives' work during this period, such as when Irene Basini, a 16-year-old girl from Ipswich disappeared. She had been bullied by local girls because she was of Italian descent, and subsequently went missing. Neighbours paid for private detectives to help locate Irene, and she was found after a week, hiding in a London convent.[5]

Private detectives continued to have a market for their work during wartime because crime continued despite the war, and because people continued to live and to love during this period. Divorces still happened; people still went missing, got into debt, or were tempted by goods they couldn't afford, or preferred to steal, in local stores. The problem of shoplifting was a perennial one, and during wartime, it is understandable that some would have been tempted either by food, during times of rationing, or by clothing that they could not afford to buy. It was not surprising that in August 1941, one Newcastle store advertised for a lady detective, asking for a woman aged between 30 and 40 who had 'a thorough experience in the handling of shoplifters and shoplifting cases'.[6] At the top end of the shopping scale, female detectives worked at Harrods throughout the war, and in 1940 were involved in the conviction of a married couple for stealing and receiving clothing and jewellery from Harrods, the Peter Jones store in Chelsea, and Barkers in Kensington.[7]

When forged tickets for greyhound races were circulated in the northeast of England, both police and local private detectives were employed in looking for the forgers.[8] However, they could also be employed working on more individualistic cases, such as in 1944, when the Reverend Hugo Dominique de la Mothe, rector of Dogmersfield in Hampshire, was convicted at the Consistory Court of frequently being drunk, and drinking in local pubs (although he was found not guilty of 'making a nuisance of yourself in the presence of women'). The reverend, who blamed the case on 'village gossip', commented that for six months prior to the case being heard, he had been 'dogged' by private detectives, employed to find evidence of him drinking.[9] Presumably, in this case the private detectives were male, as they would have found it easier to shadow the rector in various local pubs, and drink without attracting the attention of the same village gossips. Even into the mid-twentieth century, there were still some jobs that male private detectives would find easier to undertake than their female equivalents.[10] However, the female private detective did continue to work throughout the 1940s; Annette Kerner, who had been working since the end of the previous war, established the Mayfair Detective Agency – based at Baker Street, to milk the link between herself as a maverick private detective and her fictional forebear, Sherlock Holmes. However, she was one of the 'old breed', semi-retiring in 1950 due to poor sight, and stating that she was a 'retired private detective' in 1952. By this point, she had gained a liking for gambling, had got into debt, and ended being charged with obtaining money under false pretences.[11] Kerner was, in this sense, somewhat reminiscent of the less ethical late Victorian and Edwardian detectives who promulgated negative perceptions of their profession by engaging in criminal activities.

Despite, or perhaps because of, cases such as Annette Kerner's, after the end of the Second World War, attempts again began to 'professionalise' the private investigating industry. In 1946, the Association of British Detectives was formed, but it soon became clear that having two separate associations did not help the industry present a united, coherent front to the world. Therefore, in 1953, the two bodies merged, becoming a new, larger, Association of British Detectives.[12] This larger organisation continued with earlier attempts to professionalise the industry, and in 1963 laid a charter before the Privy Council which, if granted, would enable their members to receive professional status. Its president at this time, John Walsh, stated that the charter would enable the public to recognise and use a 'genuine' detective rather than one who might defraud them. However, this professional accreditation would only apply to the owners of detective agencies, and not to individual detectives or employees of agencies, thus limiting its scope.

Women were also at a disadvantage, in that all people wanting recognition would need to provide two references from 'people of professional standing' and proof of the quality of their investigative work over a minimum of two years, thus limiting accreditation to those who were able to work consistently in the field for years, and those who knew professionals who could provide references. Lingering misogyny on the part of either the Association of British Detectives or the newspapers was evident in coverage of the attempts to gain a charter, when it was noted that 'former policemen' – not policemen and policewomen – with 'exemplary records' would be admitted to the Association.[13] Given that in 1953, over 80 per cent of the Association's members were former CID detectives, and that women had been admitted to the police for a relatively limited period beforehand, it gives the impression that the Association was a largely male body that saw women as an afterthought at best.[14] Yet although women may have formed a minority of its members, and a relative minority of private detectives, their history showed that they were an important part of the business, and hence stores advertising for female detectives, and agencies boasting about their use of the same.

Part of the association's remit appears to have been to generate positive coverage in the British newspapers about what its members did. In 1968, *The Times* included a full-page piece about how to trace missing people – from husbands deserting their wives, to teenagers running away from their parents. This made clear that the commissioning of private detectives was a largely middle-class activity, because those on limited incomes could not afford to do so, and might instead ask the Salvation Army for help. However, those using private detectives had a choice of around 600 detective agencies across the 'country' (*The Times* did not specify whether it was just referring to England, or Britain as a whole), of which around 400 were members of the Association of British Detectives.[15] It was noted that 'a substantial percentage' of these agencies' work came from either divorce cases or tracing missing people – and here, it was clearly specified that these tended to be girls between the ages of 17 and 21. Locating women and girls caused detectives particular issues, as they were less likely to return home than men, and were harder to trace as they 'frequently assume another name and rarely have an obvious employment link'.[16] There would be continuing attempts to regulate the world of the private detective throughout the twentieth century – a further attempt in 1973 saw chief constables around Britain apparently reluctant to endorse any licensing of agencies, in the fear that they would be seen as putting their 'stamp of approval' on individual agencies, while the Association of British Detectives now called for a code of professional conduct.[17]

The way in which private detectives were described changed over time – in the 1960s, it was noted that they preferred to be called either private investigators or private detectives, rather than private inquiry agents or process servers ('this smacks too much of the bad old days').[18] However, the way in which female detectives were depicted in both fact and fiction changed surprisingly little over the next few decades, although fictional female detectives became more likely to be undertaking detective work alongside a day job rather than as their full-time employment – from Jemima Shore, detecting while also working as a television investigative reporter in the early 1980s, to Maddy Magellan, writer and sidekick to Jonathan Creek in the 1990s.[19] A detective who happened to be female was still sometimes referred to as a 'lady detective'; although this was done more to signify a particular gender being needed – such as a store detective working in ladies' clothing departments – even in the late 1980s, one television series was described simply as a 'lady detective series'.[20] As with the reality, a lady detective was either seen as the sidekick to the male, or as a novelty that needed singling out. Yet despite one journalist confidently stating in 1993 that 'the image of the crime novel has changed. No longer does there have to be a body in a country house with a red herring and a shrewd amateur lady detective', the likes of Miss Marple remain popular today, and the re-publication of *Revelations of a Lady Detective* and *The Female Detective* by the British Library in recent years similarly attest to an interest in the history of the female detective, whether real or fictional.[21]

In 2011, the Association of British Investigators – the successor to the British Detectives Association and Association of British Detectives – published a discussion document, where, as in the 1930s, the 'questionable antecedents' of some working in the industry were raised: 'It is possible for anyone, even criminals, to advertise and trade as a private investigator … as a result, some lack integrity, [and] many lack know-how.'[22] The document, which estimates that there are between 5,000 and 10,000 self-employed private detectives working in Britain in the private sector, and which states that women form only 8 per cent of its membership (meaning there are only around forty female members), argues for the ABI to develop into a Chartered Institute of Investigators, where individuals have to be licensed and prove their competence before being allowed to practice.[23] In 2013, Theresa May, as Home Secretary, announced that the industry would be regulated, and that being an unlicensed private detective would become a criminal offence from 2014. Yet even in 2017, the licensing of private investigators appeared to be no further forward, with one private investigator complaining that 'nothing has happened'.[24] Therefore, at the time of writing it remains that anybody can establish themselves as a private detective, and although you can undertake training via various organisations in the skills needed to be a twenty-first-century investigator, there is no mandatory course or registration required. In fact, it is in some ways easier now to become one than in the past – all you need is a laptop or smartphone, an internet connection, and perhaps a car, and you can track a variety of individuals down.

This is simplistic, of course, but one fact remains: the private detective remains seen as a somewhat shadowy, mysterious, being – one who is also a subject of fascination to press and public alike. This is especially true of the female detective, who is both more shadowy than her male equivalent, perceived as being a rarity still, and thus the focus of particular interest. In the last few years, there have been a couple of articles in the UK press where female detectives have been interviewed about why they chose to work in this field, and what they do. Just as Maud West and Kate Easton recognised that secrecy was good, but sometimes publicity was too, so too have these modern detectives tried to balance dark with light.

In August 2019, *The Guardian* published an interview with a former journalist turned private investigator, Emmanuelle Welch, who detailed both her work, and the tools she needs to do it. Social media and open-source intelligence to undertake background checks; getting details off experts in different fields such as bitcoin transaction specialists, forensic genealogists, and AI (artificial intelligence) experts – these sound very different from how the private detectives of the past worked. Yet when she detailed the basic jobs she undertakes, including cheating spouses, process serving, embezzlement and insurance fraud, the work of Emmanuelle Welch does not sound dissimilar to the Edwardian lady detectives: similar work, but with more modern tools to investigate.[25] The same month, the *Daily Mail* featured an interview with Cotswold-based Alison Harris, who became a private investigator in her forties. Like

Welch, Harris often deals with personal relationships, such as allegations of cheating; like her forebears, she has also developed an ability to pretend to be someone else – often a dog walker. ('Always have a dog lead – you can get out of any situation with a dog lead!')[26] Harris appears to deal primarily with cheaters, missing people and debtors.

These articles show that women may have always formed a minority of private detectives, but that because of this relative rarity, and the secrecy necessary to their job, they have always been an object of interest to the wider public. The need to balance secrecy with publicity, in order to gain jobs in an increasingly crowded marketplace, has led to some of these women giving interviews, although few have gone to the lengths of Maud West to create an image of derring-do and bravery. The continued interest in these women also points to a lingering misogyny, or the expectations of what is, at heart, still a patriarchal society. That women have chosen independence by undertaking what is perceived to be a masculine, dangerous job remains a source of confusion for some, and of envy, perhaps, by far more. Yet for centuries, women have displayed a keen interest in their neighbours and communities, wanting to be involved in identifying miscreants and to play their part in the regulation of societies. From the mid-nineteenth century, the new divorce law gave them new opportunities to do so, whilst earning money, while others' skills – as well as their gender – was recognised as being useful by the police. In the twentieth century, women were finally able to join the police and become police detectives – but being a private detective has always offered something different, from being self-employed and working hours to suit, to providing a sense of independence that has not always been available to women. Whether or not private detectives ever get the chartered, professional, status that has been sought for decades, women will continue to work in this field, albeit still largely in the shadows.

Notes

Introduction: 'At least as good detectives as men'
1. *Cardiff Times*, 13 March 1897, p.7
2. 'The Lady Detective', *Yorkshire Evening Post*, 28 June 1901, p.4
3. 'Floral Frascati Restaurant, London', www.jazzageclub.com/venues/flora-frascati-restaurant-london/
4. *Yorkshire Evening Post*, 24 April 1909, p.5
5. *Yorkshire Evening Post*, 28 June 1901, p.4
6. *Leominster News*, 9 September 1904, p.3
7. Kathleen Gregory Klein, *The Woman Detective: Gender & Genre* (University of Illinois Press, 1995), p.5

Chapter 1: Early Detective Work
1. 'Sarah Good, theft from a specified place, 26 February 1680', *Old Bailey Online*, t16800226-1
2. 'Catherine Griffiths, Mary Evans: theft: pocketpicking', *Old Bailey Online*, t17570526-11
3. 'Jane Wylae: theft: grand larceny, 25 June 1788', *Old Bailey Online*, t17880625-36
4. Sir John Fielding (1721–1780) was the half-brother of novelist and chief magistrate Henry Fielding. Having been blinded in an accident in his teens, he was known as the 'Blind Beak' when he was appointed as a Bow Street magistrate after his brother's death (The Editors of Encyclopaedia Britannica, 'Sir John Fielding', *Encyclopaedia Britannica*, 1 January 2020, at http://www.britannica.com/biography/John-Fielding)
5. 'Elizabeth Cooper: theft: grand larceny, 23 October 1754', *Old Bailey Online*, t17541023-28
6. Janka Rodziewicz, 'Women and the hue and cry in late 14th century Great Yarmouth' in Bronach Kane (ed), *Women, Agency and the Law, 1300–1700* (Routledge, 2016), p.88
7. *The Police Gazette, or Hue and Cry*, 19 September 1828, p.2
8. *The Police Gazette, or Hue and Cry*, 19 September 1828, p.5
9. *Ipswich Journal*, 9 August 1735, p.1. It appears there may have been a longer standing issue or even criminal partnership between the two cheese men, as the press reported that both men ended up being put in the pillory. The hue and cry had to be 'raised' by those who lived in the hundred (a small county division) where a robbery or other crime had been committed – or they would become liable to pay for any damages incurred by the victim.
10. *Newcastle Courant*, 26 July 1735, p.1
11. Heather Shore, 'Crime, Policing and Punishment' in Chris Williams (ed), *A Companion to Nineteenth-Century Britain* (Blackwell Publishing, Oxford, 2004), pp. 388–9

12. This was not the first police force in the UK, with the City of Glasgow police force, established in 1800, probably holding that title. However, the Glasgow police were more similar to the older style of policing, taking on numerous jobs outside of law enforcement, and being a small organisation. In terms of the development of modern detective work, however, the establishment of the Metropolitan Police is arguably more significant.

13. Clive Emsley, *Crime, Police and Penal Policy: European Experiences 1750–1840* (OUP, 2007), p.108

14. Heather Shore, 'Crime, Policing and Punishment' in Chris Williams (ed), *A Companion to Nineteenth-Century Britain* (Blackwell Publishing, Oxford, 2004), pp. 388–9

15. *Freeman's Journal*, in Dublin, for example described the 'detective police' as having been given a 'terrible power', in that they were not restricted to simply pursuing offenders or protecting community property: 'None of us know how soon these men may be set upon our tracks – prying into our affairs – interpreting our acts – listening to our words – recording our conversations – noticing even our looks.' (*Freeman's Journal*, 4 October 1844, p.2)

16. *Coleraine Chronicle*, 12 February 1848, p.1

17. *Globe*, 30 August 1849, p.1

18. Bryan Kesselman's biography of Pollaky that seeks to cast him as 'the real Sherlock Holmes'. However, Pollaky, as well as pre-dating the invention of Holmes by decades (he only became a private detective in the late 1850s or early 1860s) to me appears to have been a slightly more mundane figure than Kesselman's description suggests (Bryan Kesselman, *'Paddington' Pollaky, Private Detective* (The History Press, 2015))

19. John Sutherland writes that Field was consulted prior to Palmer's charging or conviction, when an insurance company became concerned at the premature death of Palmer's brother Walter, as Palmer was the beneficiary of the policy. They consulted Field who advised them not to pay the money out and challenge Palmer to take them to court. Contemporary press reports include mention of Field's extensive 'professional aid to the local constabulary' and 'six weeks' of work, but the facts focus again on him simply advising the insurers not to pay out on an insurance policy – although in this case, one involving a labourer employed by Palmer (John Sutherland, *Victorian Fiction: Writers, Publishers, Readers* (Palgrave Macmillan, 1995 rpt 2006), p.36; *Ipswich Journal*, 5 January 1856, p.3). Field irritated his former employers at the Metropolitan Police by insisting on using the title 'Inspector' subsequently, during his work as a private detective, presumably because it gave him a gravitas and professional aura.

20. Heather Shore, 'Crime, Policing and Punishment' in Chris Williams (ed), *A Companion to Nineteenth-Century Britain* (Blackwell Publishing, Oxford, 2004), p.389

Chapter 2: It Started with Kate

1. See Fred Lewis Pattee, *The Development of the American Short Story: An Historical Survey* (Biblo and Tannen, 1923), p.165. Both Oliphant and Whyte-Melville were Scottish writers; O'Brien was an Irish-American author best known for writing surrealist fiction that was seen as the precursor to science fiction; he would die of tetanus in 1862 following a Civil War skirmish (*Appleton's Annual Cyclopaedia and*

Register of Important Events of the Year: 1862 (Appleton & Co, New York, 1863), p.664). *The Living Age*, which ran from 1884 to 1941, was officially titled *Littell's Living Age*, but was popularly known by the alternative title.

2. *New York Daily Tribune*, 23 August 1856, p.1; *New York Daily Tribune*, 23 August 1856, p.5

3. '1856 Presidential General Election Results – Illinois' at https://bit.ly/IllinoisElection. Buchanan duly became president, with John C. Breckenridge as his vice-president. The Illinois Governor was also voted for this year, but unlike the presidential elections, this time, the state voted for a Republican, William Henry Bissell – the first election of a Republican governor in the history of the state (the Republican Party itself was, in 1856, just two years old).

4. This was the site of Pinkerton's office in 1855, according to adverts he placed in the Chicago press at this time (for example, the *Chicago Tribune* of 2 May 1855, p.1). By 1868, he had relocated to 92 and 94 Washington Street. In 1871, 89 Washington Street had become the real estate office of WD Kerfoot, and a photograph of the building at this time can be seen at www.chicagology.com/biographies/kerfoot. The building appears to have been little more than a single storey, wood-built, double fronted shack, with the address painted onto the exterior wall.

5. Beau Riffenburgh, *Pinkerton's Great Detective* (Penguin, 2013), p.16; 1841 census for Little Bowhill, Glasgow St James (1841/644-1/46, p.9); National Records of Scotland, OPR 644-01/420, p.536, 13 March 1842

6. Anon, 'Allan Pinkerton (1819–1884)', National Records of Scotland (2020), at www.nrscotland.gov.uk/research/learning/hall-of-fame/hall-of-fame-a-z/pinkerton-allan; Beau Riffenburgh, *Pinkerton's Great Detective*, p.16

7. Beau Riffenburgh, *Pinkerton's Great Detective*, p.17

8. Accounts vary as to whether Pinkerton started an agency in 1850, 1851 or 1852. Richard Wilmer Rowan, in *The Pinkertons: A Detective Dynasty* (Hurst & Blackett, London, 1931), p.31, gave the date as 1850; Frank Morn, in *The Eye That Never Sleeps: A History of the Pinkerton National Detective Agency* (Indiana University Press, Bloomington, 1982), p.54, says 1851. Beau Riffenburgh is more cautious, noting that Pinkerton himself used 1850 and 1852 variously in his accounts (Beau Riffenburgh, *Pinkerton's Great Detective*, p.18). The Library of Congress, which holds the records of the Pinkerton National Detective Agency, gives the start date of these records as being 1853, but adds a note stating that the agency was founded 'circa 1850' (https://www.loc.gov/item/mm75036301/). S. Paul O'Hara, though, implies that the North West Police Agency (the precursor to Pinkerton's) only started in 1855 (S. Paul O'Hara, *Inventing the Pinkertons: or Spies, Sleuths, Mercenaries, and Thugs* (John Hopkins University Press, 2016), p.16). Personally, I believe a date of 1852–3 to be the most probable, giving Pinkerton enough time to relocate to Chicago, and build up his reputation as Deputy Sheriff and perhaps unofficial private investigator, before setting up the North West Police Agency on a more formal basis.

9. Beau Riffenburgh, *Pinkerton's Great Detective*, p.18, p.19

10. Maggie MacLean, 'Kate Warne – Union Spy and First Female Private Investigator', *Civil War Women* (2011) at https://www.civilwarwomenblog.com/kate-warne/

11. Town of Erin website, at http://www.townoferin.org

12. https://en.wikipedia.org/wiki/Erin,_New_York

13. Chris Enss, *The Pinks*, p.7

14. Very little is known about Kate Warne beyond the basics, but this is the most commonly reported version of her life. Greer Macallister's fictional account of Kate, *Girl in Disguise*, creates a whole new identity for her, as the child of abusive performers who was forced into marriage to a drunkard – the reality, however, was probably more mundane (Greer Macallister, *Girl in Disguise* (Sourcebooks Landmark, 2018)).

15. Pinkerton regularly advertised in the Chicago press at this time, it was usually to advertise his own services, rather than to explicitly advertise for new staff (see, for example, *Chicago Tribune*, 2 May 1855, p.1).

16. *Chicago Tribune*, 4 August 1856, p.3

17. Erika Janik has stated, based on *The Expressman and the Detective*, that Warne 'was not... looking to be a secretary, as Pinkerton first thought' (Erika Janik, *Pistols and Petticoats: 175 Years of Lady Detectives in Fact and Fiction* (Beacon Press, 2016), p.17

18. Allan Pinkerton, *The Expressman and the Detective*, p.95

19. Richard Wilmer Rowan, *The Pinkertons: A Detective Dynasty* (Hurst & Blackett, London, 1931), p.28

20. Chris Enss also names Pryce Lewis, John Scully, John H. White, R. Rivers and man by the name of DeForest as other Pinkerton operatives at this time (Chris Enss, *The Pinks*, p.8)

21. *Janesville Daily Gazette*, 6 September 1856, as quoted in Chris Enss, *The Pinks*, p.9

22. S. Paul O'Hara, *Inventing the Pinkertons*, pp.29–30; Allan Pinkerton, *The Expressman and the Detective*, p.10

23. Allan Pinkerton, *The Expressman and the Detective*, p.96

24. Allan Pinkerton, *The Expressman and the Detective*, p.101

25. In the end, Nathan Maroney confessed to the workplace theft to his cellmate – who was himself a plant, placed by Allan Pinkerton. Maroney pleaded guilty at his trial, and was sentenced to ten years' hard labour (Colin Falconer, 'The First Female Sleuth In History' (undated), www.colinfalconer.org/the-first-female-sleuth-in-history/); Chris Enss, *The Pinks*, p.18.

26. Cleveland Moffett, 'How Allan Pinkerton thwarted the first plot to assassinate Lincoln: stories from the archives of the Pinkerton Detective Agency', *McClure's Magazine* (1894, pp.519–29), p.520 at https://archive.org/details/howallanpinkerto00moff.

27. Cleveland Moffett, 'How Allan Pinkerton thwarted the first plot to assassinate Lincoln: stories from the archives of the Pinkerton Detective Agency', *McClure's Magazine* (1894, pp.519–29), p.520 at https://archive.org/details/howallanpinkerto00moff. Webster was convicted as a spy and, despite being seriously ill, probably with tuberculosis, was executed in Richmond, Virginia, on 30 April 1862.

28. Chris Enss, *The Pinks*, p.56, citing Daniel Stashower, *The Hour of Peril: The Secret Plot to Murder Lincoln Before the Civil War* (Minotaur Books, New York, 2013), p.195

29. Chris Enss, *The Pinks*, 56; Stashower, *The Hour of Peril*, p.104, pp.195–6

30. Kate's involvement in thwarting the assassination plot only became public in 1868, nearly seven years later, when Pinkerton became frustrated by others trying to claim the glory of Lincoln's rescue from the assassins for themselves. He commissioned a letter from Harry B. Judd, which referred to Kate Warne's participation. Both this and the 1894 account acknowledge 'Kate Warn' [sic] as being present with Lincoln on his train, and the latter acknowledges Kate and another detective, George H. Bangs, as 'two of Pinkerton's most trusted detectives' (Cleveland Moffett, 'How Allan Pinkerton thwarted the first plot to assassinate Lincoln: stories from the archives of

the Pinkerton Detective Agency', *McClure's Magazine* (1894, pp.519–29), p.528, at https://archive.org/details/howallanpinkerto00moff)

31. *Buffalo Daily Courier*, New York, 13 March 1868, p.1
32. *The McArthur Enquirer*, Ohio, 19 March 1868, p.2. It copied the report and then simply stated '*Chicago Republican*' at the end, with no date provided for the original report. The *Chicago Republican* was a newspaper published by A.W. Mack in Chicago between 1865 and 1872; during 1868, it was published three times a week (https://www.loc.gov/item/sn82014236/). It was founded by the Republican financier and industrialist Jacob Bunn (1831–1920) and after it ceased publication, it was relaunched as the *Chicago Inter-Ocean*, which ran until 1914.
33. *The McArthur Enquirer*, Ohio, 19 March 1868, p.2
34. Ibid., copying an undated edition of the *Chicago Republican*.
35. *Morning Advertiser*, 7 July 1868, copying undated issue of *New York Revolution*.
36. Ibid.
37. See, for example, Anon., 'Women Spies of the Civil War', *Smithsonian.com* (2011) at https://www.smithsonianmag.com/history/women-spies-of-the-civil-war-162202679/
38. The lack of information is due to formal birth and marriage records in the US starting fairly late, sometimes decades after the UK, which had introduced such records back in 1837. There was no statewide registration of births, marriages or deaths in Kate's home state, New York, until 1880; therefore, there is no trace of Kate's parents in the official records. Neither is there any record of her own birth (as Kate or any other permutation of her name). New York State Archives, 'Birth, Marriage, and Death Records', at http://www.archives.nysed.gov/research/birth-marriage-death-records. FamilySearch reiterates this, and adds that the first Chemung County land records date from 1836 and census returns from 1840. However, there is no entry for a Hulbert family that I have been able to find for this early date (https://www.familysearch.org/wiki/en/Chemung_County, New_York_Genealogy). The 1835 and 1845 federal censuses for New York State are not available online. Similarly, although Kate was said to have married a man named Warne, who left her a widow by the age of 26 – in other words, she had been widowed by the time she approached Pinkerton – these facts cannot be proved or disproved through official records.

Chapter 3: Monitoring Morality

1. *The McArthur Enquirer*, Ohio, 19 March 1868, p.2
2. Of course, women were also recruited as searchers for the police in the UK and Australia, for example, and the newspapers of the mid-1850s record these within police numbers (see, for example, the *Sydney Morning Herald* of 20 October 1854, p.1, which records a single female searcher working for the Sydney police at a salary of £20 [sic] per year; an inspector received a basic salary of £83pa, for comparison) but they did not undertake the activities we associate with detective work. In the 1880s, it was reported that searchers might be the police superintendent's wife, or an inspector's wife or 'female relation' (Janet Horowitz and Myra Stark (eds), *The Englishwoman's Review of Social and Industrial Questions: 1887* (Routledge, 2016), n.p.).
3. *Lloyd's Weekly Newspaper*, 11 May 1851, p.5
4. *The Dundee Courier and Argus*, 12 December 1855, p.4

5. The Eastern Counties Railway's employment of female detectives was news around the UK, being recorded in the pages of the *Dundee Courier* and *Aberdeen Journal* in Scotland, *Lloyd's Weekly Newspaper* in England, *The Freeman's Journal* in Ireland, and the *Wrexham Advertiser* in Wales, as well as numerous other provincial newspapers. The story continued to make the pages of the newspapers over the course of December 1855 and January 1856, before becoming news on the other side of the Atlantic in February 1856 (see, for example, the *Buffalo Morning Express* of 7 February 1856, the *Detroit Free Press* of 10 February, and the *Chicago Tribune* of 12 February).

6. Criminal conversation was, in common law, a tort arising from adultery; it was abolished in England and Wales in 1857, but existed in Northern Ireland until 1939.

7. The case was actually heard twice; the first time, the court determined in favour of Omwell Evans; the second time, in favour of Mary Sophia Evans. Omwell Evans then sought a divorce from the Court of Arches in 1857 and failed; the following year, he petitioned for divorce, and again failed. The press report into this case merely refers to 'Grocott' in relation to the female detective hired by Field; however, legal documents from 1858 refer to 'Sarah Grocott, wife of Thomas Grocott, and Charles Frederick Field' being brought as witnesses to Mary Sophia's alleged adultery. When a case for adultery was subsequently brought at the Court of Arches, Sarah failed to appear as a witness three times, and was held to be in contempt of court. Only then did she appear and agree to give evidence. (Copy of Minutes of Arches Court of Canterbury, 12 November 1855, case of Evans, Jenner, v Evans, Laurie, within Divorce Petition of Omwell Lloyd Evans, 8 February 1858, TNA J77/16).

8. *The Examiner*, 26 August 1854, p.11. Archive information corroborates Evans' statement that he was separated soon after his marriage; the 1851 census, taken around four months after the marriage, records him living with his mother Charlotte and servants, while Mary Sophia was living with her parents in the nearby Lansdown Terrace (1851 census for Sinclair Villa, Cheltenham and 15 Lansdown Terrace, Cheltenham). Mary Sophia was living in London by 1861, and died there in 1906. The 1891 and 1901 censuses recorded her as 'widow' (1891 census for 27 The Avenue, Tottenham; 1901 census for 78 Tavistock Road, Kensington; death of Mary Sophia Evans, age 81, Jan–Mar 1906, Kensington (vol 1a p.89)). Omwell Lloyd Evans had died in Gloucestershire in 1887, and Mary Sophia must have known of this in order to be recorded as a widow (death of Omwell Lloyd Evans, 71, Oct–Dec 1887, Winchcomb district (vol 6a p.259)).

9. *The Observer*, 14 June 1857, p.7

10. *Essex County Standard*, 14 December 1855, p.2

11. 'Obtaining a Divorce', ParliamentUK (www.parliament.uk/about/living-heritage/ transformingsociety/private-lives/relationships/overview/divorce/)

12. '1857 – Matrimonial Causes Act 1857' at Population Europe Resource Finder & Archive (www.perfar.eu/policies/matrimonial-causes-act-1857)

13. *Kentish Gazette*, 22 December 1857, p.8. Others, however, saw the Matrimonial Causes Act as the means to make money – such as with the case of William Holdworth and Richard Tidswell, barristers who quickly published a guide to the Act, stating that without their information, 'the public is not much wiser for being told that a woman is entitled to a divorce if her husband be guilty of adultery, "coupled with such cruelty as without adultery would have entitled her to a divorce *a mensa et*

thoro"' (advert in the *Norwich Mercury*, 19 September 1857, p.8; their book was entitled *The New Law of Marriage and Divorce Popularly Explained*). Divorce *a mensa et thoro*, legally, meant 'divorce from bed and board' but rather than being a divorce as we understand it, simply permitted a husband and wife to live apart from each other, so being a legal separation.

14. During the divorce case, Mary Sophia Evans referred back to her husband's original suit for legal separation, and an 1857 'libel brought in or on his behalf in the Arches Court [of Canterbury] and which were attempted to be proved by witnesses', stressing that the divorce repeated the same allegations that had been dismissed four years previously. Her argument appears to have prevailed, with no divorce being granted (TNA J77/16/E3).

15. Anon, 'Divorce rates data, 1858 to now: how has it changes?', *The Guardian*, www. theguardian.com/news/datablog/2010/jan/28/divorce-rates-marriage-ons, whose data was obtained from www.ons.gov.uk/peoplepopulationandcommunity/ birthsdeathsandmarriages/divorce/bulletins/divorcesinenglandandwales/ 2014-02-06. The data used by *The Guardian* is also available to view year-by-year at https://docs.google.com/spreadsheets/d/1caHyaJSD31eMwiG-jxn5wUH6M1 7QydeeILFH3eRuX24/htmlview

16. 1873 saw 215 divorces granted; this figure was exceeded every year from 1877 onwards.

17. Martin Gill and Gerry Hart, 'Exploring Investigative Policing', *British Journal of Criminology*, 37:4 (1997), p.556

18. Martin Gill and Gerry Hart, 'Exploring Investigative Policing', *British Journal of Criminology*, 37:4 (1997), p.557

19. Between 1870 and 1879, there are 302 mentions, 1,449 between 1880 and 1889, and 2,254 between 1890 and 1899. Although the BNA does not cover 100 per cent of newspapers between these times, it provides a snapshot of the growth of private inquiry agents, and how the industry appears to have exploded in the 1880s and 1890s.

20. Benjamin Welton, 'The Case of the Vanishing Private Eyes', *The Atlantic*, 15 January 2015 (https://www.theatlantic.com/business/archive/2015/01/the-long-steady-decline-of-the-private-eye/384450/); Jeremy Agnew, *Crime, Justice and Retribution in the American West, 1850–1900* (McFarland, 2017), p.148

21. *Liverpool Daily Post*, 26 January 1860, p.3

22. Ibid.

23. *Morning Advertiser*, 18 March 1861, p.7

24. John Walton, *The Legendary Detective: The Private Eye in Fact and Fiction* (University of Chicago Press, 2015), p.48

25. Graham Nown, *Watching the Detectives* (Grafton Books, 1991), p.27

26. John Walton, *The Legendary Detective: The Private Eye in Fact and Fiction* (University of Chicago Press, 2015), p.49

27. John Walton, *The Legendary Detective: The Private Eye in Fact and Fiction* (University of Chicago Press, 2015), p.45

Chapter 4: The Female Detective: Fact or Fiction?
1. Later examples, from the Golden Age of the private detective, include, in Britain, Leonard Merrick's *Mr Bazalgette's Agent* (1888) and Catherine L. Pirkis's *The Experiences of Loveday Brooke, Lady Detective* (1894).

2. Andrew Forrester, *The Female Detective* (British Library, 2012), p.4

3. Andrew Forrester, *The Female Detective* (British Library, 2012), p.7

4. Joseph A. Kestner, *Sherlock's Sisters: The British Female Detective, 1864–1913* (Ashgate, Aldershot, 2003), p.1

5. Ibid.

6. Mike Ashley, 'Introduction', in Andrew Forrester, *The Female Detective* (British Library, 2012), p.vii

7. Andrew Forrester, *The Female Detective* (British Library, 2012), p.8

8. William Stephens Hayward, *Revelations of a Lady Detective* (British Library, 2013), p.18

9. Ibid.

10. Ibid.

11. Michelle Slung, repeated in Joseph A. Kestner, *Sherlock's Sister: The British Female Detective, 1864–1913* (Ashgate, 2003), p.5

12. Joseph A. Kestner, *Sherlock's Sisters: The British Female Detective, 1864–1913* (Ashgate, Aldershot, 2003), p.17

13. Kestner also describes how fictional works about the female detective 'inherently challenge the hierarchical power of the gaze when the subject is a female detective exercising surveillance in the pursuit of her detection' (Kestner, *Sherlock's Sisters: The British Female Detective, 1864–1913* (Ashgate, Aldershot, 2003), pp.17–18

14. *The Halifax Courier*, 11 July 1868

15. Moser was actually referring to female pickpockets in this quote; but the skills needed and displayed by women were transferrable across both sides of the criminal divide, as both criminals and detectives. (Maurice Moser and Charles F. Rideal, *Stories from Scotland Yard* (George Routledge and Sons Ltd, 1890), pp.75–6.)

16. Andrew Forrester, *The Female Detective*, p.1

17. Andrew Forrester, *The Female Detective*, pp.3–4

18. The Metropolitan Police, established in 1829, had instituted a detective department in the summer of 1842, which had become an integral part of London policing by the 1850s. In 1868, a review of the Met led to a huge increase in the number of its detectives, influenced, Shpayer-Makov notes, by the ending of transportation to Australia (which led to serious offenders now remaining in Britain) and the garrotting panic of the early 1860s (Haia Shpayer-Makov, *The Ascent of the Detective* (OUP, 2011), pp.33–5)

19. *New York Times*, 15 June 1866

20. *Oban Times and Argyllshire Advertiser*, 23 October 1869, p.4

21. *New York Times*, 3 June 1869

Chapter 5: From Amateur to Professional

1. For example, the *Ballymena Observer* of 15 July 1871, p.1, included an advertisement by a London publisher listing its popular titles. These included *Annie, or the life of a lady's maid*, *Left her Home: a tale of female life and adventures*, and *The Lady Detective*.

2. *Western Daily Press*, 3 January 1873, p.3. The youths – William Chapman, Charles Ferris, and Thomas Jones – were committed for trial.

3. See NRA 29343; the company was established by the 1820s and its records are now held by Courtaulds.

4. This may be the Eliza Bissell born in Turnham Green, London, in 1855, who in the 1901 census was living in Mile End with husband James, a farrier and corn dealer. Eliza's occupation was given as 'attends to shop', helping her husband out from their premises at Oxford Street in Mile End. If it was this woman, she would only have been around 22 years old when she was involved in the theft case. However, we know that she was married – and Mary Eliza Schermuly married James Bissell in December 1875 at Bethnal Green, and she would also have been a mother, as her oldest child, James Conrad Bissell, was born in 1876 (marriages for Bethnal Green, December quarter 1875, vol 1c p.501; birth of James Conrad Bissell, Mile End, September quarter of 1876, vol 1c, p.506). The 1911 census shows that Eliza had nine children during her marriage, of whom five had died by 1911. Eliza's husband and children were all born in East London – in the Stepney area – and after having lived in Mile End for decades, in their old age, they moved to Limehouse. Eliza died in the Mile End district in 1915, aged 70. However, two things make Eliza a bit more than an average working-class wife and mother from the East End. Firstly, she was literate – she signed her 1875 marriage register with a firm hand – and secondly, she was the daughter of a musician, Conrad Schermuly, who also signed the register as a witness. Although both he and James Bissell seem a bit more unsure in their signatures, that they were able to do so suggests more than a basic education.
5. Trial of Robert Clough, George Blacker and Edward Slow for stealing from master, 7 May 1877, *Old Bailey Online* ref t18770507-421
6. *Northern Echo*, 18 July 1870, p.2
7. Ibid., citing undated issue of *The Times.*
8. *Belfast Morning News*, 25 November 1870, p.3
9. Undated issue of *Pictorial World*, copied in the *Man Of Ross*, 28 June 1877, p.6 and elsewhere (see note 12).
10. I work on the assumption here that the reporter would likely have been male, in order to assign a pronoun to descriptions of 'him'.
11. Flag of Ireland, 4 March 1876, p.3
12. Undated issue of *Pictorial World*, copied in *Falkirk Herald*, 10 March 1877, p.4; *Worcestershire Chronicle*, 10 March 1877, p.7; *Falkirk Herald*, 15 March 1877, p.7; *Man Of Ross*, 28 June 1877, p.6, *St Neots Chronicle and Advertiser*, 30 June 1877, p.4
13. Mr Ward was based at Chandos Chambers, 22 Buckingham Street, Strand (*London Evening Standard*, 8 July 1879; *London Evening Standard*, 24 September 1880).
14. Marriage of Caroline Greenwood and William Smith, both of Lewis Place, Lewisham, on 5 July 1866, at St Mary's Church, Lewisham. The 1861 census for Willow Walk, Lewisham, lists Caroline as the daughter of George Greenwood, cordwainer, which ties in with her marriage record, which gives George Greenwood, boot-maker as her father.
15. Caroline Ann (b.1867); William Samuel (b.1869); Sydney Delamore (b.1870); Sylvester (b.1872); Bernard Edwin A. (b.1874). Caroline was born in Blackheath or Greenwich (the 1871 census says Greenwich, 1881 says Blackheath); the next three in Marylebone, and Bernard in the Holborn registration district.
16. Kelly Hager, 'Chipping Away at Coverture: The Matrimonial Causes Act of 1857', in Dino Franco Felluga (ed), *BRANCH: Britain, Representation and Nineteenth-Century History* (https://www.branchcollective.org/?ps_articles=kelly-hager-chipping-away-at-coverture-the-matrimonial-causes-act-of-1857).

17. *Islington Gazette*, 16 June 1880.
18. 1881 census for 143 Holloway Road, Islington.

Chapter 6: The Emergence of the New Woman

1. Patricia Marks, *Bicycles, Bangs, and Bloomers: The New Woman in the Popular Press* (University Press of Kentucky, 1990), p.ix
2. Greg Buzwell, 'Daughters of Decadence: The New Woman in the Victorian fin de siècle', British Library, 15 May 2014, at https://www.bl.uk/romantics-and-victorians/articles/daughters-of-decadence-the-new-woman-in-the-victorian-fin-de-siecle
3. *Birmingham Daily Post*, 25 June 1881, p.5
4. Ibid.
5. Marks, *Bicycles, Bangs, and Bloomers*, pp.ix–x
6. *Wexford People*, 17 August 1889, p.9
7. Mike Ashley, 'Introduction', *Mr Bazalgette's Agent*, p.6
8. As Judith Flanders has noted, the 'penny dreadfuls' were the successors to the early nineteenth century 'penny bloods'. By the 1840s, tales of crime and detection were starting to become popular in these, and by the mid-1860s, there was an increased focus on these subjects (Judith Flanders, 'Penny Dreadfuls', British Library, 15 May 2014, at https://www.bl.uk/romantics-and-victorians/articles/penny-dreadfuls
9. Dime Novels and Penny Dreadfuls Project Team, 'Old Sleuth, the Detective', Stanford University, at https://web.stanford.edu/dept/SUL/library/prod/depts/dp/pennies/1870_sleuth.html
10. Mike Ashley, 'Introduction', *Mr Bazalgette's Agent*, p.8
11. *Morning Post*, 24 September 1886, p.6. The English edition of Macé's book was produced by publisher and journalist Edward Vizetelly, who was seen as a 'pioneer' in translated books, but had previously been the *Illustrated London News'* Paris correspondent. Interestingly, Vizetelly had started by translating 'high literature', but this proved a financial failure – he then started publishing more 'low brow' works, such as Monsieur Lecoq, and this venture proved far more successful, indicating where the public's tastes lay (*Pall Mall Gazette*, 24 March 1888, p.2).
12. *Tower Hamlets Independent and East End Local Advertiser*, 14 February 1885, p.4; *Sporting Life*, 22 October 1884, p.1
13. *The Stage*, 14 September 1888, p.4
14. In *The Stage*'s review, it noted that 'she finds that she has disgraced the cloth of her calling by becoming a very everyday body; she falls in love with the man she is about to deliver up to justice'. This suggests that being a female detective made women 'unusual', in putting career above love, and that if they reverted to convention by falling in love, they became an 'everyday body' rather than the different individual they had been perceived as before.
15. *Dundee Evening Telegraph*, 30 May 1888, p.2; *Cork Constitution*, 4 June 1888, p.4, and numerous newspapers across northern England and the Midlands.
16. Ibid.
17. Henry Frith, 'The Hand of Destiny: or, The Mysterious Tenant of Francton Holme', in *Wexford People*, 17 August 1889, p.9
18. It should be noted that one of the canonical murders ascribed to Jack the Ripper – that of Catherine Eddowes – took place in Mitre Square, which was in the Square Mile

and therefore came under the jurisdiction of the City of London Police. However, it was the Criminal Investigation Department of the Metropolitan Police, which took overall responsibility for trying to track down the killer, that was the subject of press criticism (Richard Jones, 'Jack the Ripper – the Police Investigation', *Jack the Ripper 1888*, at https://www.jack-the-ripper.org/police-investigation.htm).

19. For more on the use of bloodhounds in the investigation, see Neil Pemberton, 'Bloodhounds as Detectives: Dogs, Slum Stench and Late-Victorian Murder Investigation', *Cultural and Social History*, 10:1 (2013), pp.69–91
20. *Sheffield Evening Telegraph*, 13 October 1888, p.2
21. Ibid.
22. Ibid.
23. *Manchester Evening News*, 30 May 1895, p.3

Chapter 7: The Golden Age Dawns
1. *St Louis Post-Dispatch*, 10 October 1897, p.43
2. Ibid. Isadore Rush, the wife of comedian Roland Reed, was a successful vaudeville and Broadway actress, who drowned off the coast of California in 1904.
3. *The Sketch*, 24 January 1894, p.704
4. Ibid.
5. *Ally Sloper's Half-Holiday*, 18 October 1870
6. Ibid.
7. Greg Buzwell, 'Daughters of decadence: the New Woman in the Victorian fin de siècle', British Library, 15 May 2014, (at https://www.bl.uk/romantics-and-victorians/articles/daughters-of-decadence-the-new-woman-in-the-victorian-fin-de-siecle); CL Pirkis, *The Experiences of Loveday Brooke, Lady Detective* (Summit Classic Press, Ohio, 1894, rpt 2014), p.4
8. Patricia Craig and Mary Cadogan, *The Lady Investigates: Women Detectives and Spies in Fiction* (St Martins, 1981, pp.23–4
9. *Burnley Express*, 22 July 1893, p.8
10. Elizabeth Burgoyne Corbett (1846–1930) was at one time a journalist on the *Newcastle Daily Chronicle*, and regularly wrote about women's position in society. She was often separated from her husband George, who was a steam engine fitter and later ship's engineer, working largely away from home. She published two collections of short stories as *Adventures of a Lady Detective* (1890) and *Secrets of a Private Enquiry Office* (1891). It is not clear from the 1893 press advert which collection is referred to, but it is likely to be the 1890 stories, with a slightly amended name.
11. 1891 census for 44 Stockwell Green, Lambeth.
12. 1901 census for 8 Bath Parade, Cheltenham; 1911 census for 11 Montpellier Villas, Cheltenham. *The Gloucestershire Echo* of 22 July 1935 records Mary Annabella Burridge's death on 20 July at 22 Lansdown Crescent, Cheltenham, aged 80.
13. As recorded in the 1881 census for 44 Sherwin Street, Nottingham. The Addey sons – Gordon and Harry – were born in Auckland in 1875 and 1877.
14. 1891 census for 112 Holsworthy Buildings, St Andrew Holborn.
15. 1901 census for 91 Illiffe Street, Newington.
16. The fact that her daughter Essie married another private detective, George Payne, in 1898, may suggest that Mary was working fairly continuously as a private detective throughout the 1890s, and that this is how her daughter met George; although it is

also possible that George Payne was an associate or colleague of Mary's son Gordon (marriage of George Henry Payne and Essie Irma Kathleen Addey at Southwark Register Office, 31 December 1898. Mary Addey was a witness).

17. 1911 census for 8 Studland Street, Hammersmith.
18. *North Wales Times*, 8 April 1896.
19. Paulowna had also previously pretended to be a baroness. Her first name may have suggested a foreign origin, but that was all that could be said. In court, her life story was described as a 'very curious one' that was clearly not believed – for good reason. However, the combination of her hiding her identity, which on its own was understandable, as being a private detective relied somewhat on the adoption of fake identities, and her desire to make more money from her job than simple fees, helped the court find against her (*Hampshire Telegraph*, 1 June 1895, p.3; *South Wales Echo*, 31 May 1895, p.5).
20. *South Wales Echo*, 31 May 1895, p.3; *Hampshire Telegraph*, 1 June 1895, p.5.
21. *Northampton Mercury*, 12 August 1892, p.3; *Worcester Journal*, 23 July 1892, p.6; Petition of Barrett, Gertrude Alexandra v Barrett, John Edward, filed 18 February 1892, dismissed 11 August 1892 (TNA J77/488/14487). The couple's marriage entry at St Pancras shows that Gertrude was 21 when she married; her husband was listed there as 35. Interestingly, both the Barretts had families involved in law and order: John's father, David William, had been a barrister, whereas Gertrude's father, Charles Henry, had been a barrister. Both fathers, however, had died by the time of their offspring's marriage. There are also some factual errors on the marriage entry, given that John had actually been born in Kurrachee, Bombay, on 21 December 1853, making him 37 when he married, and Gertrude had been born at Agra on 6 September 1872, so she was actually a minor when she married. On her baptism, her father's name is given as Daniel Henry Bird, rather than the Charles Henry Bird who appears on her marriage entry (birth and baptism details taken from Ancestry's India collection).
22. 'Henry John Clarke and Ellen Lyon: sexual offences: keeping a brothel', 25 March 1895', *Old Bailey Online*, t18950325-534
23. Ibid.
24. Ibid.
25. Keeling, a former solicitor's clerk, advertised that he employed 'none but experienced male and female detectives' at his enquiry offices at 9 Figtree Lane in Sheffield (*Lichfield Mercury*, 11 June 1898, p.1). Harrington, based at Rodgers' Chambers on Norfolk Street, appears to have been a larger operation, with a telegraphic address, 'home and colonial experience' as well as 'male and female detectives' – although one of his detectives, William Swindell, only worked for him part-time (he was not 'exclusively in Harrington's employ as he was a sawyer by trade. He worked for Harrington at night'), and so any female detectives he used were likely to have been employed on a similarly part-time or even ad hoc basis (*Lichfield Mercury*, 17 May 1898, p.1; *Sheffield Daily Telegraph*, 24 June 1898, p.6).
26. *Daily Telegraph and Courier*, 30 May 1896, p.12

Chapter 8: Fashionable Females
1. Julian Humphrys, 'A Brief History of Shopping' (*BBC History*, December 2015, https://www.historyextra.com/period/twentieth-century/history-shopping-

sales-black-friday-boxing-day-what-oldest-shop-selfridges/); Jonathan Glancey, 'A History of the Department Store', BBC, 26 March 2015, http://www.bbc.com/culture/bespoke/story/20150326-a-history-of-the-department-store/index.html

2. Jon Stobart, 'The Shopping Streets of Provincial England, 1650–1840' in Jan Hein Furnée and Clé Lesger (eds), *The Landscape of Consumption: Shopping Streets and Cultures in Western Europe, 1600–1900* (Palgrave Macmillan, 2014), p.16

3. Erika D. Rappaport, *Shopping for Pleasure: Women in the Making of London's West End* (Princeton University Press, 2000), p.5, p.135

4. Elaine S. Abelson, *When Ladies Go A-Thieving: Middle-Class Shoplifting in the Victorian Department Store* (Oxford University Press, 1989), p.11

5. It was a similar situation in the US, where Elaine S. Abelson notes three different categories of detective operating in stores by the end of the nineteenth century: shopwalkers 'acting' as detectives; detectives from external detective agencies being used, with these agencies developing a 'specialism' in store work; or a regular police officer hired in a private capacity (Elaine S. Abelson, *When Ladies Go A-Thieving: Middle-Class Shoplifting in the Victorian Department Store* (Oxford University Press, 1989), pp.129–130

6. *North Wales Times*, 4 April 1896, p.6

7. *Dundee Evening Post*, 21 November 1903, p.8

8. *Preston Herald*, 23 October 1905, p.7

9. Lilias was still working as a store detective in 1922, but was now based at the Army & Navy Stores. She appeared in court in December of that year, accusing a septuagenarian vicar of stealing books, cakes and soap from the stores after watching him for two hours. The magistrate hearing the case, although finding the vicar guilty, was lenient towards him, because 'he is not very well versed in money matters' (*Western Morning News*, 27 December 1922, p.5).

10. *Birmingham Daily Post*, 19 February 1917, p.7

11. For example, *Western Times*, 12 February 1903, p.2; *Dundee Evening Post*, 13 February 1903, p.4

12. *London Evening Standard*, 22 June 1906, p.10

13. *Daily Telegraph and Courier*, 10 January 1900, p.14

14. *Daily Telegraph & Courier*, 3 January 1900, p.4

15. *Manchester Evening News*, 21 September 1903, p.1. This lady did not provide any details such as a name or full address – the address provided was 'B 247, E. News' which sounds more like a correspondence address via the newspaper (the other adverts in the same column as this all provided home addresses, so her advert was unusual).

16. *Preston Herald*, 23 October 1905, p.7

17. This was not always the case, although it was more unusual for a man to be employed as a detective in a shop or department selling ladies' goods. This can be seen in coverage of a court case in 19011, when two detectives from the Metropolitan Police posed as shopwalkers at Swan and Edgar's store on Piccadilly. They caught a woman, Kate Graham, stealing gloves, laces, stockings, silk and a dress robe from the store, noting that she had gone 'from counter to counter, and took the articles mentioned in the charge, while purchasing something else'. (*Nottingham Evening Post*, 4 July 1901, p.2) The fact that male detectives posed as shopwalkers to catch a female shoplifter seems to have been as newsworthy, if not more so, than the actual theft and prosecution.

18. *Londonderry Sentinel*, 28 July 1903, p.7
19. Ibid.
20. *Dundee Evening Post*, 4 January 1901, p.4
21. *Barnsley Chronicle*, 20 January 1900, p.2; *Preston Herald*, 29 November 1904, p.4
22. *Liverpool Echo*, 22 July 1909, p.5
23. *Heywood Advertiser*, 25 September 1908, p.4, citing an undated issue of *Cassell's Saturday Journal*.

Chapter 9: Acting the Part
1. Peg A. Lamphier and Rosanne Walsh (eds), 'The Civil War and Reconstruction (1861–1877)', *Women in American History: A Social, Political and Cultural Encyclopaedia and Document Collection, Vol 2: Antebellum America Through the Gilded Age* (Publisher: ABC-CLIO, Santa Barbara, California, 2017), n.p.
2. Tracy C. Davis notes, in relation to the theatre, that 'the social stigma on female performers was perpetuated by the context in which they were presented on stage' (Tracy C. Davis, *Actresses as Working Women: Their Social Identity in Victorian Culture* (Routledge, 2001), p.6).
3. Peg A. Lamphier and Rosanne Walsh (eds), 'The Civil War and Reconstruction (1861–1877)', *Women in American History: A Social, Political and Cultural Encyclopaedia and Document Collection, Vol 2: Antebellum America Through the Gilded Age*, (ABC-CLIO, Santa Barbara, California, 2017), n.p.
4. Leonard Merrick, *Mr Bazalgette's Agent* (British Library, 1888, rpt 2013), pp.23–4; George Robert Sims, *Dorcas Dene, Detective, Etc* (British Library, 2010). The adventures of Dorcas Dene were originally published as two volumes in 1897 and 1898.
5. Tracy C. Davis, *Actresses as Working Women: Their Social Identity in Victorian Culture* (Routledge, 1991), p.3
6. At its worst, in the acting world, this resulted in the deaths of young, struggling actresses, one of the saddest cases being the double suicide of acting sisters Edith and Ida Yeoland, aged 23 and 21, who poisoned themselves with cocaine in their Bloomsbury lodgings in July 1901. They had struggled to find regular engagements – despite glowing press reviews of their work, particularly Ida's – and Ida had recently had a rejection from a stock company in New York. The girls decided they could not cope with the uncertainty of their acting lives, and decided to kill themselves instead (Nell Darby, 'The Sibling Suicides', *Discover Your Ancestors*, April 2020, at www.discoveryourancestors.co.uk; *London Daily News*, 17 July 1901, p.2).
7. Maud was based at Albion House, 59a New Oxford Street, almost opposite what was, at one time, the office of her rival Kate Easton. The newspapers.com blog states that Maud started work as a private detective in 1905 (Karen Lee, '3 Amazing Female Detectives You've Never Heard Of', *Fishwrap: the official blog of Newspapers.com*, 20 March 2019, https://blog.newspapers.com/female-detectives/
8. From an interview Maud gave to a Dutch language newspaper in Jakarta, 1930, as cited in Susannah Stapleton, *The Adventures of Maud West, Lady Detective* (Picador, 2019), p.315
9. A further private detective operating alongside these women, who may also have been a former actress, was Norah Desmond – an individual of this name was performing songs at the Palace Theatre in Carlisle in April 1910, and singing 'American picture

songs' at the Stoke-on-Trent Hippodrome the following month, and Norah
Desmond, private detective, was operating from Regency House, on Warwick Street
off London's Regent Street, the following year – but that the two Norahs were the
same individual cannot be proved, although suspected (*The Era*, 23 April 1910;
Staffordshire Sentinel, 6 May 1910, p.1; *Pall Mall Gazette*, 4 December 1911, p.11).

10. Marriage record at St George, Southwark, 11 September 1838, for William Mead
Easton and Sarah Carone; birth of William Alexander Mead Easton, Lambeth, 1848;
baptism of Kate Augusta Easton, born 18 June 1856, baptised 5 September 1856 at
St John the Evangelist; 1841 census for Waterloo Road, Lambeth. Kate's full name
is given as a witness at her brother William's marriage in 1872. Madeleine Elizabeth
Mead Easton, her older sister, was born in the first quarter of 1840 in Lambeth (vol
4, p.282). Kate's father William worked variously as a waterman, fireman, and then
tobacconist.

11. Madeleine was the daughter of Kate's older sister and her husband, printer Alfred
Bradley (1881 census for 125 Gaisforth Street, Kentish Town; 1911 census for 18
Patten Road, Wandsworth). Kate's brother William married pianist Louisa Ellen
Vokins, herself the daughter of a musician (marriage of William Easton and Louisa
Ellen Vokins at St Peter's, Walworth, 25 February 1872). More about Madeleine
Lucette can be found in Sherry D. Engle's *New Women Dramatists in America, 1890–
1920* (Palgrave Macmillan, 2007), p.56

12. This initial press mention is an advert for her, placed either by her or an agent:
'MISS MADELINE [sic] LUCETTE, on Tour with Mr JL Toole's Company, as
MARY BROWN in 'Tottie's', Julia in 'Spelling Bee', Laura in 'Sweethearts and
Wives', etc. Prince of Wales Theatre Birmingham. Gaiety, London, July 24th.' (*The
Era*, 16 July 1876, p.13)

13. 1891 census for 76 Southampton Row, Bloomsbury.

14. 1901 census for 24 Great Russell Street, Bloomsbury; Army & Navy Gazette issues
for 19 May 1917, 26 May 1917 and 28 July 1917.

15. *Irish News and Belfast Morning News*, 21 June 1904, p.8; *Belfast News-Letter*, 21 June
1904, p.5; *Northern Whig*, 21 June 1904, p.10; *Belfast Telegraph*, 21 June 1904, p.2

16. *Daily Telegraph & Courier*, 16 October 1905, p.15. Interestingly, three days later,
when Kate advertised again in the *Daily Telegraph*, one of the other adverts placed
in the same edition was from Maurice Moser, the former Met police detective and
Antonia Moser's former lover, who warned in his advert: 'Beware of self-styled
detective agencies. How can they possibly possess the necessary sagacity of a life-
long trained detective like Mr Moser, who has for 28 years enjoyed the confidence
of British and foreign Government departments, solicitors, merchants, and the
nobility?' (*Daily Telegraph & Courier*, 19 October 1905, p.16)

17. *Daily Telegraph & Courier*, 16 October 1905, p.15

18. There was a singer named Kate Easton who performed with her sister, Florence, but
private detective Kate Easton did not have a sister of this name.

19. *The Stage*, 16 November 1911, p.2; *Daily Record*, 30 September 1918, p.3

20. Louise A. Jackson, 'The Unusual Case of "Mrs Sherlock". Memoir, Identity and the
"Real" Woman Private Detective in Twentieth-Century Britain', *Gender & History*,
15:1 (April 2003), p.108, p.118

21. *The Era*, 7 June 1890, p.15

22. 1911 census for 13 Great Turnstile, Lincolns Inn Fields.

23. *West Sussex Gazette*, 14 May 1914, p.4; *Nottingham Evening Post*, 11 June 1914, p.3. By 1914, Margaret had moved a street away from her old accommodation at Great Turnstile, and was living at Whetstone Park, again in Lincolns Inn Fields.

24. *The People*, 25 January 1914, p.1

25. Ibid.

26. Susannah Stapleton, *The Adventures of Maud West, Lady Detective* (Picador, 2019), pp.320–1. Stapleton also suggests that Matilda had formerly worked as a railway detective.

27. *The People*, 25 January 1914, p.1. Matilda Emma Mitchell married Thomas Walter Hayward in the March quarter of 1914 in Wandsworth (vol 1d, page 780). Tom died in Cambridge in 1939; Matilda died in Hove six years later, aged 72 (1939 Register for Cambridge; National Probate Calendar for Matilda Mitchell, 1945).

28. Matilda clearly dates her retirement to her marriage in 1914; it is not possible to date Margaret Cooke's retirement as easily, although it is likely that she continued as a private detective for some time in order to maintain her daughter. We know that she was working as such for at least three years, but did not advertise her services in the newspapers – at least, not under her real or stage names – which makes it harder to track her career. The only hard piece of archival evidence for her not working as a detective any more only comes in 1939, when, in her seventies, she was a bed-bound invalid, looked after by her unmarried daughter Olga (1939 Register for 51 Swinton Street, St Pancras). Margaret died in Epson in 1942, her death registered as Margaret A. B. Cooke (Surrey, January quarter of 1942, vol 2a p.505).

Chapter 10: Press and Publicity

1. *Morning Post*, 23 May 1907, p.1

2. Susannah Stapleton, *The Adventures of Maud West, Lady Detective* (Picador, 2019), p.17. The first advert for Antonia Moser as an independent 'detective expert' that exists in the British Newspaper Archive comes from the *Morning Post* of 4 January 1905.

3. Antonia was 19 when she was baptised at St Giles in the Fields on 5 June 1875. She was baptised alongside her younger sisters Louisa Georgina (born 1858), Maria Elizabeth (born 1860) and Ada Catherine Wilhelmina (born 1863), who all took Sarah as their new first names.

4. Marriage of Charlotte Antonia Williamson and Edward James Clarendon Williamson at St Bride's Fleet Street on 9 March 1882. The couple had two children – Margaret Welburn Williamson, born on 7 October 1882 (suggesting that she may have been conceived before the couple's marriage), and Richard Wagner Williamson, born 6 September 1884 (TNA J77/433/3201, p.36).

5. Keeping things within the very close Williamson family, Antonia's former husband – and first cousin – Edward was accused by her of having had an affair with her youngest sister, Ada, since March 1887, which he denied. However, he was soon living with Ada and had a child by her; they would not marry, though, for years, until the legislation that forbid a man from marrying his wife's sister had been repealed. (TNA J/77/433/3201, p.29)

6. *Derby Daily Telegraph*, 22 July 1890, p.4

7. Moser's career details are taken from his summary of police service, which shows that he joined, aged 24, on 23 July 1877 as a PC in B Division, was a sergeant in

the CID from December 1877, and left, on 24 January 1887, as an Inspector in A Division (Summary of Police Service for Maurice Moser, warrant number 61710, from the Metropolitan Police Heritage Centre). Maurice and Antonia claimed to be married – with Antonia later stating that they had married in Chicago in 1891. She also stated that she was owed maintenance under their deed of separation, which again suggests that a marriage had taken place. However, there is no evidence of this, and Antonia also claimed that she married as a widow, when in fact she was divorced (*London Daily News*, 24 October 1902, p.9). In 1908, though, Antonia claimed to have changed her surname from Williamson to Moser by deed poll, which would suggest that she had never legally married Moser (and if she had, she had not divorced him). However, no record of a deed poll name change – as would be expected in the pages of *The London Gazette* – can be found for her either (the only *London Gazette* entry for Antonia is the announcement that the partnership existing between 'Charlotte Antonia Williamson and Maurice Moser, carrying on business under the style of Maurice Moser's Detective Agency' had been dissolved. The use of Williamson here again suggests that Antonia had never formally changed her name, nor married Moser (*London Evening Standard*, 28 August 1908, p.10; *The London Gazette*, 16 February 1892, p.869).

8. Antonia stated at Bow Street Police Court that she had gone to visit Moser at his office to remind him that he owed her £50 in maintenance, he having allegedly taken 'her jewellery, furniture and money, and had left her practically penniless'. He then verbally abused her, threatened to shoot her, and then slapped and kicked her. Moser had then called a policeman and doctor, and organised for Antonia to be forcibly confined as a lunatic, falsely claiming that she had tried to kill herself. It had taken forty-eight hours for her to be examined, found to be sane, and released (*London Daily News*, 24 October 1902, p.9).

9. Private detective William Pierrepont similarly used this line.

10. Another example was 'S White, late Inspector CID, Metropolitan Police', who was working as a private inquiry agent in Belgravia in the late 1890s, and who boasted that he 'personally conducted' divorce and other cases for moderate terms (*London Evening Standard*, 26 May 1896). This was likely to have been Stephen White, who was listed in the 1891 census as a police detective, and in 1901 as a retired police inspector (1891 census for 55 Bromehead Street, Whitechapel; 1901 census for 57 Senrab Street, Stepney Green). The male detectives dominated the classified ads, and by the end of the nineteenth century, the agencies run by Henry Slater, Attwood (based at Catherine Street, off the Strand) and Simmonds (on King Street, Cheapside) were particularly ubiquitous. Attwood promoted his confidential approach – 'secrecy in all cases' – and his free initial interviews, as well as his skills in watching 'suspected employees' and tracing 'lost friends'. Slater placed several ads in the same paper, highlighting different skills, but also using hyperbole in an unsurpassed way: 'If you desire an object accomplished, a mystery cleared up, or the doings of a person secretly ascertained, consult Slater, "the greatest detective of the age"' read one of his adverts in 1896, above another that read 'Slater's Detectives – for ascertaining where people go, what they do, the company they keep, whether the club is responsible for late hours, and if shopping alone occupies so much time' (*London Evening Standard*, 25 May 1896, p.1). Others were more circumspect, such as the individual who advertised in 1899: 'A thoroughly experienced private

detective, with established reputation, will be glad to undertake INQUIRIES and obtain EVIDENCE in delicate matters: communications treated confidentially. Address JB, care of Watson's, 150 Fleet Street, EC.' (*Morning Post*, 20 April 1899, p.1).

11. *London Evening Standard*, 8 July 1879; *London Evening Standard*, 24 September 1880.

12. *Daily Telegraph*, 19 September 1905, p.16; *Morning Post*, 20 November 1906, p.1. Barclay's rather rashly also promised 'guaranteed inviolable secrecy'.

13. Although Slater was novel in explicitly promoting lady cycling detectives, the concept of the cycling detective per se was not unknown. In 1894, the head of the Parisian police was said to be thinking about 'creating a body of cycling detectives' (*Essex Standard*, 15 September 1894, p.7), and a 'special corps of cycling detectives' were employed in Birmingham to patrol the streets on lampless bikes in 1899, although these appear to have also been part of the local police (*Sevenoaks Chronicle*, 3 November 1899, p.6; Kentish Independent, 4 November 1899, p.6). Slater's attempts were greeted with mixed responses (the *Clarion* commented: 'A famous private detective office recently advertised for lady cycling detectives. Which was a smart move, for every woman is a born detective. And finds out more than she ought to' (*Clarion*, 28 November 1896, p.7)), and appear to have been both short-lived and restricted mainly to the Brighton area.

14. *Daily Telegraph*, 24 February 1910, p.20

15. *Lichfield Mercury*, 27 January 1905, p.5; *Daily Telegraph*, 19 September 1905, p.16

16. *Evening Standard*, 28 August 1908, p.10

17. Ibid.

18. *Morning Post*, 8 December 1909, p.1; *Daily Telegraph*, 21 February 1910, p.20

19. His advert was for 'Mr Maurice Moser, officially and privately engaged in detective work for the past 30 years', and he stated that he was 'prepared to undertake every description of confidential missions at home and abroad'. Maurice was now in new offices at Palace Chambers, Westminster – 'opposite Big Ben', as he wrote in his advert – and still on a mission to carry out detective work in his sixties (*Daily Telegraph*, 19 October 1909, p.20).

20. *Daily Telegraph*, 19 October 1909, p.20. One of Pierrepont's first press mentions, back in November 1905, was altogether different; this was a disclaimer he had asked the *Pall Mall Gazette* to include, following the appointment of a more infamous namesake: 'Mr William Pierrepont, private inquiry agent, of 27 Chancery Lane, asks us to say that he is in no way connected with the Mr Pierrepont, who, it is stated, has recently been appointed to the post of public executioner.' (*Pall Mall Gazette*, 9 November 1905.)

21. Ibid. William Pierrepont advertised his office in a more subtle way in the Post Office Directory; in 1915, for example, his advert stated, 'Pierrepont William, confidential agency & inquiry office, 27 Chancery Lane, WC, TA 'Bullseye, London'; TN 10972 Central, refs to leading London solicitors.' On the same page was a shorter entry: 'Easton, Miss Kate, 10 Warwick Court, High Holborn, WC'. Kate was the only female private detective listed in the 1915 directory. (*Post Office London Directory*, 1915, p.1357, originally via London Metropolitan Archives, on Ancestry.)

22. *Daily Telegraph*, 19 September 1905, p.16

23. *Army & Navy Gazette*, 30 June 1917, p.11

24. During the Edwardian period, when she was still relatively new to the business, Maud's press coverage was largely traditional, in that it consisted of classified adverts placed by herself. However, from the mid-1920s onwards, she changed tactic to sell the dramatic illustrated stories of her 'cases' – including the Dope Fiend Mystery (*Liverpool Echo*, 22 February 1930, p.6), the German Spy Case (*Liverpool Echo*, 8 February 1930, p.6), the Remarkable Clairvoyant Case (*Liverpool Echo*, 25 January 1930, p.14), A Remarkable Office Robbery (*Liverpool Echo*, 1 February 1930, p.14), and the Strange Country House Case (*Liverpool Echo*, 8 March 1930, p.12). Another paper also included 'leaves from the notebook of the private woman detective, Maud West' that detailed 'scoundrels who make love to and deceive women' (*Liverpool Echo*, 1 March 1930, p.6). In 1926, she released three photographs of herself – one of her in her office, and two of her in disguise, firstly as an older woman (looking rather like the police photograph of baby farmer Amelia Dyer) and secondly as a man in a bowler hat (very similar to Charlie Chaplin, then of course one of the biggest movie stars). These were published as a standalone piece in the *Birmingham Daily Gazette* (5 February 1926, p.4). The articles succeeded in publicising the London lady detective to a provincial audience, making her well known across England.

Chapter 11: Frauds and Fakes

1. *Aberdeen Evening Express*, 28 July 1893, p.3; *Cheshire Observer*, 29 July 1893, p.8
2. *Birmingham Daily Post*, 9 October 1895, p.8
3. *The Scotsman*, 16 August 1892, p.6
4. *Cumberland and Westmorland Herald*, 16 October 1886, p.6
5. 1881 and 1891 census for Culcheth; 1901 census for Glazebury, Culcheth
6. *Manchester Evening News*, 20 January 1902
7. *Manchester Evening News*, 16 January 1902, p.2
8. *Manchester Evening News*, 20 January 1902
9. *Durham County Advertiser*, 14 March 1902, p.6. Prison records for HMP Wakefield, where Ada was sent, suggests that she was born in America in 1878, and that she also used the name Alice Boulby. She was a literate woman, unlike many of the women listed with her, and had formerly worked as a governess (West Yorkshire Prison Records, 1801–1914, on Ancestry).
10. The former Helen Mabel Bird had married George Juniper on 7 October 1899 at Inworth, Essex; her age was given as 22, five years younger than George – but she was actually just 20 years old at the time. What the accounts of her crime don't mention is that she was also a mother, trying to maintain her son Cyril – then barely 2 years old – after her husband's desertion (1901 census for Elmstead Village, Essex; marriage of Helen Mabel Bird and George Juniper, Essex Church of England Parish Registers, Essex Record Office, on Ancestry; birth of Helen Mabel Bird, Jul–Sept 1879, Colchester vol 4a, p.384). It's not clear what happened to Helen, but as her sister Daisy and both her parents emigrated to Canada, it's possible that Helen did too.
11. *Barking, East Ham and Ilford Advertiser*, 31 May 1902, p.1
12. *Coventry Evening Telegraph*, 6 January 1931, p.3
13. Mary's family can be found in the 1881 census for 34 Broadwell Street, Burslem, Stoke-on-Trent (with Mary present); the 1881 census for Burslem (with Mary present); the 1901 census for 77 Lower Mayer Street, Hanley, Stoke-on-Trent; and

the 1911 census for 2 Wilson Street, Hanley, Stoke (where her parents state that they have one child who is still alive – but Mary cannot be found). Mary Walsh married Charles Thomas Dean at Burslem on 19 October 1891, when she was 18 and he was 20. James Vincent Scully married Evelyn Threlfall on 21 March 1897 at Everton, and had eight children with her by 1911; the final decree in Charles Dean's divorce was issued on 5 June 1899.

Chapter 12: Spiritualism and Scepticism

1. Kathryn Hughes notes that from Jane Austen's time onwards, 'well-educated girls' were encouraged to 'soften' their 'eruption with a graceful and feminine manner', and that later in the nineteenth century, when women were able to get a university education, 'many families refused to let their clever daughters attend for fear that they would make themselves unmarriageable' (Kathryn Hughes, 'Gender Roles in the Nineteenth Century' (British Library, 15 May 2014, https://www.bl.uk/romantics-and-victorians/articles/gender-roles-in-the-nineteenth-century))
2. Srdjan Smajic, *Ghost-seers*, p.3
3. Roger Luckhurst, 'The Victorian Supernatural', British Library (2014), https://www.bl.uk/romantics-and-victorians/articles/the-victorian-supernatural
4. Roger Luckhurst, 'The Victorian Supernatural', British Library (2014), https://www.bl.uk/romantics-and-victorians/articles/the-victorian-supernatural
5. Srdjan Smajic, *Ghost-seers*, p.115
6. Srdjan Smajic has noted how the 'fictional detective is a master-semiotician adept at reading visual language' (Srdjan Smajic, *Ghost-seers*, p.93)
7. Srdjan Smajic, *Ghost-seers*, p.131
8. Roger Luckhurst, 'An Occult Gazetteer of Bloomsbury: An Experiment in Method', in Lawrence Phillips and Anne Witchard (eds), *London Gothic: Place, Space and the Gothic Imagination* (Continuum, London, 2010), p.54. Roger Luckhurst, 'Passages in the invention of the psyche: mind-reading in London, 1881–84', in Roger Luckhurst and Josephine McDonagh (eds), *Transactions and Encounters: Science and Culture in the Nineteenth Century* (Manchester University Press, 2002), p.123.
9. ParliamentUK, 'Religion and Belief: Witchcraft', on http://www.parliament.uk/about/living-heritage/transformingsociety/private-lives/religion/overview/witchcraft/, accessed 29 January 2018.
10. The Fraudulent Mediums Act was 14 & 15 Geo VI, c.33). http://www.legislation.gov.uk/ukpga/1951/33/pdfs/ukpga_19510033_en.pdf
11. In a later charge, Martha Stephenson's name was given as Mary Stevens, although she was still performing as Madame Keiro. This may either be a press error – which was common amongst newspapers – or an attempt by the Stephensons to obfuscate their past by altering their names just enough to cause confusion (see *Western Times*, 5 March 1917, p.4). In reality, Martha's birth name was the rather lovely Martha Faircloth. She had married Charles Yates Stephenson in Ormskirk in 1888, when Charles was 30, and Martha may have been 32 (her origins are rather obscure, but a Martha Faircloth was born in 1856 in North Witchford, Cambridgeshire, and I cannot find anyone else of this name who would have been of the right era to have married Charles (births for North Witchford, March 1856, vol 3b p.575). Although Keiro was a genuine Scottish surname, it seems likely that the Stephensons chose it as a stage name more because of its similarity in sound to Cairo, with there being a

keen interest in Egypt in *fin de siècle* England – it being seen as a place of mystery and other-worldliness – and Egyptology reaching a zenith in popularity with the unearthing of Tutankhamun's tomb by Howard Carter in 1922 (Sharla Hutchinson, 'Marie Corelli's *Ziska*: A Gothic Egyptian Ghost Story', in Sharla Hutchinson and Rebecca A. Brown, *Monsters and Monstrosity from the Fin de Siècle to the Millennium: New Essays* (McFarland & Co, 2015), p.34). Prior to forming a partnership with Martha, south Londoner Charles had worked variously as a reporter in Brighton and a 'masseur and medical electrician' in Lancashire (1881 census for Cumberland Mansion, 27 Kings Road, Brighton; 1891 census for 53 Adelaide Street, North Meols, Lancashire). As 'Charles Keiro', he was listed in Post Office directories throughout the 1910s as a medical galvanist, or medical electrician, still based on Regent Street (see for example, the *Post Office London Directory* for 1910, p.1890, and for 1915, p.1019). After their prosecution, the couple also wrote and published books on palmistry and clairvoyance, separately – with Charles also writing the 'memoirs' of his 19-year-old tabby cat, Mephistopheles (published by Messrs Jarrold and Sons in 1907).

12. *Globe*, 26 October 1904, p.6
13. *Leeds Mercury*, 18 August 1904, p.5
14. Ibid.
15. Under her maiden name of Annie Lange, Annie Betts is listed as a detective (police) in the 1901 census; it looks as though the census enumerator has added the 'police' later, as a descriptor of the industry under which 'detective' usually fell. Annie married Robert Betts, a clerk of works, and a widower nearly twenty years her senior, at Pimlico in September 1903, when she described herself as a lady detective (1901 census for 136 Tachbrook Place, Pimlico; marriage at St Saviour, Pimlico, on 30 September 1903).
16. Annie and Robert Betts had a daughter, Ellen Jessica Betts, who was born on 7 May 1906 at Barnes. Although Robert had been married before, his first wife, Florence, died after just five years of marriage, in 1894, and I can't find evidence of any children born of this marriage.
17. *St James's Gazette*, 1 September 1904, p.16
18. *Western Times*, 5 March 1917, p.4
19. See, for example, the Fletcher case, which is mentioned in the *Dundee Evening Telegraph* of 21 February 1881, p.2; details of the trial, at the Central Criminal Court on 28 March 1881, are at *Old Bailey Online* (ref t18810328-406). The case was brought by Juliet Ann Theodora Heurtley Hart-Davies against Susan Fletcher. Fletcher was convicted on six charges relating to obtaining goods by false pretences; one of the charges was 'obtaining property by witchcraft and sorcery'. She was sentenced to twelve months in prison. Juliet Hart-Davies was born Juliet Ann Theodora Heurtley, the son of Richard Walter Heurtley, Esq, and married James Penrose Hart-Davies at Hampton Wick on 22 January 1878, when she was already 35 years old, and her husband 39 (marriages for St John the Baptist, Hampton Wick, on Ancestry). The marriage was not happy, and Juliet brought divorce proceedings against her husband just three years later, in 1881, citing his impotence and subsequent non-consummation of the marriage – 'the said James Penrose Hart-Davies [sic] was at the time of the said marriage and has ever since been wholly unable to consummate the said marriage owing to the chronic weakness and condition of his parts of

generation' (TNA J77/263/7646A). She died at 4 rue Donizetti, Paris, on 19 April 1912, her status given as widow. She may have been targeted due to her evident wealth; after she died, her effects were valued at £27,980 0s 5d (National Probate Calendar, 1858–1966, on Ancestry, 30 January 2018).

20. She was baptised on 17 May 1868 at the parish church in Sutton Coldfield (Warwickshire County Council/Ancestry).

21. *Birmingham Daily Gazette*, 17 January 1868, p.1. Edwin Cornelius Middleton, of 13 Cannon Street, Birmingham, architect and surveyor was adjudged bankrupt on Christmas Eve, 1869 (*The London Gazette*, 11 January 1870, p.261). In 1871, the family was listed on the census as living in Moseley, then part of Worcestershire.

22. 1891 census for Harborne, Staffordshire; *Barnet Press*, 20 April 1907, p.7; *Manchester Times*, 16 November 1850, p.2. Edmond's factory dried the swim bladders of sturgeon, cod and other fish, producing a substance that was pressed into sheets or shredded, and which could be used for clarifying beer or made into glues. Given that Edmond also manufactured glucose (from wheat, corn or potatoes), commonly used to sweeten confectionery and ice-creams, it is likely that his isinglass was used in sweets and puddings – such as jellies and blancmange – to help set them. Both isinglass and gelatine had been marketed for invalids in the mid-nineteenth century, as having a restorative purpose akin to Bovril in the early twentieth century; but by the time Edmond was in business, sweets for children were the more popular use for his products (see 'Orange Isinglass Jelly', in Eliza Acton, *Modern Cookery in all its Branches* (John E. Potter, 1860), accessed at http://chestofbooks.com/food/recipes/Modern-Cookery/Isinglass-Jellies.html; The Foods of England, 'Table Jelly' (www.foodsofengland.co.uk/tablejelly.htm) and Historic Food, 'Jellies and Creams' (www.historicfood.com/Jellies.htm), for more information about isinglass production and uses).

23. 1901 census for 87 Oak Hill Park, Hampstead, on Ancestry. Edmond Victor Parkes Thompson's birth was registered as taking place in Smethwick on 27 May 1894.

24. Victoria Park opened in 1902 ('Victoria Park, Finchley', Parks & Gardens UK (www.parksandgardens.org/places-and-people/site/8134).

25. An advert placed in the *Hendon & Finchley Times* in 1905 stated 'For sale: 20 in Green's lawn mower, in good condition; also a number of fowls, 2s each. La Turbie, Seymour Road, Church End, Finchley'. The combination of items for sale sounds a bit random; but perhaps the family simply wished to upgrade their lawn mower; and perhaps their chickens had multiplied and they wished to reduce their numbers in a humane way (*Hendon & Finchley Times*, 17 November 1905, p.3). There would have been servants at La Turbie, as there were still commonly at this time; one of the Thompson neighbours, living at Grenside on Seymour Road, advertised in 1905 for a 'good general servant wanted; strong; good character indispensable; wages £16 to £18; must understand plain cooking; Sunday evenings out, and one evening a week and monthly holiday; help given; boy for boots; no children; no washing' (*Hendon & Finchley Times*, 2 June 1905, p.4).

26. *Barnet Press*, 20 April 1907, p.7; *Barnet Press*, 2 February 1907, p.4

27. *Barnet Press*, 20 April 1907, p.7. Edmond's will was proved on 9 March 1907 at the High Court of Justice in London by Rosalie Thompson 'of La Turbie, Seymour Road, Finchley, aforesaid widow' and Edward Thomas Ridge of Lloyds Bank House, Summerfield, Birmingham, a bank manager.

28. National Probate Calendar (Index of Wills and Administrations), 1858–1966, for Edmond Thompson, 9 March 1907. The equivalent sum of money today would be over £2 million (calculated via www.moneysorter.co.uk).

29. Louisa Hadley, *Neo-Victorian Fiction and Historical Narrative: The Victorians and Us* (Palgrave Macmillan, 2010), p.87

30. As Ann D. Braude notes, 'Spiritualism epitomised the Victorian fascination with the dead and the hereafter' (Ann D. Braude, 'Spirits Defend the rights of Women: Spiritualism and Changing Sex Roles in Nineteenth-Century America', in Yvonne Yazbeck Haddad and Ellison Banks Findly (eds), *Women, Religion and Social Change* (State University of New York Press, 1985), p.428).

31. Marriages for Lambeth district, December 1899, vol 1d, p.924, on FreeBMD.org. uk, accessed 26 February 2018. The 1881 census for Kirton, Lincolnshire, records John William's father, William, as a farmer of 13 acres, employing three labourers; his 15-year-old son is recorded as 'teacher in school'.

32. *Yorkshire Evening Post*, 26 November 1908, p.3

33. London and Surrey, England, Marriage Bonds and Allegations, 1597–1921, appearance of John William Dennis on 5 July 1909, on Ancestry, accessed 26 February 2018. The 1911 census records J.W. Dennis as now being a landowner, and living with second wife Betsy – along with their butler, cook and housemaid – at 28 Albert Hall Mansions, Kensington. The census shows that J.W. was born in 1866 in Freiston, Lincolnshire; Betsy (nee Onions), a year his senior, was originally from Birmingham, the daughter of a bedstead manufacturer; she had married silk dyer William Keith at St Pancras Parish Church on 16 April 1892. Betsy died whilst at 7 Mandeville Place, London, on 6 July 1912, leaving effects worth nearly £15,000; probate was granted to John William Dennis, 'merchant' (National Probate Calendar (Index of Wills and Administrations), 1858–1966, on Ancestry). John William lived on until 1949, dying there in Devon (Deaths for Tiverton, Devon, Sept 1949, vol 7a, p.643).

34. *Hampstead & Highgate Express*, 3 July 1909, p.6

35. 1911 census for Marylebone. Walsh and Stockley were the two former detectives James Stockley and John Walsh. Walsh retired from Scotland Yard in 1907, having joined the Met in 1878, and one of his successes was in – temporarily at least – breaking up the notorious criminal gang known as the Forty Thieves (*Newcastle Evening Chronicle*, 15 April 1907, p.4). When Stockley died in 1954, one obituary described him as a 'retired Chief Detective Inspector who took part in the Jack the Ripper murder hunt, and became bodyguard to an American millionairess' (*Belfast Telegraph*, 29 June 1954, p.8). The 1911 census confirms that by this point, James Stockley was a private inquiry agent (1911 census for 31 Blandford Road, Bedford Park, Chiswick). John Walsh, though, is listed in the same census simply as a pensioned police inspector (1911 census for Granada Hotel, Granada Road, Southsea).

36. *Leeds Mercury*, 15 March 1911, p.3

37. Ibid.

38. Ibid.

39. Alvin Wee, 'Nineteenth-Century Psychology: An Introduction', *The Victorian Web* (2005), http://www.victorianweb.org/science/psych/psych.htm; C. James Goodwin, in *A History of Modern Psychology* (Wiley, 2015, 5th ed), p.47, notes that

'psychology did not just pop out of the ground in the late nineteenth century', but it is at this point, arguably, that it 'evolved into a scientific discipline'.

40. Again, the basis for biological theories of criminality had their basis earlier, in the late eighteenth and early nineteenth centuries, with the development of phrenology (Robert Morin, 'Phrenology and Crime', *The Encyclopaedia of Theoretical Criminology* (online 2014), at http://onlinelibrary.wiley.com/doi/10.1002/9781118517390. wbetc103/abstract?), by the late nineteenth and early twentieth century, Cesare Lombroso's theory of the 'born criminal' and his attempts to classify criminals according to their physical attributes were capturing the imagination (Diana Bretherick, 'The "born criminal"'? Lombroso and the origins of modern criminality' (*BBC History*, 14 February 2015, http://www.historyextra.com/period/victorian/ the-born-criminal-lombroso-and-the-origins-of-modern-criminology/). The combination of such approaches as Lombroso's, and the development of psychological approaches led to an interest in understanding both the physical and mental reasons that might lie behind the criminal behaviour of an individual.

Chapter 13: Suffragist Agents

1. Grace Wood, 'Actresses' Franchise League: The 100-year-old feminist theatre coalition that's inspiring writers today', *The Stage*, 20 July 2018, at https://www. thestage.co.uk/features/2018/actresses-franchise-league-the-100-year-old-feminist-theatre-coalition-thats-inspiring-writers-today/ and Isobel Hamilton, '100 years ago, my ancestor was an actress fighting for the same thing Time's Up wants today', *MashableUK*, 9 March 2018, at https://mashable.com/2018/03/09/ actresses-franchise-league-times-up/?europe=true

2. More men were included as a result of the 1867 Second Reform Act, and the 1884 Third Reform Act – see www.parliament.uk/about/living-heritage/transforming society/electionsvoting/womenvote/overview/earlysuffragist

3. Ibid.

4. Karen Manners Smith, 'Women's Social and Political Union', *Encyclopaedia Britannica*, 17 March 2017, at www.britannica.com/topic/Womens-Social-and-Political-Union

5. John Simkin, 'The Vote' (1997), accessed via http://spartacus-educational.com/ WvoteJ.htm

6. Anon, 'Suffragette Newspapers', *British Newspaper Archive*, 1 February 2018, https://blog.britishnewspaperarchive.co.uk/2018/02/01/suffragette-newspapers/

7. *The Vote*, 30 December 1911, pp.13–14

8. *The Vote*, 9 May 1913, p.10

9. *Votes for Women*, 24 December 1908, p.3

10. *Globe*, 31 May 1913, p.3

11. Ibid.

12. Susannah Stapleton, *The Adventures of Maud West, Lady Detective* (Picador, 2019), pp.87–8

13. Alex Cox, '5 Defiant Suffrage Statements Found in the 1911 Census', *Findmypast*, 1 February 2018, at https://www.findmypast.co.uk/blog/discoveries/suffragettes-in-the-1911-census

14. 1911 census for 83 Queens Road, Wimbledon.

15. 1911 census for Warwick Mansions, 15 Warwick Court, London WC. Madeleine Lucette had, in 1902, stated 'I am most anxious always to stand on my own merits, and to dissociate myself, as far as may be, from my petticoats. I don't want to take refuge behind the fact that I am a woman.' (quoted in Sherry D. Engle, *New Women Dramatists in America, 1890–1920* (Palgrave Macmillan, 2007), p.55

16. 1911 census for 13 Great Turnstile, London WC.

17. His death merited a brief obituary in the *Shoreditch Observer* of 7 June 1913, stating 'Mr Maurice Moser, a famous detective in the eighties, has passed away at Boulogne-sur-Mer at the age of sixty-one'.) Somewhat bizarrely, it was an Oxfordshire newspaper – in an area not associated remotely with Moser and his work – that gave a fuller obituary, although with several mistakes, which was not unusual in late nineteenth century and early twentieth century obituaries. This again suggested that he was part of an old world, one in which detective work involved chasing down criminals who had 'taken refuge abroad'. Moser was 'a famous detective 30 years ago'; 'the last survivor of inspectors of Old Scotland Yard' (*Banbury Advertiser*, 12 June 1913, p.2). He had passed the baton onto his son by Harriet Moser, Gustav, who was now part of the new generation of private detectives, working from a former office of his father's at Palace Chambers in London.

18. *Pall Mall Gazette*, 20 August 1913

19. Ibid.

20. *Lloyd's Weekly News*, 19 May 1907, p.6, and cited in Susannah Stapleton, *The Adventures of Maud West, Lady Detective* (Picador, 2019), p.38. Kate, though, also stated that she had started her career as a wholesaler's correspondence clerk, undertaking bits of sleuthing work for him before working for a solicitor and then a male private detective – only then did she open her own agency. However, she failed to note at all here that she had been in a different career altogether initially.

21. *Western Daily Press*, 12 June 1914, p.5

22. *The Suffragette*, 19 June 1914, p.10

23. *Daily Record*, 29 June 1914, p.8

24. *Birmingham Daily Post*, 5 August 1914, p.5

Chapter 14: War and Peace

1. Marriage at All Souls Church, St Marylebone, on 7 October 1900. Charles was aged 26 when he married, and a bachelor; Dorothy was 'of full age' – she appears, from the 1921 Canada census, to have been three years his senior. At the time of their marriage, in Marylebone, Charles Senior was a lieutenant in the Royal Navy, based in Devon; his wife, who was living in London, was the daughter of the late James Mason Houghton, a lawyer.

2. *The People*, 13 December 1914, p.8

3. Sir Henry Bargrave Finnelley Deane (1848–1919) was known as Bargrave Deane.

4. *Western Daily Press*, 18 February 1915, p.4; *Western Mail*, 18 February 1915, p.9

5. This more complex depiction of women was also hinted at in Anna Katharine Green's story *The Golden Slipper* – one of her tales featuring New York-based female detective Violet Strange – which was published in 1915. In it, Violet has to investigate a group of female friends, who suspect one of their own number of stealing from them. The story ably shows the sometimes difficult dynamics of female friendship, and how women might turn on each other to advance their own agendas (Anna

Katharine Green, *The Cases of Violet Strange* (e-artnow, 2018, originally published 1915).

6. What happened to the female detective in this case, or even who she was, remains unknown. Employed by the British Slingsby brothers, she may have been British herself, and sent to investigate in the US, or they may have used their contacts to find an American based detective. What happened to the Slingsbys is better recorded. They remained together, but emigrated to Canada, where the 1921 census recorded them as living in Oak Bay, British Columbia with their only child, the disputed Charles, and Dorothy's older brother, Charles Warner (1921 census for 2187 Oak Bay Avenue, Oak Bay, Newcastle, British Columbia). They remained in Oak Bay, in fact in the same house, for the next twenty years. Charles Slingsby Senior died on 29 March 1941; his son, whose parentage had been so debated in 1914 and 1915, lived until 1972. Charles died at the Royal Jubilee Hospital in Victoria, leaving an estate of nearly £45,000 (National Probate Calendar). A private family tree by Ancestry user @Chaletjuderuth, accessed 12 June 2018, records Charles Eugene Edward Slingsby as dying in 1972, although it records his birth as 1908 rather than 1910.

7. 'ABI origins', https://www.theabi.org.uk/about/abi-origins. Harry Smale had joined the Metropolitan Police in 1887 as a constable in T Division, and retired as a CID superintendent in 1908 (TNA MEPO 4/343/83). When he died in 1939, aged 75, he was remembered primarily as a freemason and 'also president of the British Detectives Association' – the association sent a floral tribute to his funeral (*West Briton and Cornwall Advertiser,* 13 July 1939, p.8). I have not been able to ascertain who the detectives Harry Smale initially met with were, although it is likely they were male detectives drawn from Harry's former Met contacts.

8. In 1912, there had actually been a fraud involving a bogus York detective agency, which claimed to be called the British Detectives Association. When a 26-year-old man named William Halton was charged with obtaining money by false pretences (by advertising for men to become private detectives for his 'association' by paying him), he said, 'I'll tell you the truth. I AM the society.' Presumably, when Harry Smale established his own British Detectives Association, he was unaware of its previous, fraudulent, iteration (*Hartlepool Northern Daily Mail*, 7 May 1912, p.3).

9. 1911 census for 25 St Barnabas Road, Sheffield. Robert Graham was boarding at 284 Shoreham Street at the time.

10. Plymouth War Memorial details; Royal Navy and Royal Marine War Graves Roll, 1914–1919 on Ancestry.

11. Imperial War Museum, 'Nine women reveal the dangers of working in a munitions factory', 31 January 2018, at https://www.iwm.org.uk/history/9-women-reveal-the-dangers-of-working-in-a-first-world-war-munitions-factory

12. *Yorkshire Post and Leeds Intelligencer*, 6 December 1916, p.7

13. Mary Perkins was from the small community of Roeburndale near Lancaster, but in 1911 was living with her husband in Usk, Monmouthshire, where he was chief prison warder. They then moved to Leeds, where Mary was living in 1916, at 24 Hawthorne Terrace, New Wortley, Leeds (*Yorkshire Post and Leeds Intelligencer*, 22 November 1916, p.3). She was George's second wife, and had only married him around two years earlier, his first wife, also called Mary, having died, leaving George with a toddler daughter to look after. In 1922, Mary was a witness at her

stepdaughter's wedding, and still living in the family home at Hawthorne Terrace. At the time of her 1916 press mentions, she was in her mid-forties

14. *Western Mail*, 20 April 1916, p.2
15. *Western Daily Press*, 4 December 1917, p.7
16. *Pall Mall Gazette*, 8 March 1913, p.8; *Leeds Mercury*, 10 March 1913, p.3. Matilda worked under the direction of Percy Alfred Best, the manager of Selfridge's.
17. *Dundee Courier*, 14 July 1919, p.8
18. Joseph Walker Madigan was a former detective inspector at Scotland Yard (he was listed as such in the 1911 census for 4 The Crescent Gardens, Wimbledon Park. He had only retired in November 1913 (Metropolitan Police Registers, entry for 24 November 1913, on Ancestry); in December 1914, he appeared in court to claim damages for libel from the *Daily Sketch*. The day he retired from the Met, the *Sketch* had published his photo, with the text underneath: 'Detective Inspector Madigan, who retires from Scotland Yard today. For some years past his particular duty has been to watch international cardsharpers and confidence trick swindlers, all of whom he knows.' A few days later, another description of him was published, describing him at an event as 'a famous detective, possessed of a great sense of humour, was entertaining a score of cardsharpers and crooks, all of them flash men and very well dressed'. In coverage of the court case, it was noted that Madigan was now a private detective; William Kemp gave evidence that he had been at the event referred to by the *Daily Sketch*, and had sung 'Down in the Deep' at it. The *Daily Sketch* was found to have committed libel, and Madigan won damages (*Gloucestershire Echo*, 4 December 1914, p.4). Mentions of Annie Betts as a Whiteleys store detective can be found in the *Central Somerset Gazette*, 25 December 1914, p.8; *Taunton Courier*, 27 January 1915, p.8; *Dundee Evening Telegraph*, 16 August 1915, p.2; and *The People*, 3 October 1915, p.7, for example.
19. This was a case brought against Thomas Morgan, who told fortunes at premises on Edgware Road under the name 'Professor Melini', advertising his services as 'excellent service during war time'. Annie had posed as a customer, and detailed in court how Morgan had told her 'she had three children, then two – as a matter of fact she only had one – and said she was separated from her husband, whereas she was living with him happily.' (*Globe*, 29 December 1916, p.5).
20. *Evesham Standard & West Midlands Observer*, 4 July 1914, p.1; and *Hull Daily Mail*, 14 August 1915, p.4.

Chapter 15: Roaring into the Post-war Era

1. Louise A. Jackson, 'The First World War and the first female police officer', *History of Government*, 17 June 2014, at https://history.blog.gov.uk/2014/06/17/the-first-world-war-and-the-first-female-police-officer/
2. Louise A. Jackson notes that Smith's role in moral regulation and the surveillance of women's behaviour caused some feminists to end their involvement with the movement to employ female police officers (Louise A. Jackson, 'The First World War and the first female police officer', *History of Government*, 17 June 2014, at https://history.blog.gov.uk/2014/06/17/the-first-world-war-and-the-first-female-police-officer/)
3. 'Celebrating 100 years of female officers in the Met', 22 November 2018, http://news.met.police.uk/news/celebrating-100-years-of-female-officers-in-the-met-333878

4. 'History of the Force', http://www.avonandsomerset.police.uk/about/history-of-the-force/
5. 'Celebrating 100 years of female officers in the Met', 22 November 2018, http:// news.met.police.uk/news/celebrating-100-years-of-female-officers-in-the-met-333878
6. *Western Daily Press*, 21 November 1923, p.6
7. Louise A. Jackson, 'The unusual case of "Mrs Sherlock". Memoir, Identity and the "Real" Woman Private Detective in Twentieth-Century Britain', *Gender & History*, 15:1 (April 2003), p.108
8. *The Mysterious Affair at Styles* (1920 US, 1921 UK); *The Secret Adversary* (1922); *The Murder on the Links* (1923); *The Man in the Brown Suit* (1924); *The Secret of Chimneys* (1925); *The Murder of Roger Ackroyd* (1926); *The Big Four* (1927); *The Mystery of the Blue Train* (1928); *The Seven Dials Mystery* (1929).
9. 'Tommy and Tuppence: A detective series by Agatha Christie', *The Sketch*, 24 September 1924, p.10
10. *Ally Sloper's Half-Holiday*, 7 July 1923, p.6
11. Ibid.
12. *The Graphic*, 30 April 1927.
13. Metropolitan Police Pension Registers, 1852–1933, on Ancestry (TNA MEPO 21). Kersey had married Julia Agnes McGuinness in Homerton on 19 September 1903 (LMA P79/BAN1/016). She was not incarcerated all the time, but instead seems to have had spells in and out of asylums. In 1928, she was subject to a record in the London settlement records to determine her place of settlement, which might suggest that she had needed to be an inmate again at this point. However, in 1930, she is listed at both 2 Osborne House, St Mary's Terrace, W2 and at 130 Baker Street with her husband (LMA electoral registers for St Marylebone). Julia Kersey died in Romford in 1934 (Romford deaths in the March quarter of 1934, vol 4a, p.702), and within months of her death, Charles married again, to Emmeline Weavers, in Southend (marriages in Rochford, September quarter of 1934, vol 4a, p.2368). Charles died in Southend in 1942 (deaths in Southend, September quarter of 1942, vol 4a p.636).
14. Benjamin Welton, 'The Case of the Vanishing Private Eyes', *The Atlantic*, 15 January 2015, at https://www.theatlantic.com/business/archive/2015/01/the-long-steady-decline-of-the-private-eye/384450/
15. *Nottingham Journal*, 31 January 1920, p.5
16. *Leeds Mercury*, 11 October 1924, p.7; *Illustrated Police News*, 18 October 1928, p.7. There is no mention of Annie as a detective in the press after 1928, and she does not appear to have ever given an occupation to census enumerators after 1901 (in other words, she did as a single woman on the census, but not as a married woman). As she was usually employed by others, rather than working on her own or establishing her own agency, there are no press adverts for her services either. However, at some point, she and her husband relocated from Barnes, where they had lived for decades, to the Sunningdale area of Berkshire, and this may have been to retire. Annie died there on 14 March 1949, seven years after her husband (death of Robert A. Betts, 82, March quarter of 1942, Windsor, vol 2c, p.1041; death of Annie Betts, 72, March quarter of 1949, Surrey NW, vol 5g, p.826; National Probate Calendar entry for Annie Betts, 13 May 1949).

17. *Morning Post*, 10 August 1908; *Daily Telegraph & Courier*, 15 September 1911, p.16
18. *West London Observer*, 10 December 1920, p.12
19. *Western Daily Press*, 4 January 1924, p.4; *Gloucester Citizen*, 6 February 1924, p.2; *Western Morning News*, 23 April 1921, p.2; *West Sussex Gazette*, 15 May 1924, p.1. Not all agencies employed women at this time, however; for example, the Western Inquiry and Detective Agency, based in Bristol, proudly advertised only its 'experienced men' in 1924 (*Horfield and Bishopston Record*, 18 April 1924, p.1).
20. *Chelmsford Chronicle*, 9 January 1925, p.7
21. Stewart's was based at 101 St Vincent Street, and Macdonald's at 19 Waterloo Street, both in central Glasgow (*The Scotsman*, 1 December 1923, p.2). The Wynnecliff agency was at 43 Castleford Road, Sparkhill, and managed by John Marshell [sic], DSSA (*Illustrated Sporting and Dramatic News*, 23 February 1929, p.74).
22. See *The Scotsman*, 1 October 1923, p.1. Stewart's was based at 101 St Vincent Street, and Macdonald's at 19 Waterloo Street, both in central Glasgow (*The Scotsman*, 1 December 1923, p.2)
23. *The Bioscope*, 15 August 1928, p.42. Harry Piel was also the film's director. The film's title for its German release was *Mann Gegen Mann – Man Against Man*. Interestingly, given its German provenance, the lady detective is the only character given a British name – Miss Gladys Norton – suggesting that the female private detective was perceived as singularly British, rather than European, occupation.
24. *The Tatler*, 4 January 1928, p.22
25. *The Sketch*, 15 August 1928, p.25
26. Quoted in *The Sketch*, 13 June 1928, p.32
27. Death certificate from General Register Office. Dorothy died at 45 Eton Avenue, Hampstead, on 10 June 1928. The certificate states that at the time of her death, she was working as a solicitor's process server – a common job undertaken by private detectives – and that she died of heart disease, bronchitis, lung congestion and heart failure.
28. On 12 May 1920, Rosalie Thompson married at Marylebone Register Office. Her new husband was Leo Thomas Kennedy, nine years her junior. In reality, it seems that Rosalie had stopped working as a private detective by 1914, when she is first recorded as living in South Africa; however, she seems to have only returned to London to marry, and then returned to South Africa. Interestingly, she had spent at least a few of the years prior to her marriage referring to herself as Rosalie Kennedy, despite no marriage having yet taken place, suggesting that, like many private detectives, she was quite a modern, forward-thinking individual. Rosalie died in Durban on 22 February 1940; Leo, now in his sixties, remarried a year later, and died in 1975 – a week before the anniversary of Rosalie's death. Perhaps Leo Kennedy did not approve of his new wife working – unlike Edmond Thompson, who presumably accepted his wife's work as a spiritualist, and Robert Betts, Annie Betts' much older husband, who also appears to have been happy with his wife working throughout their marriage. Alternatively, and more likely, she may now have had the financial security to stop work; however, it is also probable that the peripatetic nature of her detective work suited her lifestyle as a widow with an adult child, but not the life of a newly wedded wife, the spouse of a mobile American businessman. Rosalie's case showed that the work of a private detective was best suited to a woman in need of money and a challenge, but who did not have a husband or young children to

look after; it is significant that back in the 1860s, the fictional lady detectives were vague about their marital status, or suggested that they were widowed or single, just as many of the real lady detectives of the 1890s and 1900s were similarly on their own. The lifestyle did not suit everyone, but it best suited women who could move around, and who had fewer domestic commitments. There is another aspect of Rosalie's case to consider, however. The lady detective sought, and found, variety, changes in scene and in the people one came into contact with, through her detective work. When Rosalie found other situations that could give her this same variety – life in the US and South Africa – her boundaries expanded, and she may have simply no longer needed detective work, for she had found other sources of variety and mental satisfaction.

29. *The Sunday Post*, 14 March 1926, p.11
30. Ibid.

Chapter 16: The Dirty Thirties

1. See Chapter 11 for more detail on the National Detective Agency scam. The Slater's Agency case, which caused the closing of the agency in 1904, involved a divorce sought by Kate Pollard, whose husband Thomas was both an alcoholic and unemployed, whereby several of Slater's detectives sought to fabricate evidence of Thomas's adultery when they could not find any; this included procuring a woman for that purpose. Slater, his solicitor, and four of his detectives were arrested on charges of conspiracy, and tried at the Old Bailey in a long, well-publicised trial. Four of the detectives were found guilty; although Slater himself wasn't, he was ridiculed in court and his career did not survive the case ('Henry Scott alias Henry Slater: perverting justice, 17 October 1904', *Old Bailey Online*, t19041017-788, at www.oldbaileyonline.org). The 1912 case involved 26-year-old William Halton, who advertised for men to join his 'British Detectives Association', but in answer to applications, asked for money 'to cover the cost of inquiries'. He was charged with obtaining money by false pretences, and, following a trial at York, sentenced to three months' hard labour (*Northern Daily Mail*, 7 May 1912, p.3).
2. *Yorkshire Evening Post*, 21 September 1933, p.9. The proposed bill was promoted in the *Police Chronicle*, with other newspapers then picking up on it. The *Western Daily Press*, which headlined a brief piece on the bill with 'My dear Watson!', highlighting the continued association of private detective work with Sherlock Holmes, noted that this would be a 'legal charter for the recognition of private detectives in the same way as lawyers, accountants, dentists, and other professional workers' (*Western Daily Press*, 1 September 1933, p.8).
3. Anonymous British Detectives Association official, quoted in the *Daily Herald*, 3 September 1933, p.6. This official was likely to have been president Harry Swale, who provided quotes at other times, such as in the *Daily Herald* of 7 August 1933, p.7
4. *Daily Herald*, 3 September 1933, p.6. In 1950, it was noted that most members of the British Detectives Association were ex-police officers, including its then president, Tom Webster, who had been a private detective since around 1930 (*Lincolnshire Echo*, 11 October 1950, p.4).
5. *Dundee Evening Telegraph*, 20 February 1930, p.2
6. *The Sketch*, 21 January 1931, p.123

7. 1939 Register for 43 Haslemere Avenue, Mitcham; 8 Victoria Square, Westminster; St George's Square, Westminster; Duke of York Cottage, Harpers Bridge Road, Guildford.
8. 1939 Register for 104 South View Crescent, Sheffield; marriage of Mary V. Ayres and William E. Holmes, June quarter of 1938, Sheffield (vol 9c, p.1575); marriage of Mary Holme and Herbert K. Spence, 10 October 1946, Wharfedale district (vol 2d p.1845).
9. 1939 Register for 9 Fairfax Road, Hampstead
10. O'Donovan was the Conservative MP for Mile End from 1931 to 1935; he would attempt a return to parliament in 1950, but lost to Dr Edith Summerskill, and died in 1955, aged 68. He was something of a maverick; his obituary in *The Times* described him as an 'amusing and fearless speaker' who attracted hostility, and that he 'loved a fight'. It seems unlikely that he was very interested in private detection per se – he was seen as making 'contributions to a wide range of subjects', mainly medicine-related, as befitted the professional dermatologist (*The Times*, 15 January 1955, p.8).
11. *Lancashire Evening Post*, 22 April 1935, p.7
12. Ibid.

Chapter 17: From Licences to Dog Leads
1. *Lincolnshire Echo*, 11 October 1950, p.4
2. Ibid.
3. *Lancashire Evening Post*, 4 April 1945, p.2; *Lancashire Evening Post*, 1 September 1947, p.2. These adverts predominantly involve former police detectives, again highlighting men's predominance in private detective circles post-Second World War. Another individual was Thomas E. Hoyland, former detective constable and member of the BDA, who was working in Bradford immediately after the war (*Yorkshire Post*, 30 November 1948, p.3; 1939 Register for 207 Beacon Road, Bradford).
4. See, for example, the *Belfast News Letter* of 19 April 1948 p.4. The classified ads section of this paper also advertised the services of both 'male and female expert private detectives' working at the Private Detective Bureau on Belfast's Donegall Street, who could trace or shadow anyone 'night or day, anywhere'.
5. *Daily Herald*, 7 October 1941, p.3; *Daily Herald*, 9 October 1941, p.3
6. *Newcastle Evening Chronicle*, 20 August 1941, p.6. Another advert after the end of the war, in 1948, specified the need for a 'fully experienced lady detective, used to police court work' and with experience in a similar role in a retail store, was needed for department stores in the Liverpool area; in return, such women could expect a permanent, well-paid job with paid holidays (*Liverpool Echo*, 13 October 1948, p.1).
7. The couple was 51-year-old Harold Wigg and his wife Berta, 37. Although the male detective from Barkers was named in press coverage, the two female detectives from Harrods were not (*Chelsea News and General Advertiser*, 31 May 1940, p.3).
8. *Newcastle Evening Chronicle*, 24 July 1941, p.5
9. *Daily Herald*, 7 December 1944, p.4
10. Female detectives continued to be popular in fiction and in theatrical or film productions. Examples during the 1940s include the Cyril Campion play *Ladies In Waiting*, featuring a lady detective, the female detective Daphne Wrayne, who featured in Mark Cross's stories, and the MGM film *Sky Murder*, billed as a 'new

type of feminine comedy' and starring Joyce Compton as a lady detective (*Waterford Standard*, 5 July 1941, p.2).

11. Louise A. Jackson, 'The unusual case of "Mrs Sherlock". Memoir, Identity and the "Real" Woman Private Detective in Twentieth-Century Britain', *Gender & History*, 15:1 (April 2003), pp.108–109

12. Different sources have varying details about how and when this took place. A 1993 article in *The Independent* stated that the British Detectives Association merged with the Association of British Detectives in 1970 to become the ABI (Cal McCrystal, 'No prying eyes as the gumshoes gather', *The Independent*, 9 May 1993, at https://www.independent.co.uk/news/uk/no-prying-eyes-as-the-gumshoes-gather-2321883.html). However, Nigel South refers to 'The Association of British Detectives (founded in 1945) and the British Detectives Association (founded in 1919)' and states that the ABI was formed from a merger of these two organisations in 1953 (Nigel South, *Policing for Profit: The Private Security Sector* (Sage, London, 1988), p.74). Louise A. Jackson states that the BDA was formed in 1913, the Federation of British Detectives in 1949, and that the two amalgamated as the ABI in 1953 (Louise A. Jackson, 'The unusual case of "Mrs Sherlock". Memoir, identity and the "Real" woman private detective in twentieth-century Britain', *Gender & History*, 15:1 (April 2003), p.115).

13. 'Private detectives seek charter', *The Times*, 20 February 1963, p.15

14. Ibid.

15. However, later in this article, it is stated that the Association has '260 members in the United Kingdom and 150 associate members abroad' ('Private detectives seek charter', *The Times*, 20 February 1963, p.15)

16. Rosemary Simon, 'Who can help you find a missing relative?', *The Times*, 9 August 1968, p.11

17. 'Limited law against harassment and pestering being examined', *The Times*, 14 July 1973, p.4

18. 'Private detectives seek charter', *The Times*, 20 February 1963, p.15

19. *Liverpool Echo*, 8 June 1983, p.2

20. *Liverpool Echo*, 23 February 1974, p.27; *Dublin Evening Herald*, 17 April 1989, p.23. A press report in an Irish newspaper in 1973 relating to a case of shoplifting at Dunnes Stores in Dundalk recorded that it was the store's 'lady detective' who had apprehended the suspected shoplifter and referred to her as such twice – she was neither named, nor simply referred to as the store detective, even though her gender was of little relevance to the case (*Drogheda Argus and Leinster Journal*, 6 July 1973, p.8).

21. *Liverpool Echo*, 17 April 1993, p.24. *Revelations of a Lady Detective* was republished by the British Library in 2013; *The Female Detective* in 2014. *Mr Bazalgette's Agent* was also republished by the British Library in 2013.

22. Tony Imossi/The Association of British Investigators, 'The Self Regulation of Investigators in the Private Sector: A Discussion Document' (The Association of British Investigators, 2011), p.4

23. The document also states that 40 per cent of its 500-strong membership is drawn from retired police officers (Tony Imossi/The Association of British Investigators, 'The Self Regulation of Investigators in the Private Sector: A Discussion Document' (The Association of British Investigators, 2011), p.5, p.15

24. Anthony Smith, 'Has Theresa May forgotten about the licensing of private investigators?', *Huffington Post*, 31 March 2017, updated 1 April 2018, at https://www.huffingtonpost.co.uk/anthony-smith/private-investigators_b_15707332.html

25. J. Oliver Conroy/Emmanuelle Welch, 'Gadgets, drug mules and a French accent: my life as a private investigator', *The Guardian*, 2 August 2019, at https://www.theguardian.com/lifeandstyle/2019/aug/02/private-investigator-life-drugs-cheating-husbands-pi

26. Hayley Richardson, 'Former carer who trained as a private investigator in her 40s reveals why social media and a spare dog lead are her best tools for tracking down cheating spouses and missing people', *Daily Mail*, 12 August 2019, at https://www.dailymail.co.uk/femail/article-7348471/Private-investigator-reveals-social-media-dog-lead-key-tools-success.html

Select Bibliography

Books

Abelson, Elaine S. *When Ladies Go A-Thieving: Middle-Class Shoplifting in the Victorian Department Store* (Oxford University Press, 1989)

Acton, Eliza. *Modern Cookery in all its Branches* (John E. Potter, 1860)

Agnew, Jeremy. *Crime, Justice and Retribution in the American West, 1850–1900* (McFarland, 2017)

Cox, Pamela and Annabel Hobley. *Shopgirls: True Stories of Friendship, Hardship and Triumph from Behind the Counter* (Arrow, 2015)

Crone, Rosalind. *Violent Victorians: Popular Entertainment in Nineteenth-Century London* (Manchester University Press, 2012)

Davis, Tracy C. *Actresses as Working Women: Their Social Identity in Victorian Culture* (Routledge, 1991)

Durie, Bruce (ed). *The Pinkerton Casebook: Adventures of the original private eye* (Mercat Press, 2007)

Emsley, Clive. *Crime, Police and Penal Policy: European Experiences 1750–1840* (Oxford University Press, 2007)

Engle, Sherry D. *New Women Dramatists in America, 1890–1920* (Palgrave Macmillan, 2007)

Enss, Chris. *The Pinks: The First Women Detectives, Operatives, and Spies with the Pinkerton National Detective Agency* (TwoDot, 2017)

Flanders, Judith. *The Invention of Murder: How the Victorians Revelled in Death and Detection and Created Modern Crime* (HarperCollins, 2011)

Forrester, Andrew. *The Female Detective.* (British Library, 2012 (original publication date 1864))

Furnée, Jan Hein and Clé Lesger (eds). *The Landscape of Consumption: Shopping Streets and Cultures in Western Europe, 1600–1900* (Palgrave Macmillan, 2014)

Goodwin, C. James. *A History of Modern Psychology* (Wiley, 2015, 5th ed)

Green, Anna Katharine. *The Cases of Violet Strange* (e-artnow, 2018 (original publication date 1915))

Haddad, Yvonne Yazbeck and Ellison Banks Findly (eds). *Women, Religion and Social Change* (State University of New York Press, 1985)

Hadley, Louisa. *Neo-Victorian Fiction and Historical Narrative: The Victorians and Us* (Palgrave Macmillan, 2010)

Hayward, William Stephens. *Revelations of a Lady Detective* (British Library, 2013 (original publication date 1864))

Horan, James D. *Desperate Men: Revelations from the sealed Pinkerton files* (Hammond, Hammond & Co, 1952)

Horowitz, Janet and Myra Stark (eds), *The Englishwoman's Review of Social and Industrial Questions, 1887* (Routledge, 2016)

Hutchinson, Sharla and Rebecca A. Brown. *Monsters and Monstrosity from the Fin de Siècle to the Millennium: New Essays* (McFarland & Co, 2015)

Janik, Erika. *Pistols and Petticoats: 175 Years of Lady Detectives in Fact and Fiction* (Beacon Press, 2016)

Kane, Bronach (ed). *Women, Agency and the Law, 1300–1700* (Routledge, 2016)

Kayman, Martin A. *From Bow Street to Baker Street: Mystery, Detection and Narrative* (Macmillan, 1992)

Kesselman, Bryan. *'Paddington' Pollaky, Private Detective: The Mysterious Life and Times of the Real Sherlock Holmes* (The History Press, 2015)

Kestner, Joseph A. *Sherlock's Sisters: The British Female Detective, 1863–1913* (Ashgate, 2003)

Klein, Kathleen Gregory. *The Woman Detective: Gender and Genre* (University of Illinois Press, 1988)

Lamphier, Peg A. and Rosanne Walsh (eds). *Women in American History: A Social, Political and Cultural Encyclopaedia and Document Collection, Volume 2: Antebellum America Through the Gilded Age* (ABC-CLIO, 2017)

Ledger, Sally and Roger Luckhurst. *The Fin de Siècle: A Reader in Cultural History, c1880–1900.* (Oxford University Press, 2000)

Luckhurst, Roger and Josephine McDonagh (eds), *Transactions and Encounters: Science and Culture in the Nineteenth Century* (Manchester University Press, 2002)

Macallister, Greer. *Girl in Disguise* (Sourcebooks Landmark, 2018)

Marks, Patricia. *Bicycles, Bangs, and Bloomers: The New Woman in the Popular Press.* (University Press of Kentucky, 1990)

McKay, James A. *Allan Pinkerton: the Eye who never slept* (Mainstream, 1996)

Merrick, Leonard. *Mr Bazalgette's Agent.* (British Library, 2013 (original publication date 1888))

Mitchell, Elizabeth. *The Fearless Mrs Goodwin: How New York's First Female Police Detective Cracked the Crime of the Century* (Kindle, 2011)

Morn, Frank. *'The eye that never sleeps': a history of the Pinkerton National Detective Agency* (Indiana University Press, 1982)

Moser, Maurice and Charles F. Rideal. *Stories From Scotland Yard* (George Routledge and Sons Ltd, 1890)

Nown, Graham. *Watching the Detectives* (Grafton Books, 1991)

O'Hara, S. Paul. *Inventing the Pinkertons; or, Spies, Sleuths, Mercenaries, and Thugs: Being a story of the nation's most famous (and infamous) detective agency* (John Hopkins University Press, 2016)

Pattee, Fred Lewis. *The Development of the American Short Story: An Historical Survey* (Biblo and Tannen, 1923)

Phillips, Lawrence and Anne Witchard (eds). *London Gothic: Place, Space and the Gothic Imagination* (Continuum, 2010)

Pinkerton, Allan. *The Expressman and the Detective* (Dodo Press, 2008)

Pinkerton, Allan. *The Somnambulist and the Detective* (Lector House, 2019)

Pirkis, Catherine Louisa. *The Experiences of Loveday Brooke, Lady Detective* (Dover Publications, 1986 (original publication date 1894))

Pirkis, Catherine Louisa. *The Experiences of Loveday Brooke, Lady Detective.* (Summit Classic Mysteries, 2014 (original publication date 1894))

Queen, Ellery (ed). *The Female of the Species: The Great Women Detectives and Criminals* (Little, Brown & Co, 1943)

Rappaport, Erika D. *Shopping for Pleasure: Women in the Making of London's West End* (Princeton University Press, 2000)

Ricca, Brad. *Mrs Holmes: Murder, Kidnap and the True Story of an Extraordinary Lady Detective* (Amberley, 2018)

Richardson, Angelique and Chris Willis. *The New Woman in Fiction and Fact: Fin-de-Siècle Feminisms.* (Palgrave Macmillan, 2000)

Riffenburgh, Beau. *Pinkerton's Great Detective: The Rough-and-Tumble Career of James McPartland, America's Sherlock Holmes* (Penguin, 2014)

Shpayer-Makov, Haia. *The Ascent of the Detective: Police Sleuths in Victorian and Edwardian England* (Oxford University Press, 2011)

Sims, George Robert. *Dorcas Dene, Detective, Etc* (British Library, 2010)

Skene-Melvin, David (ed), *Investigating Women: Female Detectives by Canadian Writers* (Simon & Pierre, 1995)

Slung, Michele B. *Crime on her Mind: Fifteen Stories of Female Sleuths from the Victorian Era to the Forties* (Penguin, 1977)

Smajic, Srdjan. *Ghost-seers, Detectives, and Spiritualists* (Cambridge University Press, 2010)

South, Nigel. *Policing for Profit: The Private Security Sector* (Sage, 1988)

Stapleton, Susannah. *The Adventures of Maud West, Lady Detective: Secrets and Lies in the Golden Age of Crime* (Picador, 2019)

Stashower, Daniel. *The Hour of Peril: The Secret Plot to Murder Lincoln Before the Civil War* (Minotaur Books, 2013)

Summerscale, Kate. *The Wicked Boy: An Infamous Murder in Victorian London* (Bloomsbury, 2017)

Sutherland, John. *Victorian Fiction: Writers, Publishers, Readers* (Palgrave Macmillan, 1995, rpt 2006)

Walton, John. *The Legendary Detective: The Private Eye in Fact and Fiction* (University of Chicago Press, 2015)

Williams, Chris (ed). *A Companion to Nineteenth-Century Britain* (Blackwell, 2004)

Wilmer Rowan, Richard. *The Pinkertons: A Detective Dynasty* (Hurst & Blackett, 1931)

Journal articles

Gill, Martin and Jerry Hart. 'Exploring Investigative Policing: A Study of Private Detectives in Britain', *British Journal of Criminology*, pp.549–67

Holmes, Ann Sumner. 'The Double Standard in the English Divorce Laws, 1857–1923', *Law & Social Inquiry*, 20:2 (Spring 1995), pp.601–620

Jackson, Louise A. 'The Unusual Case of "Mrs Sherlock". Memoir, Identity and the "Real" Woman Private Detective in Twentieth-Century Britain', *Gender & History*, 15:1 (April 2003), pp.108–134

Kisby, Anna. 'Vera "Jack" Holme: cross-dressing actress, suffragette and chauffeur', *Women's History Review* (2014), 23:1, pp.120–36

Pemberton, Neil. 'Bloodhounds as Detectives: Dogs, Slum Stench and Late-Victorian Murder Investigation', *Cultural and Social History*, 10:1 (2013), pp. 69–91

Shpayer-Makov, Haia. 'Journalists and Police Detectives in Victorian and Edwardian England: An Uneasy Reciprocal Relationship', *Journal of Social History* (Summer 2009), pp.963–88

Shpayer-Makov, Haia. 'From menace to celebrity: the English police detective and the press, c.1842–1914', *Journal of Historical Research*, 83:222 (November 2010), pp.672–93

Online articles

Anon, 'Allan Pinkerton (1819–1884)', *National Records of Scotland*, 2020, https://www.nrscotland.gov.uk/research/learning/hall-of-fame/hall-of-fame-a-z/pinkerton-allan

Anon, 'Divorce rates data, 1858 to now: how has it changed?', *The Guardian*, 28 January 2010, www.theguardian.com/news/datablog/2010/jan/28/divorce-rates-marriage-ons

Anon, 'Nine women reveal the dangers of working in a munitions factory', Imperial War Museum, 31 January 2018, https://www.iwm.org.uk/history/9-women-reveal-the-dangers-of-working-in-a-first-world-war-munitions-factory

Anon, 'Private detectives to need licence', *BBC News*, 31 July 2013, https://www.bbc.co.uk/news/uk-23519690

Anon, 'Suffragette Newspapers', *British Newspaper Archive*, 1 February 2018, https://blog.britishnewspaperarchive.co.uk/2018/02/01/suffragette-newspapers/

Anon, 'Women Spies of the Civil War', *Smithsonian.com*, 2011, https://www.smithsonianmag.com/history/women-spies-of-the-civil-war-162202679/

Bretherick, Diana. 'The 'born criminal'? Lombroso and the origins of modern criminality', *BBC History*, 14 February 2015, https://www.historyextra.com/period/victorian/the-born-criminal-lombroso-and-the-origins-of-modern-criminology/

Buzwell, Greg. 'Daughters of Decadence: The New Woman in the Victorian fin de siècle', British Library, 15 May 2014, https://www.bl.uk/romantics-and-victorians/articles/daughters-of-decadence-the-new-woman-in-the-victorian-fin-de-siecle

Conroy, J. Oliver and Emmanuelle Welch. 'Gadgets, drug mules and a French accent: my life as a private investigator', *The Guardian*, 2 August 2019, (https://www.theguardian.com/lifeandstyle/2019/aug/02/private-investigator-life-drugs-cheating-husbands-pi

Cox, Alex, '5 Defiant Suffrage Statements Found in the 1911 Census', *Findmypast*, 1 February 2018, https://www.findmypast.co.uk/blog/discoveries/suffragettes-in-the-1911-census

Darby, Nell. 'The Double Event', *Discover Your Ancestors*, April 2020, http://www.discoveryourancestors.co.uk

Falconer, Colin. 'The First Female Sleuth in History' (undated), http://www.colinfalconer.org/the-first-female-sleuth-in-history/

Flanders, Judith. 'Penny Dreadfuls', *British Library*, 15 May 2014, https://www.bl.uk/romantics-and-victorians/articles/penny-dreadfuls

Glancey, Jonathan. 'A History of the Department Store', *BBC*, 26 March 2015, http://www.bbc.com/culture/bespoke/story/20150326-a-history-of-the-department-store/index.html

Hager, Kelly. 'Chipping Away at Coverture: The Matrimonial Causes Act of 1857', in Dino Franco Felluga (ed), *BRANCH: Britain, Representation and Nineteenth-Century History*, https://www.branchcollective.org/?ps_articles=kelly-hager-chipping-away-at-coverture-the-matrimonial-causes-act-of-1857

Hamilton, Isobel. '100 years ago, my ancestor was an actress fighting for the same thing Time's Up wants today', *MashableUK*, 9 March 2018, https://mashable.com/2018/03/09/actresses-franchise-league-times-up/?europe=true

Hughes, Kathryn. 'Gender Roles in the nineteenth Century', *British Library*, 15 May 2014, https://www.bl.uk/romantics-and-victorians/articles/gender-roles-in-the-nineteenth-century

Humphrys, Julian. 'A Brief History of Shopping', *BBC History*, December 2015, https://www.historyextra.com/period/twentieth-century/history-shopping-sales-black-friday-boxing-day-what-oldest-shop-selfridges/

Jackson, Louise A. 'The First World War and the first female police officer', *History of Government*, 17 June 2014, https://history.blog.gov.uk/2014/06/17/the-first-world-war-and-the-first-female-police-officer/

Jones, Richard. 'Jack the Ripper – the Police Investigation', undated, *Jack the Ripper 1888*, https://www.jack-the-ripper.org/police-investigation.htm

Lee, Karen. '3 Amazing Female Detectives You've Never Heard Of', *Fishwrap: the official blog of Newspapers.com*, 20 March 2019, https://blog.newspapers.com/female-detectives/

McCrystal, Cal. 'No prying eyes as the gumshoes gather', *The Independent*, 9 May 1993, https://www.independent.co.uk/news/uk/no-prying-eyes-as-the-gumshoes-gather-2321883.html

MacLean, Maggie. 'Kate Warne – Union Spy and First Female Private Investigator', *Civil War Women*, 2011, https://www.civilwarwomenblog.com/kate-warne/

Moffett, Cleveland. 'How Allan Pinkerton thwarted the first plot to assassinate Lincoln: stories from the archives of the Pinkerton Detective Agency', *McClure's Magazine*, 1894, https://archive.org/details/howallanpinkerto00moff

Murawski, Lewis. 'What Can UK Private Investigators Legally Do To Trace You?', *Diem Legal*, undated, https://www.diemlegal.co.uk/can-private-investigators-uk-legally-trace/

Richardson, Hayley. 'Former carer who trained as a private investigator in her 40s reveals why social media and a spare DOG LEAD are her best tools for tracking down cheating spouses and missing people', *Daily Mail*, 12 August 2019, https://www.dailymail.co.uk/femail/article-7348471/Private-investigator-reveals-social-media-dog-lead-key-tools-success.html

Simkin, John. 'The Vote', 1997, http://spartacus-educational.com/WvoteJ.htm

Smith, Anthony. 'Has Theresa May Forgotten the Licensing of Private Investigators?', 1 April 2018, *Huffington Post*, https://www.huffingtonpost.co.uk/anthony-smith/private-investigators_b_15707332.html

Smith, Karen Manners. 'Women's Social and Political Union', *Encyclopaedia Britannica*, 17 March 2017, www.britannica.com/topic/Womens-Social-and-Political-Union

Torley, Pete. 'Are Private Investigators Regulated in the UK?', undated, *PrivateDetectiveLondon*, at https://www.privatedetective.london/are-private-investigators-regulated-in-the-uk/

Wee, Alvin. 'Nineteenth-Century Psychology: An Introduction', *The Victorian Web*, 2005, http://www.victorianweb.org/science/psych/psych.htm

Welton, Benjamin. 'The Case of the Vanishing Private Eye', *The Atlantic*, 15 January 2015, https://www.theatlantic.com/business/archive/2015/01/the-long-steady-decline-of-the-private-eye/384450/

Wood, Grace. 'Actresses' Franchise League: The 100-year-old feminist theatre coalition that's inspiring writers today', *The Stage*, 20 July 2018, https://www.thestage.co.uk/features/2018/actresses-franchise-league-the-100-year-old-feminist-theatre-coalition-thats-inspiring-writers-today/

Woodfine, Katherine. 'Behind the Scenes: The Edwardian Lady Detective', 6 September 2019, http://followtheyellow.co.uk/2019/09/behind-the-scenes-the-edwardian-lady-detective/

Miscellaneous publications and websites

Anonymous. *Appleton's Annual Cyclopaedia and Register of Important Events of the Year: 1862* (Appleton & Co, New York, 1863)

Dime Novels and Penny Dreadfuls Project Team, 'Old Sleuth, the Detective', Stanford University, undated, https://web.stanford.edu/dept/SUL/library/prod/depts/dp/pennies/1870_sleuth.html

Imossi, Tony. 'The Self Regulation of Investigators in the Private Sector: A Discussion Document' (The Association of British Investigators, 2011)

Morin, Robert. *The Encyclopaedia of Theoretical Criminology* (2014), at https://onlinelibrary.wiley.com/doi/abs/10.1002/9781118517390.wbetc103

Index